# Shut Up and Say Something

# Shut Up and Say Something

## Business Communication Strategies to Overcome Challenges and Influence Listeners

KAREN FRIEDMAN

 PRAEGER

AN IMPRINT OF ABC-CLIO, LLC
Santa Barbara, California • Denver, Colorado • Oxford, England

**Library of Congress Cataloging-in-Publication Data**

Friedman, Karen, 1956–
   Shut up and say something : business communication strategies to overcome
challenges and influence listeners / Karen Friedman.
      p. cm.
   Includes bibliographical references and index.
   ISBN 978-0-313-38585-8 (alk. paper) — ISBN 978-0-313-38586-5 (ebook)
1. Business communication.   2. Communication—Psychological aspects.   I. Title.
   HF5718.F75   2010
   658.4'5—dc22        2010031842

ISBN: 978-0-313-38585-8
EISBN: 978-0-313-38586-5

14   13   12   11   10        2   3   4   5

This book is also available on the World Wide Web as an eBook.
Visit www.abc-clio.com for details.

Praeger
An Imprint of ABC-CLIO, LLC

ABC-CLIO, LLC
130 Cremona Drive, P.O. Box 1911
Santa Barbara, California 93116-1911

This book is printed on acid-free paper ∞

Manufactured in the United States of America

To my loving husband and two extraordinary sons who always
have something to say
To Mom and Dad, my biggest cheerleaders

# Contents

# Author's Note

When I was writing this book, the television show *American Idol* was approaching its ninth season. As my son and I watched from week to week, I couldn't help but continually notice the similarities between mesmerizing singers and powerful presenters who immediately grab our attention and magnetically hold us in their grip. Like lyrics that capture the main message in just minutes, commanding speakers are able to do the same. They make you feel their words and believe that they believe what they are saying even if you don't. They understand that the only way to connect with an audience is to be connected to what you're saying.

Like memorable entertainers who aren't afraid to be a bit vulnerable and let their personalities shine through, great speakers are true to themselves and invite listeners to be active participants in an effort to create engaging and meaningful experiences for their audiences.

# Acknowledgments

So many of the stories, examples, and lessons shared on the following pages are from savvy, talented professionals whom I've had the pleasure to work with throughout my career. I am so thankful to have had the opportunity to learn so much from so many and am humbled to share that knowledge with others. I could not have completed this book without them.

Special thanks also goes to my husband David, who picked up the slack at home while I was behind closed doors pounding away at the keyboard. Additionally, I am grateful to my dear friend and best-selling author Suzanne Bates for her encouragement and guidance and to my brother Jordan Friedman, whose advice and know-how first got me started. I also want to thank Judy Hoffman, who is always so willing to share her expertise. Brainstorming with my speaker buddies Marsha Egan and Terry Adams was simply the best along the way. Special thanks go to my literary agent Ken Lizotte, whose expertise was instrumental far beyond helping me develop my book proposal. I continue to value his insight as a thought leader. I am also appreciative of my editor Brian Romer and the wonderful people at Praeger Publishing for their belief in and support of this project.

Lastly, it's important to note that, while all of the personal experiences and stories shared in this book are as authentic as I remember them, out of respect of confidentiality agreements and meaningful relationships established over many years, in numerous cases, I do not feel it is appropriate to divulge names of certain individuals or companies whose situations I've shared. In these instances, I have simply left the names out or labeled examples Company X or Company XYZ. Any familiarity to people you know may be purely coincidental.

# Introduction

I have been talking about writing this book for at least 10 years. I've written it in my head. I've shared its contents with colleagues, and I've named it as many times as I've thought about writing it. The truth is, I was overthinking it instead of sharing valuable information from countless coaching sessions, speaking engagements, training programs, a run for political office, and lessons learned from 20 years in television.

Most of the people I work with are not exceptional orators. However, they are bright, capable, and dedicated professionals who are expert in their field and desperately want to articulate their vision to accomplish goals and make a difference. Like most of us, they aren't always sure how to communicate so people will listen and often fear boring listeners, embarrassment, or not making a good impression when it really counts.

I can't even begin to tell you how many times management has confided that someone is terrific but says if he or she can't learn to command attention and respect when they speak, their career will suffer. Yet even the most senior bosses will privately admit they're no longer sure how to be effective in a world where slides are king and attention spans are dwindling. Furthermore, when you barely have time to sort through your e-mails and read what you want to read, it's not likely that you'll actually read a another epic-like book on improving communication skills no matter how good it may be.

This is not that book. *Shut Up and Say Something* is a practical problem-solving approach to business communications. The backward Z-to-A format reminds readers to keep the end goal (Z) in mind when faced with daily communication challenges that are frequently met with resistance and skepticism. Each chapter examines a different communication topic and offers the reader instant problem-solving strategies to make important listeners care about what they have to say. Packed with real-life stories, easy-to-apply tips, techniques, best practices, and personal review notes from thousands of coaching and training sessions, *Shut Up and Say Something* provides specific examples of good and not-so-good communications, showing readers how to think and speak differently in order to engage participants and sell ideas. It does not have to be read in order of chapters.

As importantly, because communicating is about connecting with others, this book urges readers to draw on their unique strengths and personal styles to stay true to themselves even in the most difficult situations.

I am a firm believer that, like successful companies that encourage customer interaction, good communicators actively involve listeners when they speak. From the mailroom to the boardroom, the results-focused strategies found in this book can be instantly applied to a wide variety of circumstances on a daily basis. Sometimes that means knowing when to zip it, which is where we'll start!

# CHAPTER 1

# Zip It

> Half the world is composed of people who have something to say and can't, and the other half who have nothing to say and keep on saying it.
>
> —*Robert Frost, American poet*

Not too long ago, I was helping a prominent doctor prepare for an upcoming appearance on a network television program. An expert in his field, he conducted a terrific videotaped interview about potential medicines that might one day eliminate the common cold. When the interview was over and the camera crew was packing up, a crew member looked up and said, "Hey Doc, what do you do when you get a cold?" The doctor laughed and said, "Well, quite frankly, I usually pour myself a shot of Jack Daniels." Perhaps he was joking or perhaps not, but that off-the-cuff remark was written into the story and attributed to him for millions of Americans to see. Not because anyone wanted to make the doctor look bad, but because most people out in TV land could probably better relate to a shot of whiskey than to medical mumbo jumbo.

In business, as in life, even a seemingly harmless remark can backfire. Think about it—how many times have you hit *send* and wished you could get that e-mail back? How many times have you regretted something you said that hurt someone or positioned you poorly in an important meeting? It happens to all of us, including those in the public eye, who can be embarrassed on a far bigger stage. It's a reminder to all of us that we are responsible for what we say, which is why it's so important to keep the end result in mind.

Example:   Speaking about her experience in Bosnia, then Democratic presidential candidate Hillary Clinton said she landed in Bosnia and had to run from sniper fire. Not only was the very public statement proved false with supporting video to refute the remark, but some observers believe the embarrassing high-profile blunder played a factor in Clinton's losing campaign.

Example:   Actor Michael Richards, who portrayed Kramer on the hit TV show *Seinfeld*, was caught saying the *N* word via cell phone video at a comedy club. Even if he was just joking as comedians do, Richards learned that there are some things you just don't say out loud. That clip remains the number-one video on YouTube when searching for "Michael Richards."

Example:   President Obama's White House Chief of Staff Rahm Emanuel blasted a plan by liberal special-interest groups to run ads against conservative Democrats not supportive of health care reform as "f—retarded." Despite his apology, the remark drew outrage from many, including former Alaska Governor Sarah Palin, whose son has Down syndrome. On her Facebook page, she called for him to be fired.

Example:   When actor Alec Baldwin left an angry voicemail message for his daughter that went viral, it tainted his image on the world stage. Baldwin was so upset he told a reporter he thought about killing himself. He said he feels the consequences of his remarks every single day.

Example:   MSNBC's *Imus in the Morning* host Don Imus referred to the Rutgers University women's basketball team, which included eight African American and two white players, as "nappy-headed hos." Even though he repeatedly apologized, many listeners and guests have permanently changed the channel.

Example:   Hollywood heartthrob Mel Gibson made a similar mistake when he let loose anti-Semitic remarks and blamed it on being drunk. Drunk or sober, this is a perfect example of when to zip it.

The blunders are endless and spark different degrees of offensiveness. Learning how to better handle slipups and prevent future errors in judgment can help you turn negatives to positives.

For example, a television reporter I know aired a scathing report about broken security cameras at one of the United States' busiest airports. The report was loaded with inaccuracies but did not threaten public safety. Instead of calling management and blasting the reporter as airport executives wanted to do, we took a different tack to try to help them change the end result. Airport communications professionals phoned the number-one local television station in town and offered it an exclusive behind-the-scenes look at airport security. The station jumped on the chance to have a private tour, which resulted in a positive story watched by a much larger audience. If executives had simply reacted and called to complain, they might have generated more negative publicity by creating an even bigger controversy. The lesson: Think about the outcome you seek, and program your internal GPS to take you there before you shift into gear.

> Think about the outcome you seek, and program your internal GPS to take you there.

The age of social media has intensified what can happen when people lash out without thinking. Consider the Nestlé social media debacle of March 2010. Greenpeace, an environmental activist group, had been pressuring the food giant to stop using palm oil, which it said was harmful to forests, and supporters had started posting comments to Nestlé's Facebook fan page. CNET reported that a Nestlé representative responded by writing sarcastic remarks on the Facebook trail and even mildly threatened to delete critic's comments. The Nestlé spokesperson later apologized, but the incident is an example of how an open public forum can quickly backfire when you are so quick to lash out that you fail to acknowledge criticism, complaints, or suggestions in a grown-up way.

A similar incident occurred during the 2008 presidential primary campaign, when a student reporter from the University of North Carolina aired a report on campus television about the high-rent location of Democratic candidate John Edwards's Chapel Hill, North Carolina, office. When a staffer from the campaign asked the station to pull the report and management refused, the staffer reportedly threatened to sever ties with the university should Edwards get the presidential nod. A professor learned about the exchange and was so outraged that he started blogging and thrust the story into the spotlight. In three days, an online newscast normally viewed by approximately 1,500 people received more than 50,000 hits. The end result could have been much different if the staffer had checked his arrogance at the door and recognized that blogs, tweets, and Internet postings have dramatically changed the rules and outcomes.

An international candy company we work with almost learned a similar lesson the hard way when a local paper reported that the company was outsourcing work to China. The story was neither positive nor negative, but the company president thought the newspaper should have presented more of the company's viewpoint. He wanted to call and request that the paper run another story about his company's commitment to quality and providing products at an affordable cost around the world. The following advice is from selective e-mail conversations between the client and me.

- I understand your desire to defend the company decision to outsource jobs to China. But the story was already published. Leave it alone. Why would you want to help it resurface, especially when it's such a hot potato and can generate more attention than ever during the holiday season? Just because you don't think the reporter presented enough of your side of the story is not a reason to call. Stories are written every day of the week that we don't like—it is not the reporter's job to tell the story you want told or write what you want written. If you call him, you have to have a darn good reason, strong messages, and think through potential outcomes.
- Unfortunately, doing your job or what's in the best interest of your customers is not the story. What matters to you doesn't always matter to the audience. The story they care about is: taking jobs away from the United States and safety concerns regarding imports and production. I strongly advise you to leave this alone.

Ultimately, the company did leave it alone and the story died. Yet, too often, companies with bruised egos overreact instead of thinking through how their words and actions can affect outcomes. Before picking up a phone or texting a publication to set the record straight as you see it, it's important to take this quick true-or-false test:

**True or False:** This has nothing to do with my ego; it's about providing critical information for readers that could affect their safety or well-being.

Yes, the statement is almost always false. Just because you don't like the tone of a report is not cause for you to keep talking.

That leads to a story that didn't have such a happy ending, when a leading expert in homeopathic medicine agreed to do an interview with John Stossel, cohost of ABC-TV's *20/20.* The title of the segment, "Gimme a Break," should have been his first clue. Refusing media coaching, the spokesperson decided he was fully capable of debunking myths and handling any tough questions that might come his way. And they came. When Stossel stated that perhaps homeopathic medicine was for "suckers," the spokesperson said, "you can choose to call us suckers, but we have experience that suggests otherwise." Not only did he inadvertently validate what Stossel suggested by repeating negatives, but those words became his words, which were devoid of message.

As you can imagine, the spokesperson was outraged at the edited television program, which he claimed misrepresented a scientific study of homeopathy in its visual portrayal of how homeopathy works. In a memo to colleagues, he labeled it a "story of science fiction" and "reality television" to "discredit homeopathic medicine." He wanted to demand a retraction from ABC and the BBC, which had aired a similar story, and send letters to the editors of numerous national publications denouncing both broadcasts. We advised against it. Below are selected excerpts from our communications advice provided to the spokesperson and his organization following the television broadcast.

- While most people in your field would likely not appreciate Stossel's report, he is doing his job, which is to raise questions and deliver an interesting report that addresses viewer concerns and fits into the format of his show. It is not his job to explain homeopathy in great detail, to promote it, say nice things, or report what was reported in a scientific journal.

- While his visual description of dropping droplets into pools and oceans to describe homeopathy might be a bit out there or not even entirely accurate, it works for his program. Television is visual. Their job is to make complex information easy to understand in visual terms. You can't ask someone to apologize just because you don't approve of what they said. Unless he delivered glaring inaccurate information that could harm viewers, they are not going to retract anything.

- Responding by demanding retractions, sending out inflammatory letters or press releases will actually do more harm than good. You simply further perpetuate and give credibility to some people's feelings that homeopathy is a bunch of baloney. Your goal should be to gain greater control over interviews so you can deliver strong, powerful messages that resonate with the public.

- There were numerous missed opportunities to deliver key facts about homeopathic medicines and how those medicines have benefited millions. For example, you might have said, "Homeopathic medicines are widely used by millions of people around the world. From ear infections to the flu, homeopathic products have become one of the most effective ways to treat both acute and chronic conditions." That's up to you, not the reporter.

- It's important to realize that what is upsetting and considered a big deal to you because you are intimately involved in this is not as big a deal to those who saw the piece. But when someone then writes emotionally charged letters with titles like "Junk Science" and "Junk Journalism," you are keeping the negative alive instead of looking for ways to educate people, share the positives of homeopathy, and position the industry in a credible light. Until you start focusing on what you can control, you will never further your own agenda.

---

| Until you start focusing on what you can control, you will never further your own agenda. |
| --- |

---

## COACHING NOTES

Regardless of your audience, if you hope to make others care about what you have to say, the secret is to put yourself in their shoes so you can speak from their perspective. When you do that, you are more likely to shut up and say something that addresses their concerns whether they agree with you or not. The following notes are from a variety of different coaching sessions that focused on helping communicators zip it by recognizing the consequences of their actions.

- You don't think closing this store is that big of a deal because it's a sound financial business decision. But you can't publicly say it's not a big deal because that will offend employees who are losing their jobs and alienate members of the community who have shopped here for more than 60 years. So let's look for ways to explain the situation honestly and let them know that they remain a priority.

- You know that people will lose their jobs and they know that many of them will lose their jobs, even though you can't say that and they know you can't say that. But, to us, words like *consolidation*, *streamlining*, and *navigation* make you and your company sound cold and calloused. Think about how you would feel if you were them. Let's look for ways to soften what you're saying so you speak to them as openly and honestly as possible but with a lot more compassion.

- I can only imagine how hurtful an accusation (anti-Semitic) like that must be, especially for someone as warm and caring as you are, not to mention how you have bent over backward to try to help this person when you didn't have to and how you have tried so hard to do the right thing. He's trying to get to you by threatening to try to ruin your reputation even if he didn't say that directly. It's so important to remember not to take this personally even though all communication really is personal. In this case, I think it's best to say as little as possible. Given the matter is now being handled by lawyers; we can go to our "zip it" statement that simply says here's the situation and why we can't talk.

Clearly, we've all made mistakes and have said things that unintentionally offended others without stopping to think about why the words we use or context we use them in is inappropriate. People sometimes use words like *gay* or *retarded* in contexts that have no relevance to homosexuals or challenged individuals without realizing how hurtful and offensive these words are to others or how what's acceptable and unacceptable changes according to the times.

As an example, the word *gay* used to mean merry, and flight attendants used to be called stewardesses. Administrative assistants were secretaries and housekeepers were once called maids. It used to be okay to refer to someone as "the Korean woman," which could be interpreted as a racial slur today. It is far more appropriate to identify that person as "the dark haired woman in the green dress" instead of referring to her ethnicity.

So when a celebrity or politician says something offensive, in an oddly positive way, the remarks call attention to right versus wrong and should redirect all of us to think before we speak in an effort to prevent blunders that can have long-lasting results. As former White House Press Secretary Marlin Fitzwater once said, "You don't have to explain what you don't say."

You don't have to explain what you don't say.

## ZIP IT FIXES

I once heard a speaker say, "Shutting up is an art." How many times have we heard spokespeople drone on and on, repeating the same information over and over again? Successful speakers make points and shut up. Successful salespeople understand silence is more than golden; it's how they often close a deal. They learn to ask a closing question, and then zip it to put the pressure on the prospect. Here are several strategies to help you apply your own zip it fixes.

- **20-second rule.** Practice stating your main point in 20 seconds or less. State that point first to prevent rambling or burying the lead. The longer it takes you to answer, the more likely you will say something you didn't intend to say.
- **Need versus want.** Differentiate between what you think you *need* to tell audiences and what they really *want* to know. Learning to do this will help you speak to their wants and needs. For example:

    If you're an auto mechanic, does your customer really *need* to know the long-winded nitty-gritty details of how you replaced the fuel pump, or does she *want* to know that it's now working safely?

    If you're selling technology to management, do they *need* to know the inside workings of the software, or do they *want* to know how the program will save them time and money?

- **Don't wing it.** Just because you are expert at your subject doesn't mean you can speak clearly and concisely. It's critical to pick your points in advance to focus your message and limit others from using your own words against you.

Comedian Jimmy Durante once joked, "My wife has a slight impediment in her speech. Every now and then she stops to breathe." If you have the gift of gab, as some call it, and struggle to come up for air, this can work for you or against you depending on the circumstances. In social situations, talkers can break the ice and draw less chatty individuals into conversation. In business, however, people may perceive chatty people as full of themselves and not very interested in what others have to say.

So think about the communication traits you really admire in friends, associates, family members, or newsmakers. In a brief online survey we conducted with about two dozen clients from multiple industries, we asked that question. Although the answers varied and included "being a good storyteller," "having passion," "presence," "able to engage people," "the ability to condense complicated information," and "they get in touch with the way other people feel," one answer was repeated six (25%) times. To paraphrase, these people said, "People who communicate well also stop long enough to hear what others have to say."

They also noted that, when you act as if you are being publicly observed or quoted at all times, you are more likely to zip it and avoid embarrassing or high-profile blunders.

**If you don't have something constructive to say, zip it!**

# CHAPTER 2

# You're On

You know what they say, "You don't sell the steak, you sell the sizzle."

—*Kramer in "The Bizzaro Episode" of* Seinfeld

Make no mistake about it. Every time you walk into a meeting, talk to your boss, or address an audience of one or one thousand, you're on! Whether you like it or not, even delivering a simple update at a staff meeting is a performance and can affect your ability to succeed in an organization. If you want to have presence, you must be present.

I work with a global brand manager who told me one of his rising stars is smart as a whip but too laid back at meetings and doesn't instill confidence in people. He said, "Mike comes across as if he doesn't care, when I know he's passionate about his work." Shortly after, Mike and his colleague Carol were both asked to quickly update the senior team on two potentially promising products that would require additional funding. Mike's product was the stronger of the two, but Carol was so energizing, passionate, and convincing that she was granted more money than expected and, to Mike's surprise, his budget was cut. Mike eventually left the company and once complained to me that "presentation skills at this company were too high of a priority."

While I am not suggesting you deliver a motivational speech in the boardroom or smile in the face of bad financials, I am telling you to treat every meeting, conversation, speech, interview, or presentation as an opportunity, which is exactly what happened at Viropharma, a publicly traded biopharmaceutical company. When a promising drug was not initially approved, the stock dropped, investors became wary, and the CEO had some explaining to do. Vincent Milano could have gone on the defensive and talked about things from the company's point of view, but he did just the opposite. Milano talked about those who were most affected and placed the burden back on himself by saying, "We are extremely disappointed by the outcome of this pivotal study . . . our disappointment is no doubt shared by physicians and transplant patients, who must today contend with this terrible disease . . . we still have a significant amount of work to do."

Milano clearly understood the need to inform, motivate, and lead people every time he spoke. He is passionate about his work and not afraid to let it show. If you want to excite other people, then act excited. If you care about your message, then show your feelings so other people care too! Deliver your thoughts with expression, conviction, and energy. Use your hands instead of putting them in your pockets. Look people directly in the eye. Instead of backing into important conversations or presentations, grab the audience's attention by coming out of the gate at a gallop instead of a sprint. For example:

| | |
|---|---|
| Sprint: | "I am going to outline our strategy moving forward to show you how we plan to do better than we did last year. The first slide shows . . ." |
| Gallop: | "This is an exciting product with great potential to address a huge unmet need, and we have a strategic plan in place to hit one billion in sales by 2010." |
| Sprint: | "So, let me take you through the RFP process that can be accessed online by vendors." |
| Gallop: | "Good morning. We are very proud of the online RFP system that is now up and running and can be accessed by hundreds of vendors." |
| Sprint: | "Our technology is better than our chief competitor because it offers multiple heterogeneous operating system versatility." |
| Gallop: | "Because we can securely handle thousands of data transactions on a single server, customers benefit from more power and efficiency, reduced costs, and can spend more time concentrating on their business, which gives us an edge over the competition." |

Grab their attention by coming out of the gate at a gallop instead of a sprint.

Thanks to so many choices and instant access to more information than ever before, like children, we expect immediate gratification. We want the home page to load faster, the images to appear clearer, and the transactions completed sooner. If we turn on the TV and don't see something we like, we're just a click away from another option.

A published study determined that Americans, compared to other nations and to themselves, suffer from dramatically short attention spans. The report concluded that, on average, people have six applications open on their computer at any one time and that the active window switches or a new window opens every 50 seconds. It has become such a problem that a federally funded effort to counteract what some medical professionals have termed the "epidemic-level shortness in the attention spans of American citizens" has been launched with the backing of the Congressional Task Force for Making People Pay Attention.

From my vantage point inside numerous companies, this has directly impacted the way business leaders rush through communicating without realizing how it impacts workplace morale and the way others hear them.

I recall working for a news manager at a local TV station. He was personable and likeable but overwhelmed with daily tasks and continually looked up at the clock or out his office window when you spoke to him, making you feel that you better speak quickly because he had something much more important to do than talk with you. He also gave off mixed signals. At quarterly employee meetings, he typically made a point of saying "my door is always open" yet his door was usually closed, and the only people routinely invited in were other managers or high-profile anchors.

What signals do you send when you communicate? Do you look people in the eye when you speak? Do you appear approachable, or are your arms crossed over your chest? Do you come across as confident, or are you tapping your foot and drumming your pen on the table? What about the e-mails and text messages you send? Do you think about their voice? Are they clear and concise? Could they be misinterpreted?

While the success of organizations most certainly depends on business performance, research repeatedly reveals there is a direct connection between morale and the way management communicates. From the way we pass by someone in a hallway, glance away at a meeting, talk on the phone, or even stand while conversing, verbal and nonverbal communications continually impact others. In short, you're always on. How you engage, connect, and share ideas on a daily basis determines how you make others feel. Great leaders empower others by making them feel important so they want to follow.

> Great leaders empower others by making them feel important so they want to follow.

Benjamin Franklin once said, "Words may show a man's wit but actions his meaning." Coming from a world of television where newscasters are local celebrities, I got a taste of how important actions were and what it was like to be on even when you wanted to be off. Someone always silently noticed you sweating at the gym, grocery shopping, or even scolding your child and then they embellished what they saw in a whisper-down-the-lane style, so it was important to make a good impression both on and off the air.

When the Philadelphia Phillies faced the Toronto Blue Jays in the 1993 World Series, I had the honor of co-reporting on the series with Tug McGraw, the beloved hall of famer Phillies relief pitcher who later died of brain cancer. We both worked for WPVI TV, the ABC affiliate in Philadelphia. Tug was covering the game. I was reporting on the fan pandemonium. Tug was one of the most upbeat, charismatic, larger-than-life men I have ever met. After a long, exhausting day of editing and filing reports, we went to grab a quick bite at a bar near the stadium. Tug was highly recognizable, and the fans—some of whom were loud and a bit inebriated—wouldn't leave him alone as he smiled, joked with them, and signed autographs. I looked at him and whispered, "why don't you just politely tell them to bug off?" And I've never forgotten what he said. He replied, "It's okay; they mean well. You gotta treat people the way you want to be treated."

> You gotta treat people the way you want to be treated.

Contrast that to a very different experience when traveling to Israel as an impressionable teenager. I was sitting in a restaurant with my family and excitedly noticed that actor Michael Caine was seated at the table next to us. I was afraid to bother him, but my parents said it was okay.

So, being a huge fan, I tentatively walked over to his table and nervously asked for his autograph. In a booming voice, he said, "Can't you see I'm eating dinner and don't want to be bothered? I don't give autographs." Imagine my teenage embarrassment. To this day, I have never again watched a Michael Caine film.

You may wonder how these two experiences relate to communicating in the workplace. Very simply, it's about the mood or atmosphere you choose to create by what you say or don't say. Like Tug McGraw or Michael Caine, you can achieve celebrity status in your own world. It's up to you to decide what kind of impression you wish to convey.

## COACHING NOTES

- Even though you were only asked to provide an update, you are still being judged by others, so it is critical to engage and influence. This does not mean showing off, because I know that is not your personality. Smile when you can so you appear approachable, which you are. Here are some other tips:

  - **Stronger start.** Toss out the tentative phrases and disclaimers that make you come across as unsure of yourself. Instead of using passive phrases such as "It seems" or "I think," replace these soft words with stronger language such as "I am committed" or "I believe" so others see you as someone who really does believe in what he is saying.
  - **Be your own cheerleader.** While it's important to give credit to others, it's equally important to step up to the plate. Self-promotion is not bragging. It's taking ownership and credit for your hard work so people notice you, especially when you have contributed to a project's success.
  - **Stand tall.** Positive body language draws positive attention. It's important to stand tall; make steady, direct eye contact; and make sure your body language says "I want to be here." Project as if you are speaking to the people in the back of the room. Use pauses to position yourself as thoughtful and confident.

- You clearly care about your subject but appear reluctant to let others see how much it means to you. People need to feel your enthusiasm and energy. You don't have to scream from the rooftops, but if you believe this therapy can change lives, it's up to you to speak with passion and make others believe too.

- It takes approximately seven seconds for someone to form an impression of you based on your appearance, body language, facial expressions, and mannerisms. These first impressions set the tone and can determine what a prospect thinks of you even before you speak. So when you greeted me in the lobby today and didn't smile, walked in front of me without speaking, and didn't acknowledge anyone you passed, you came across as unfriendly and a bit arrogant when indeed you are not like that at all.

- When you first walked into the room, you went right to the podium with your back toward the room, stepped up, and grabbed onto it as if you were steering a ship. I realize you were nervous, and it showed. Try arriving a bit early so you can say hello to people, make eye contact, and perhaps shake their hands. They won't seem like strangers, and you'll give your nerves a break. If someone speaks to you, look directly at her and pay attention so she feels you care about what she has to say.

- Try to avoid swaying, rocking in your chair, drumming your fingers, biting your nails, crossing and uncrossing your legs, and playing with notes. Fidgeting makes you appear anxious and unsure of yourself and can be distracting to others. When sitting, cross your legs at the ankles to prevent tapping. You can also try putting one hand on top of the other to keep the other hand from moving.

- When it's your turn to speak, put your papers down and look up and out at the audience to give them your full attention. You don't need slides or notes to greet the group and set the agenda for the day. Don't forget to smile. They want to like you, and you have a better chance of making that happen if they think you want to be here and are happy to share this information with them.

- When you are being interviewed by phone, stand up and imagine the person you are talking to is in the room. You will convey more energy and excitement, and your voice will have more power than it does when sitting down. You will be more likely to smile and gesture just as you would if you were having a face-to-face conversation. Just because you aren't in front of someone doesn't mean you're not on.

- Your attitude is essential in both good times and bad. It also speaks volumes about a leader's perceived ability to instill confidence, navigate issues, and create an environment where people feel valued professionally and personally. So speak to your employees as if you were the listener. Be warm. Be real. Laugh a little, smile—let them relate to you. That will produce a far greater outcome than a long-winded slide show or reading from a script with lots of text and little of you.

I'm frequently asked what level someone should speak to when an audience has varied expertise. Typically, the presenter is afraid of being too simplistic or over someone's head. The answer is a middle-lane approach. If you're in the left lane, you may go too fast and leave some people behind. If you're in the right lane, you could travel too slowly for others. The middle of the road allows everyone to keep pace. Remember, you're there for everybody, not just a select few.

## YOU'RE ON FIXES

- **Pal practice.** Work with a friend or coach who can stage mock drills on videotape so you can see how others see you. People often do things they are not even aware of, such as licking their lips, swallowing frequently, and blinking.
- **Hands have it.** People always ask me if they should talk with their hands. If you normally talk with your hands, the answer is yes. In fact, using your hands to gesture and illustrate points will help you come across as more animated, expressive, and interesting and can help bring material to life.
- **Speak up.** If you want to be heard, speak up! Not only are your first words important, but how well you project will enable you to command attention and appear self-assured. To do that, try to talk to the people in the middle and the back of the audience. Practice by having someone put their hand up to their ear or signal you when they can't hear you.
- **Watch the pros.** Trailing off at the end of a sentence is a problem for many presenters. Listeners struggle to hear you and eventually tune out. To help keep your voice up, try observing radio and television announcers who consistently enunciate and slow down when they talk. You can do the same thing by trying hard to articulate and stopping to pronounce consonants like *t* and *b*.
- **TV tactics.** Taking a page from television anchors, also notice what syllables and words get emphasis. Practice by reading a newspaper and exaggerating your inflection by emphasizing important words the way you would if you were reading a bedtime story to a child. For example, using the same sentence as illustrated, emphasize the

word that is underlined to hear how the meaning changes every time you read the sentence.

The <u>brown</u> fox jumped over the lazy dog.
The brown <u>fox</u> jumped over the lazy dog.
The brown fox <u>jumped</u> over the lazy dog.
The brown fox jumped <u>over</u> the lazy dog.
The brown fox jumped over the <u>lazy</u> dog.

It's important to remember that everywhere we go, someone is evaluating us. Whether it's a subordinate, a colleague, a boss, or a potential boss, put your game face on because you never know whose impression can ultimately make or break your career.

**When you are fully engaged, you engage others.**

# CHAPTER 3

# X-ray Vision

> In the absence of communication, rumor and innuendo fill the gap and become reality.
>
> —*Jonathon Bernstein, crisis manager*

When individuals or companies are publicly accused of wrongdoing, we always advise being as transparent as possible. Like an X-ray or a magnetic resonance image, it's important to show people you have nothing to hide.

For example, I once covered a story about a person with AIDS who sued a health club for not letting him join. Lawyers advised club management not to talk to the media. Instead of explaining why they couldn't comment, management ignored media phone calls, ducked from reporters who showed up at the door, and one employee called a cameraperson a name. We had a field day. Make no mistake about it, reporters love confrontation! If you want to get on the evening news or on the front page of the paper, then make a scene. It works every time. The reporters were not deliberately trying to make club owners look bad, but they were trying to cover the story. They simply reported what they saw and heard. If management had cooperated by explaining why they couldn't answer questions and realized reporters were just doing their job, the story would have been far less sensational.

The same rules apply in the workplace. If you aren't talking, that means someone else is. In the absence of information, rumors take over. Rumors aren't simply repeated; they're refined and embellished so they can fill in the blanks that aren't being communicated.

For example, I worked with a senior-level executive whose company was being acquired by another company. He was privy to confidential details but not permitted to discuss them with employees who were worried about their jobs and futures. So, how could he be open and transparent when he was not allowed to talk about the impending deal?

1. **Communicate often.** Even though you can't provide specifics, it's not advisable to act clueless. Use this as an opportunity to dispel rumors by stating what you are permitted to discuss and explaining why you can't offer more details.
2. **Address fears.** Instead of only talking about the merger itself, address people's fears, concerns, and anxieties. Let them ask questions or talk so they know you care enough to listen. They want to know you understand even if you don't have immediate answers.
3. **Convey confidence.** You can't always control what's happening, but you can show confidence during tough times without making promises or guarantees that you can't deliver.
4. **Speak calmly.** If you look panicked or scared, you will cause alarm and increase the anxiety of others.

In today's world of instant communications and social media, the old rules no longer apply. A simple rumor that was confined to the office can now hit the Internet at lightning speed, sending what you could have controlled completely out of control. Anyone can pen their opinion about your company or products on blogs and sites like Facebook and Twitter, which fuel conversation and blur the lines between fact and fiction. Consumers and employees have easy access to millions of video clips, some which might unfairly bash brands. Look no further than a video put to music posted on YouTube showing a Comcast repairman falling asleep on a homeowner's couch, which logged more than a million views and prompted customers to cancel service.

It is more critical than ever to pay attention to what's being said about your business to determine whether you want to add to the conversation or correct information that might threaten your brand or reputation. The longer you wait to communicate, the more likely the story will be told from someone else's viewpoint, which can unfairly paint you as uncaring or guilty of some wrongdoing even if you're not.

In April 2009, a hoax video uploaded to YouTube showed two fake Domino's employees mutilating pizza and sandwiches. Initially, the company said nothing, fearing it would only fuel the viral hoax that quickly spread to more than a quarter million viewers. Domino's realized there is no longer a time lag when it comes to communicating and that they needed to join the conversation in the space where it was taking place. The company released its own online video in which the president apologized and outlined what actions the company would take. Speaking directly to the online community that had watched the damaging video enabled Domino's to preserve its hard-earned reputation by sharing accurate information and communicating openly with its customers.

Another excellent example of the importance of being visible occurred during the Christmas holiday several years ago when US Airways passengers were treated to mounds of missing luggage piled sky high at Philadelphia International Airport's baggage claim. As local photographers captured the images and angry passengers publicly vented, airport personnel ran to the rescue; handing out coffee, taking names and cell phone numbers, and trying to reunite passengers with their bags. That became part of the story, and it portrayed airport employees as caring, compassionate, and proactive. They demonstrated that how you attempt to fix a problem can often leave a more lasting impression than the problem itself.

> How you attempt to fix a problem can often leave a more lasting impression than the problem itself.

When respected journalist Mike Wallace of *60 Minutes* was asked what he would do if he were at a company that got a call from his news show, he said, "If I were running a company that got a call from *60 Minutes*, I'd say 'come in. Ask me anything you want.'" While you can't give journalists, employees, or anyone else unescorted access to the executive suite, Wallace's message is dead on. If you get a phone call, return it. If you're asked a question, answer it. If you're not available, provide someone who can help the reporter meet his deadline. If you receive an e-mail, respond. If the truth hurts, tell it anyway. By communicating internally or externally (when appropriate), you create an environment of openness and honesty. The seemingly unimportant journalist who works for a barely read community paper today could land at the *New York Times* tomorrow, just as the employee who is a thorn in your side today could be your boss next week.

When you fail to acknowledge your problems and are slow to admit mistakes, you risk long-term effects, which include alienating important audiences and harming public perception of your brand. But when you proactively explain what happened, even if you don't have all the details, and then state what you are going to do to fix it, you can change the story that's being told and ultimately change perceptions. Here are some recent examples.

Story:       Data from a three-year clinical study involving a widely used painkiller medication called Vioxx revealed an increased risk for cardiovascular disease.

Perception:  The public was angry, but the data were only part of the reason. The public perceived that the pharmaceutical company that manufactured the drug withheld information.

Story:       When members of the Catholic Church were accused of inappropriate sexual conduct, at first leaders danced around the problem and were slow to talk about it.

Perception:  Because the church was defensive, the public perceived leaders as covering up. If the church had faced the accusations immediately and stated any behavior of this kind is unacceptable, it would have been easier for people to forgive.

Story:       Perhaps you remember the spinach scare of 2006, when E. coli found in the leafy green prompted a recall, but not before it killed three people and sickened hundreds.

Perception:  The industry posted Web site directions, offered deepest sympathies to those affected, took out full-page ads in national newspapers, gave out discount coupons, hired extra people to staff toll-free phone lines, eliminated certain food packers, created an education Web site to take people through stages of bagged salad, and distributed leaflets at supermarkets. By keeping consumers informed on a consistent basis, the public was reassured that the industry had their best interest at heart.

Story:       When a severe Valentine's Day storm grounded hundreds of flights across the country and stranded tens of thousands of passengers, JetBlue travelers, including small children, were trapped on planes at Kennedy airport in New York with no food, overflowing toilets, and little, if any, information for more than 10 hours as an angry public watched.

Perception:      The airline turned crisis into opportunity by publicly admitting mistakes, taking responsibility, and ultimately restructuring the company, which included a passenger bill of rights. Not only was the public forgiving, but the media had a new and positive story to tell the public.

American philosopher Jim Rohn once said, "Effective communication is 20% what you know and 80% how you feel about what you know." I love the quote because it underscores the importance of taking the emotional temperature of those affected by a situation. As reporters, we would keep stories alive for days, even weeks, if people continued to vent their fears, anxieties, or anger. Emotional sound bites make a good story and unfortunately promote exaggerated panic. The only way to slam on the brakes is to be as open as possible by telling people as much as you can as often as you can.

That was certainly the case with a chemical company executive I prepared for an interview on CBS's *60 Minutes.* The program was investigating possible connections to brain cancer at some of the company's sites. To the company's credit, it said it had nothing to hide and wanted to talk to the investigative journalist, even though there were no certainties that the story would turn out in their favor. The spokesperson, who I'll call David, was a doctor. When we first got together, he passionately told me his company did the right thing and that if there was any question about wrongdoing, he would have done everything he could to shut the place down. He was passionate, believable, and terribly upset about the people who were suffering. Yet during our interview practice sessions, that raw human transparency was missing. He was so focused on getting his company's story out that he appeared stiff and unfeeling. After multiple practice sessions, the real David was coming through. He appeared ready for game day.

But when that day came, David was clearly nervous, fearing that CBS would side with the alleged victims and try to smear him and his company. He was sweating, overexplaining, rambling, and straying from his message. We were dreading the outcome and called for a break. That's when we overheard the reporter and producer talking. The producer was pushing the reporter to ask tougher questions and to make David squirm. The reporter refused and said he thought David was really credible because he could see the tears in his eyes when he was asked about the people suffering from brain cancer. When the interview was over, I exchanged several e-mails with the company:

Company:   I was thinking what we might do to counter what may and probably will be a very negative characterization of the company. What if we did our own version and ran it on the Web site before CBS ran its story?

Me:   I think that could be a huge mistake. There is no reason to believe CBS won't be fair. Sure, they could do a crummy edit and make you look bad, but they could also do a very fair and balanced piece and pick really genuine sound bites.

    I do not think David did as well as he could have done, but he was credible, answered the questions honestly, and it was clear the company has been trying to find out what caused the brain cancers even though all its studies to date haven't found anything. It's all a guessing game on your part, and you could be pleasantly surprised as well. So just wait.

So they waited, and, when the piece aired, it was accurate and balanced. David and his company were portrayed as open, honest, and caring and continue to communicate frequently and proactively today.

Like an X-ray or MRI, the more you open up and let others see a caring compassionate person who believes in what she is saying, the more likely it is that they will also believe you and perhaps cut you some slack. When communicating internally or externally, honesty remains the best policy because it reinforces that you have nothing to hide even if you

> "People will forgive a screw up, but they won't forgive a cover up."

may have done something wrong. As a colleague once quipped, "People will forgive a screw up, but they won't forgive a cover up."

People also have longer memories than you might imagine, which is why there is a lesson to be learned from famed football coach Vince Lombardi, who said, "winning isn't everything; it's the only thing."

Lombardi would be proud of what transpired behind closed doors at Villanova University as Scottie Reynolds plunged a last-second basket to give the men's basketball team a stunning 78–76 victory over Pittsburgh, sending the Wildcats to their first NCAA Final Four season-ending tournament in 24 years. That's when my phone rang and my university communications colleague said, "let's be prepared for all possible scenarios so we can be as open as possible."

You may wonder why a communications director would want to plan for the worst when nothing could be better than the glee of that moment. But this director was far more forward thinking than the campus celebration that spilled into the streets during the wee hours of that Sunday morning. While there was no cause for alarm other than a small trashcan fire that was quickly extinguished, officials and the surrounding community clearly remembered the raucous celebration that spilled into the same streets when Villanova won the tournament more than a quarter of a century earlier.

The prominent institution wanted to be as transparent as possible about its plans to ensure a safe and responsible celebration should the Wildcats move to the final championship game. While most of the problems back in 1985 occurred off campus, which is under police jurisdiction, by reaching out to key stakeholders, including students, media, police, and community, Villanova was able to communicate expectations and plans for civilized festivities without dampening the euphoria.

In the end, the Wildcats lost the game and did not move on to the championship game, but the university scored a big win by benefiting from the loyalty and trust it created by continually communicating, answering questions, and listening to the concerns of others. The experience generated goodwill among the media and community that resulted in many positive stories showcasing the institution.

## COACHING NOTES

- It is critical to temper your excitement with expectations when creating and delivering messages. You can show your excitement and say you are excited about the team, but always temper that message with a reminder for students to put their best foot forward in this age of instant and social media.

- Honesty is still the best policy. Aside from the fact that lying is wrong, unethical, and can damage your reputation, it will come back to haunt you. Somewhere down the line, someone will remind a potential employer, reporter, or associate of the past even if the wrongdoing has been corrected. It's always better to tell the truth and explain why you did what you did, even if your explanation is shaky.

- Focus on the big picture and what you want to say. You can't control what someone else says, what the media prints, what some blogger writes, what you like or don't like, but you can focus on your actions and statements. Be as visible and transparent as possible without compromising security. For example, you can talk about the massive coordination between Villanova and all of the other partners, but the security details should come from the police.

- Unfortunately, no one cares about your problems. When a plane lands after passengers have spent several hours sitting in cramped seats, they want to get off the plane. So when a gate isn't available or a jetway isn't connected, they don't want to know why, because, frankly, they don't care. They don't want excuses. They want you to take responsibility and make sure it doesn't happen again.

Pennsylvania Secretary of Transportation Al Biehler learned that lesson firsthand when an unexpected snowstorm blanketed Interstate 78 on Valentine's Day several years ago. To everyone's surprise, eight inches of snow and three inches of ice quickly stranded hundreds of passengers, some up to 24 hours in the bitter cold. When a local newsman asked the official how it might be prevented from happening again, Biehler honestly replied, "We don't know that we could have done something differently." The public was livid, which prompted the governor to step forward and publicly apology to motorists and promise to take full responsibility, find out what happened and fix it.

- Regardless of the situation, it is critical to be a human being first. In difficult situations, people sometimes forget to empathize and show concern. Although you don't want to fall to pieces in front of employees or other key audiences, being human can make your message much more believable.

- Even if you've explained the information before or if someone has written about your business before, don't assume they completely understand your issues, remember what you said, or know what you know. If you want someone to know something, tell them even if you've told them before. It's up to you to deliver the information you want told.

- Add these words back into your vocabulary: "I don't know." Just because you're the boss or leading expert doesn't mean you have to have all the answers. It's okay not to know what you don't know. Confucius said, "When you know something, say what you know. When you don't know something, say that you don't know. That is knowledge." It's also called leading.

## X-RAY VISION FIXES

- **Do what you say.** If your company promises something, it's important to deliver. If you can't deliver, explain why.
- **Show compassion.** Never lose sight of those who are affected. Even if you've done nothing wrong, do not make light of someone else's problem. Show concern and compassion.
- **Admit mistakes.** If you made a mistake, say so. Explain why that mistake occurred and what you are doing to fix it and prevent it from happening again.
- **Keep it in check.** Try to avoid being argumentative, defensive, confrontational, or attacking someone personally. Show restraint and respect.
- **Two-way talking.** Two-way conversations create healthy, open-door environments where straight talk is expected on all levels. People are more apt to trust when they understand what's being said.

Clearly, every culture is different, but thanks to the increased use of social network tools and easy access to information about almost everything, transparent communicating will eventually become more and more customary. That does not mean every company or executive needs to answer every criticism or question. However, with so many tools at our fingertips, the public will hold organizations and the individuals that run them more accountable than ever before. Some, like Tony Hsieh, CEO of Zappos, are way ahead of the curve. Hsieh, who turned a start-up online shoe business into a $1 billion empire says he built his company on transparency, happiness, and passion for customer service. At a speech he gave on organizational culture, he stunned many when he said he would let any of his thousands of employees talk to the press. While this may fly in the face of traditional corporate communications, which typically stresses the importance of limiting spokespeople, Zappos clearly subscribes to a new culture of "we have nothing to hide and are more than happy to bare it all." The result is clearly an open, honest, and proactive environment that builds goodwill and loyalty.

**Honesty is always the best policy.**

# CHAPTER 4

# What's the Story?

Stories are as unique as the people who tell them.
—*Nicholas Sparks, author*

I am a proud alumna of the Pennsylvania State University, so you can imagine my excitement when graduating students asked me to deliver the commencement speech at one of the campuses. I probably spent more time preparing this speech than any I've ever given because it was so close to my heart and so important to me to share pearls of wisdom that graduates might draw on and remember as they entered the next phase of their lives. Many of my friends and family were also attending, so that only amplified my jittery nerves.

It was a day I will always remember, and over the years I've heard from a few of those former students who tell me they still remember some of what I said. Obviously flattered, but mostly curious, when I've asked what they recall, they've all said the same thing. They said they remember the stories I told.

Before every talk, presentation, meeting, interview, or slide show it's essential to think about the story you want to tell and how stories within that story can bring your content to life. What is the goal of your talk or presentation? What are the key takeaways you want your audience to remember? What do you want them to feel, do, or know when you are done speaking? Your story must be clearly defined to help listeners understand how your ideas and insights can address their challenges and help them accomplish their goals. To do this, you must look for ways to personalize information.

An insurance company president I worked with was preparing to deliver a keynote address to several thousand colleagues who were edgy about significant challenges facing their business. He really wanted to shine so he hired a professional speechwriter and then asked me to help him with style, delivery, and speaking techniques. While I have written more than a few speeches in my day, I am not an executive speechwriter. That said, when I read the speech, something about it really bothered me, so I decided to be as blunt as possible even though I knew it might upset him given the time and money he had already invested. Here is part of an e-mail I sent to him:

> The speech sounds like it's trying to convince people to feel optimistic . . . instead of really being optimistic. It uses negative words instead of energizing and tries too hard to add little pithy analogies and quotes that miss the mark. Most importantly, it does not have personality and doesn't capture who you are—warm, caring, proud . . . and it certainly doesn't tell the story your audience wants to hear . . . , It seems to talk at them, instead of having a conversation with them. I believe speeches should be personal; you have to bring people into the fold and make them feel that you get them ... that you really understand your audience . . . you have to humanize your thoughts and words so it truly reflects who you are and tells the story you want to tell.

What resulted was a different approach; a brainstorming session to identify the story and create a theme, which was simple: "Imagine the possibilities. Once you know the story you want to tell, everything else

**Figure 4.1**
**Message Buckets**

| Problem overview | Change isn't always bad |
|---|---|
| Stakeholder participation | Imagine the possibilities |

will fall into place. In this case, we used some of what was already written but divided the script into four squares. Each square contains a central message referred to as a bucket.

We filled every bucket with anecdotes, personal experiences, vignettes, and examples that listeners could relate to so the messages would stick. Using some excerpts from the speech, here's how it worked.

Message Bucket:  Change isn't always bad, it's just scary.

Message Filler:  I will tell you like most people I am a creature of habit. Every morning on my way into work I stop at the local Dunkin Donuts shop to get my extra large black coffee, no sugar. I can actually begin to taste it about two blocks away. When they see me at the front door they are already filling the container. Last week I arrived one day to find that they were closed due to a power outage. I was not happy! It threw off my entire routine—I was adjusting all day to drinking another brand of coffee. You may be thinking, well, if that's the worst thing to happen, then you're lucky! The point is I know firsthand how easy it is to be out of sorts when what's familiar and comfortable is no longer at arm's length.

Message Bucket:  Imagine the possibilities.

Message Filler:  Some of us probably remember those futurist books of the late 1950s with titles such as *Into the Atomic Age* or my personal cartoon favorite, *The Jetsons*. Remember George, Judy, Jane, Elroy, Mr. Spacely, wise-cracking robot Rosie the maid, and let's not forget sky dog Astro!

Surely, you remember how they moved about their sky-pad apartment complete with an atomic kitchen, stood in their one-stop morning wake-up sky bubble to shower, shave, brush teeth, and get coffee all at once, before hopping onto the conveyor-belted sidewalks that took them to their rocket car—our imaginations soaring to the future.

But, think about it—what you didn't see were women headed to the office or a modern generation complete with iPods, Blackberrys, PDAs, game boys, cell phones, hybrid cars, plasma screens, and HDTV. And if there was a mouse in the picture, it went *squeak*—not *click!*

So many things we only imagined—or thought we could only imagine—have become very real now in the 21st century. And that is where we will find our opportunities, for without imagination we can never really move forward.

Without vignettes and stories, a speech or talk is nothing more than a bunch of words void of meaning and impact. In fact, across all academic levels, storytelling is used to spread news, teach lessons, and learn about cultures and history. It's something that comes naturally to all of us, because we do it every day without even thinking about it—in hallways, at the bus stop, at home, and at social gatherings. But because many of us fear not being taken seriously or risking credibility, instead of using stories to enhance understanding and achieve outcomes, we often lapse into what I call presentation mode which is typically boring and robotic.

Here's another example.

After serious concerns about effectiveness were raised over a well-known therapy used by millions of people worldwide, sales plummeted and the pharmaceutical company that manufactured the product began looking toward a lower-dose next-generation therapy that offered the same benefits. During a series of brainstorming sessions designed to identify important facts and explain them in simple terms, the brand team consistently struggled trying to separate past from present. They were hung up on years of often inaccurate and negative news stories that had created misperceptions. Every time they spoke, they started by talking about the past instead of the present. They could not understand that the story is the garden you are growing, not the weeds still stuck in the mud.

| | |
|---|---|
| Question: | What makes this new product safer than the old one? |
| Weeds Answer: | The ABC study was incorrect when it said that . . . |
| Garden Approach: | Today's product works differently than the traditional therapy because it combines components A and B without the risk of X and demonstrates fewer side effects. |

Question:   If there is still skepticism, how will you change the mindset of patients?

Weeds Answer:   The profile of the traditional product that was criticized in mainstream media . . .

Garden Approach:   It's believed more than 40 million people suffer from this condition, which affects their relationships, ability to work, and the quality of their everyday lives. This new therapy is a safe and effective option that provides relief of these debilitating symptoms and also protects against . . .

---

The story is the garden you are growing, not the weeds still stuck in the mud.

---

In this case, the new story was about an improved lower-dose therapy that could safely and effectively manage disease symptoms and improve patient lives.

Using the same message bucket approach, the story frame looked like this:

**Figure 4.2**
**Story Frame**

| Disease impact on patients | New therapy differences |
|---|---|
| Safety profile and data | Talk to your doctor to see what's right for you |

Once you frame out the story so the central ideas are clear, you can fill in the buckets with carefully chosen details and supporting information that are essential to the story. The examples, vignettes, and analogies will bring the details to life and make the story more emotionally relevant to listeners. Taking a page from my days as a journalist, tight writing is key to maintaining focus and attention. Only in high school when I wrote for a regional newspaper did I get paid by the word, so naturally I tried to make every article as long as I possibly could. However, as a journalist, if the details didn't help the listener better understand the story they were edited out.

Not only will fewer words maximize attention, but time-challenged listeners will probably thank you.

## COACHING NOTES

- Think story. What is the story you want to tell? When I asked you that, you said this is a great opportunity for investment in a strong company with strong financials positioned for growth. In short, the story boils down to six words: Company X is a great investment.

- Remember to tell the story as opposed to going through all the details on the slide. Do they really care about all of the mathematical formulas you used to assess the risk of hospital infections? Or is the real story that infection rates have dropped? As discussed, a few of your slides looked like math problems, which are way too complicated for board members and lay people.

- Keep it simple. Limit the information and think audience. What does management really want to know versus everything you think you need to tell them? They don't need all the code numbers and legislative details. This is what they want to know and you only have 10 minutes to tell the story:

  - This is what customers will be reimbursed for.
  - These are the steps they need to take to get their money back.
  - This is what will change in the future.
  - This is how we can work more effectively with providers, payers, and patients.

- The blessing and the curse is that you know a lot! But not everyone wants to know what you know. For example, they don't need to know the details of the new insurance laws and probably don't care. What they care about is keeping their health insurance and being able to pay for treatment. So it's really critical for you to understand the story your audience came to hear in order to address their concerns.

- You said you wanted these visiting dignitaries to know what's important to your company. Why do they care what's important to you? Isn't the story what's important to them? If they learn about energy issues such as nuclear power and climate change, what can they do with that knowledge? How can they apply it back home? That's what they care about.

- When you talked about the agency's new name, new model, and new direction, you assumed that customers knew how this was different from your old company, but you didn't make clear what will be different for them. What will they receive that you weren't offering before? How will the new model change current practices for your clients? I know you know, but you can't assume they know. In other words, what's in it for them? They want to know why they should choose your agency over all the others.

Stories are not what you care about. Stories are what other people care about.

---

Stories are not what you care about. Stories are what other people care about.

---

Stories aren't about the airplanes that take off and land safely every day. They're about the ones that don't. They're not about the thousands of surgical procedures that save lives. They're about the ones that fail. The next time you have to give a speech, sell an idea, educate an audience, or speak to slides, ask this simple question: What's the story?

## WHAT'S THE STORY FIXES

- **Fire alarm approach.** If the fire alarm went off as soon as I started speaking and my audience could only hear one thing, what would they hear? For example, workers around the country spent the past 10 years collecting census data. The statistics and volumes of information are endlessly complex, but their fire alarm message is short and simple: Fill out the form.

- **Recipe rule.** After you frame your story and fill each bucket with necessary facts and details, list analogies, vignettes, examples, anecdotes, and stories in each bucket you could use to make the facts more relevant and personal to the listener. When you blend facts with emotional content, you provide context and meaning. Record yourself delivering it both ways and when you play it back, notice the differences.

- **Tell and show.** Look for places where you can tell and show. For example, when trying to assure the public that drinking water is safe despite the presence of pharmaceutical compounds (specifically acetaminophen found in painkillers); simply stating the facts does not tell the story. But when you state it visually by saying "if somebody were to drink eight eight-ounce glasses of water every day for over 11,000 years, that's what it would take to reach the infant dose of acetaminophen"—people can picture what you're saying, and it makes your point more effectively.

- **K-i-p-s.** Instead of relying on that well-known phrase "keep it simple, stupid," change your mantra to "keep it people, stupid." Do your message buckets contain stories or examples about real people and real experiences that are unique to you? What story can you tell that only you can tell because you were there? Keep a journal of the stories or experiences you naturally and often unexpectedly share with friends, family, and colleagues so they listen to you because they want to, not because they have to.

**Stories create experiences that motivate and inspire others.**

# CHAPTER 5

# Visual Overload

My belief is that PowerPoint doesn't kill meetings. People kill meetings.

*—Peter Norvig, director of research at Google*

A professor at Yale University said, "If your words or images are not on point, making them dance in color won't make them relevant." Yet every one of us has been treated to visual diarrhea mistaken for communication. You've seen these people. You've probably been in their audiences. They have 495 slides which they *read* to you one by one in a monotone voice with no facial expression and expect you to follow along in a font that even your ophthalmologist couldn't translate.

I read an article in the *Wall Street Journal* that quoted Robert Gaskins, the co-creator of PowerPoint, who said, "A lot of people in business have given up writing the documents. They just write the presentations, which are summaries without the detail, without the backup. A lot of people don't like the intellectual rigor of actually doing the work."

While I agree with Gaskins that people get hung up preparing the presentations, most of the professionals I work with spend painful hours, sometimes weeks, gathering the information needed to deliver a presentation that is typically smothered with too many details. The problem is PowerPoint has become a speaker's script, and too many business speakers have forgotten how to talk.

So let's clear up a few things:

1. Creating a slide show is not communicating.
2. According to the dictionary, communicate means to converse, to impart, or to connect. The only thing connective about most

slide shows is the plug you stick into the socket to make the projector run.

3. Slides are not place cards for you. Slides are for your audience.
4. If you have something to say, you should be able to say it without a slide.
5. You should not follow your slides. The slides should follow you.

Most importantly, no one came to see a slide show. If they can get what they need without you, then you might want to consider e-mailing the deck to them and saving them the time and trouble of sitting through another eyes-glazed-over presentation.

However, given that slides are standard and required in many business settings, as always, think about how you can best tailor your visuals to audience needs so your slides reinforce what you're saying.

To begin, before creating a single slide, think about the purpose of the presentation. Are you trying to sell a product to a customer? Are you hoping to secure funding? Are you educating people about a new technology? As a presenter, your job is to facilitate understanding. If the slides crashed, could you still tell the story? If your answer is no, then you don't truly own your material. That's why it's important to write or outline your talk first and then think about how you can use the slides to reinforce what you're saying.

For example, I worked with a team of executives who were putting together a massive presentation for a marketing and sales meeting. When we first got together, they had a rough slide deck in hand but hadn't really thought through the story they wanted to tell. When I asked them to tell me the single most important takeaway, they began to go through their slides, so I shut the projector off. After some grumbling and complaining, they said they were unveiling a new promotional campaign that contained much simpler messages to make it easier for sales people to market and sell to prospects. That's the takeaway!

Before tackling the slides, we developed our four message buckets, printed them, and laid them out on a table. Like pieces of a puzzle, we then matched the corresponding slides to each message. We were able to clearly see repetitive slides and look for places to replace text with visuals and bullet points, which made the information easier to remember and helped presenters explain instead of read. Then we looked at every slide and applied a three-step approach to explaining each one that I call FRAME. It stands for **F**rame the issue to make it **R**elevant to the **A**udience, and then pack it with **M**eat and **E**xamples:

1. Frame: State the issue, problem, or central idea.
2. Meat: Include picture data, information, results, charts.
3. Examples: Personalize information with specific examples.

Here's how you can apply the model. Instead of reading the slide or discussing it point by point, frame the issue by stating the problem, idea, or main point first so the audience understands why they should care. To do this, think of each slide as a picture frame. When you walk into a gallery and first look at a painting, you only see the big picture or one main idea. It isn't until you move in closer that you really observe the details. Slides are similar. Each slide should convey a high-level idea or big picture viewpoint that will be supported by more detailed proof points that you can back up with examples, charts, and relevant data.

Here is one slide example from the sales and marketing meeting.

|  |  |
|---|---|
| Frame: | As you can see from these pictures, this is a devastating disease that robs people of their quality of life such as walking, holding grandchildren; things so many of us take for granted. |
| Meat: | In the past 10 years, medication X has helped more than a half million people worldwide with sales capturing more than 20 percent of the marketplace. Not only does it continue to have a superior safety profile, but we have new safety data that are even more impressive and can help patients maintain treatment for longer periods of time. |
| Example: | Specifically, here's what the data showed: [more detailed data illustrated in graphs and charts that build on the slide and are further explained by the speaker]. |

In the next example, the presenter wanted investors to understand why his company was such a great buy. One of his slides showed patients in varying disease states that could now be helped by a new product his company developed. However, he made an assumption that potential investors were better versed than they actually were. His slide contained a lot of text in visually unappealing small font that was scanned to the slide from a medical journal and this is how he first explained it. "The C1 esterase inhibitor that was approved is indicated for the routine prophylaxis against angioedema attacks in adolescent and adult patients with hereditary angioedema have been extremely effective."

Even if the words are understood by the audience, they do not provide context. It would be far more effective to show pictures of patients or even a simple diagram illustrating how the missing protein is put back into the body, and it might then be explained like this:

Frame: Until last month, patients had two options. They could not manage their disease or they could take steroids. Neither was a great option. Today, there is a new option that replaces the missing protein these people lack.

Meat: Here's how it works. [In this case, the presenter created little video figures and showed them flowing through the bloodstream.]

Personalize: Provide specific examples.

Before you switch to the next slide, briefly summarize or use a transition phrase such as "given these facts, we plan to begin a new study in 2014" to take you to the next slide or next portion of the presentation. That is more effective than saying "the next slide shows . . ." or "Now, I want to talk to you about . . ." For example:

**Slide summary.** A single mutation in one gene is responsible for the problem.

**Transition.** This is very important in our understanding of this disease.

**New slide.** Which allowed us to map all of the mutations as illustrated in this chart.

While every slide doesn't have to stand alone, it must have a reason for being there such as helping a listener visualize a process. If there is too much text, audiences will try to read the slide. If they're reading, they're not listening. In a sense, you're asking them to make a choice between you and the slide. Unfortunately, the slide always wins.

Even though so many business presenters regretfully agree their slides are not viewer friendly, they continually create slides bleeding text with the excuse "this is the way we have to do it here." No, you don't. Text is boring. As a communicator, your job is to facilitate learning. We don't think in text. We think in pictures. If your friend invites you to play golf, do you visualize the letters *g-o-l-f*? Certainly not! You picture swinging that club. So if your slide lists new regulations to reduce emissions, why wouldn't you include pictures of cars or pollution to illustrate the point?

If you have a lot of necessary technical information on a single slide, then consider revealing or building the information, which allows you to present it in chunks so you focus attention where you want it. Additionally, when there are multiple images or bar graphs on a screen, you want to control where people look. For example: "As you can see the left half of the brain is white, which indicates healthy tissue. But the right side is smaller and contains deposits that are not healthy. That is what this disease looks like."

> PowerPoint has become a speaker's script, and speakers have forgotten how to talk.

Advice offered by experts such as marketing guru Seth Godin recommend never putting more than six words on a slide and to avoid handing out hard copies of the slides. While I wish everyone would follow his advice, unfortunately changing the "this is how it's done" corporate culture is not likely to happen by the time this book is published. It's also important to note that many industries like the pharmaceutical and chemical industries require significant amounts of complex data to be presented, and at many companies presenters are required to use slides prepared and approved by other colleagues. While this is certainly a drawback, it is also reality, so the key is to figure out how to own the information you're presenting and help your audience understand what you're saying.

I recently sat in on a presentation where a medical director for a specialty products company did that very well. He had to deliver a canned slide presentation outlining a shortage of obstetricians and gynecologists in Massachusetts. The numbers on the slides were important, but the message was not compelling until he drove it home with a story about a woman in labor who drove 35 miles by herself in a blizzard to deliver her baby at the hospital. It's doubtful his audience will remember the numbers, but they will most certainly recall that story.

However, there is one important point Godin makes that no one should argue with. He says, "If you believe in your idea, sell it. Make your point as hard as you can and get what you came for. Your audience will thank you for it, because deep down, we all want to be sold."

> Slides won't sell your ideas and won't make or break the deal. Only you can do that.

The truth is, slides won't sell your ideas and won't make or break the deal. Only you can do that. Regardless of how exciting data may be, if you don't convey energy and excitement, you risk putting your audience to sleep. When presenting complex information, it is important not to assume that listeners will completely grasp what you have studied for weeks, months, or even years, which is why presenting too much detail is confusing to people. It is your job to help listeners make sense of the information on the slides.

## COACHING NOTES

- Think of your slide as a Broadway production. Sometimes a single stage will contain lots of little stages, which are spotlighted according to what the director wants you to watch. It is up to you to focus your audience's attention where you want it.

- If you are worried that you won't remember what you wanted to say, prepare index cards for each slide that list two or three key points. This will be more helpful than writing sentences in the note page or trying to memorize what you want to say.

- Think of every presentation as a huge opportunity to inform, persuade, or sell your point of view. If the slides have been designed for you, you should still look for ways to personalize the information and create memorable moments for your listener. Below are two examples. Example A is not very engaging. Example B offers perspective and showcases the speaker's expertise.

  Example A.  These are new IDSA/SHEA treatment guidelines, and I will go through them one by one.

  Example B.  To understand the significance of the new guidelines, it's important to understand how they differ from the old ones and what this ultimately means to the patient. As a researcher on this project, I can personally tell you that we observed . . .

- Highlight key messages that carry through your entire slide set, and repeat them in each message bucket. In your talk, the words *sustainable*, *repeatable*, and *differentiation* were key, so repeat them where you can. They don't have to be on a slide for you to say them and reinforce your message.

- When you show the chart representing the reasons so many people are moving into lifestyle communities, it is not necessary to go through all 12 reasons and assigned percentages. You might explain it by saying "We surveyed over 3,000 people to get a clearer picture of why they move into our communities. This chart represents their reasons, with lifestyle being number one followed by location and access to things like shopping, restaurants, and theater. As you'll notice, due to the age of the people surveyed, schools and employment ranked at the bottom."

- Maintain a consistent format. If you capitalize the headline on one slide, then capitalize it on all the slides. The same holds true for font type and layout. If you are picking and choosing slides from multiple presentations, keep the format the same so your slides are as consistent as your message.

- Your audience has a limited attention span and will not remember everything on those slides, so the fewer slides the better. However, if you must include everything, I'd rather see you put it on two slides so it's simple and easier to follow. Remember, the slides are not your script. Slides are for the audience. Ideally, you should have two sets of slides, one for your verbal presentation and another with details for handouts.

- Even though you deal in complicated concepts such as portfolio management, it was very confusing because you were still talking about information on one slide when you had moved on to the next. Make sure what you are saying matches the slide. If you forget what's coming up, don't panic. Simply pause while you click to the next slide.

Earlier in this chapter I asked you if you could still deliver your presentation if your slides crashed. That actually happened to me while presenting at a technology conference in Disneyworld Florida when the power went out. What made it worse was that the entire presentation was a series of photographs that brought my story to life. I'm not advising you to do what I did, but it's certainly an option. I asked two men to help me up onto a chair and hold it steady so I could keep my balance when I held my computer, which still had battery power high above my head so people could see the pictures as I finished my talk. I received a lot of unintentional laughs and that audience probably remembers my antics as opposed to my message. My message to you: You're the show, not the slide.

## VISUAL OVERLOAD FIXES

- **Talk, don't read.** Reading is for the eye. Listening is for the ear. It's important to create slides that speak in phrases, not sentences, so you can talk without reading. Eliminate words such as, *if, the, in, on,* and *of* to help you create bullets instead of sentences.

- **You lead.** Instead of saying "this slide says" or "as this slide shows you," explain the information to the audience as if you were telling them a story or having a focused conversation with a colleague. Let the slide follow you instead of you following the slide.

- **Think visual to be visual.** If you want to show people a balance sheet, consider giving them a handout with more details, but be very clear about what you are calling their attention to on the slide. You might consider highlighting information you want to draw them to.

- **Back of the room.** Create slides with people in the back of the room in mind so they can see clearly. Replace study data or financials with colorful charts, graphs, comparative tables, and pictures that highlight the facts, evoke emotion, and make the information more understandable. Use color, big fonts, bullet points instead of sentences, and contrast to provide depth.

- **Hit them over the head.** Your first few words determine whether your audience tunes in or out. So why do people need a slide to tell the audience what they are going to talk about? When you open your mouth, hit them over the head with a story or example that engages and grabs attention so they understand why they should care? Ask what's in it for them?

- **Pause and switch.** It's important to give people a chance to digest what you are saying and one way to do that is to pause as you finish one slide and switch to another. This will also help you talk to the slide only while it is on the screen.

- **The W and B keys.** If you want to turn your audience's attention away from the slide and back to you, hit *B* for black. This will black out the screen. If you press *B* again, your slide will pop back up. If you hit *W* for white, the slide will also disappear, but the background will be white. Hit the key again and your slide returns.

- **Chunk it out.** Write down the three or four key messages you want to deliver. Like a game of cards, print your slides and place each one under the appropriate message. This will help you organize your slides, eliminate slides, examine presentation flow, and smoothly transition from one segment to the next.

To avoid visual diarrhea, the following grade school PowerPoint checklist can be found at www.classroomhelp.com/lessons/cclark/Trekkers/ppchecklist.htm.

## VISUAL OVERLOAD CHECKLIST

### Text

easy to read
bold-faced type
readable font
appropriate size
clear color and style
four or fewer brief sentences or bullets on each slide
spell check
proper punctuation
no "hanging words" (i.e., a centered line with one word on the next line)
consistent text transitions throughout the show

### Graphics

appropriate to the slide
clear, not blurry
proportionally sized (do not look stretched out)
enhance the text on the slide
limited use of clip art, relied on photographs throughout

### Transitions and Background Color

background enhances each slide
consistency to each background (same color range)
limited to a few select transitions for all slides
transitions occur quickly
titles appear first before text and graphics

**In the absence of information, slides should not fill the gap.**

# CHAPTER 6

# Understand Your Audience

*My play was a complete success. The audience was a failure.*
—*Ashleigh Brilliant, English author*

Every book ever written on the subject of speaking and presenting will—or should—advise you to know your audience before you speak. But I'd like to approach this a bit differently.

Let's say you've written a book on global warming. Your message is the same regardless of your audience. Simply put: global warming has profound effects on our environment and we must do something about it. But that doesn't mean you should say it the same way every time you speak.

For example, when former presidential candidate Al Gore appeared on *Oprah* to talk about his documentary *An Inconvenient Truth*, which is about the consequences of global warming, he had the opportunity to connect with the audience on a one-to-one level. After all, Oprah's viewers relate to emotional topics, human suffering, heroes, and causes you want to believe in. Yet, instead of showing pictures of melting glaciers or cuddly polar bears that might one day face extinction, Gore talked about infrared radiation while he flipped through his slides at warp speed. (Perhaps he had not read the previous chapter.) It reminded me of former Exxon chair Lawrence Rawl's mistake when the *Exxon Valdez* ran aground and spilled 11 million gallons of crude oil into Prince William Sound. Instead of taking the first jet to Alaska and shaping public perception—perhaps allowing photojournalists to capture his grave concern as he observed oil-slicked wildlife—like Gore, Rawl did not fully understand his audience and what they cared about.

Dale Carnegie, author of one of the greatest communication books ever written titled *How To Win Friends and Influence People*, said, "The royal road to a man's heart is to talk to him about the things he treasures most."

To fully understand your listeners, you need to become them. That means sit in their seats to think like them. To do that, it is essential to ask the following two questions:

1. What does this mean to them?
2. Why should they care?

If you read a story in the morning paper about oil-slicked geese, would you care about the oil company's problem? Of course not. You care about the animals and the environment. If you are an investor in a company and the stock drops, would your first concern be for the CEO who will take a bonus hit? The answer is obvious. You would care about your own financial loss. People care about what affects them. They care about their parents, children, friends, and loved ones. While it's important to have a message, it's more important to have a message that means something to your listener. That means appreciating the audience's needs so you can address their concerns. Here are a few examples:

> While it's important to have a message, it's more important to have a message that means something to your listener.

Company challenge:   An international candy company with long-time ties to the local community makes a business decision to outsource some of its manufacturing operations to China. This comes at a time when China is under scrutiny for export safety with reports of Chinese-made toys and food being linked to contaminants. The story hit the national wires and quickly died. Weeks later, as Christmas approaches, the company president wants to revisit the issue and invite reporters to talk with him again. The president thinks it's an opportunity to discuss how important it is for the company to outsource in order to continue providing products at an affordable cost. We advise against it.

Audience concern:    While well intended, the president does not fully understand his audience—in this case, readers. Readers don't care about his costs; they are concerned with losing jobs, safety issues, and the potential effects of cheap production. Furthermore, since toys and food are a big deal during the holidays, the story has the potential to generate even more attention.

Company challenge:    A company that owns and operates power generation plants is under intense criticism for polluting the environment. The issues it faces are very complex and will not be remedied quickly. Spokespeople frequently address community meetings and talk about generation issues, legal hassles, regulations, and pending legislation. They are often unintentionally defensive, which angers residents, and meetings repeatedly erupt into shouting matches between company officials and residents.

Audience concern:    Though listeners understand words such as "clean coal technology" and "repowering initiative," they may not fully comprehend what that means or how it affects them. They are more concerned with potential rate hikes, health and safety issues, and the environment. They are frustrated that company spokespeople don't appear to address their concerns. For example, at one meeting, a spokesperson commented, "Rate caps come off in the spring." But he failed to explain what that means and how it may save or cost customers money in the future.

Company challenge:    A manufacturing plant located in a remote and economically disadvantaged area of New York State is going to shut down. It is one of the largest employers in the region. Because the closure will extend over several years and

|                      | some manufacturing will be transferred out of state, there is ample time for negative reaction, rumors, and strained relationships with management, as worried employees continue to ask difficult questions and fear for their futures. |
| -------------------- | --------------------------------- |
| Audience concern:    | The plant manager who must address employees is backed by a company that is providing generous support, training, and continued benefits during the transition. But it was the plant manager's ability to understand his audience because he was one of them that made all the difference. Instead of simply delivering facts from a management perspective, he was not afraid to show emotion, echo employee and community fears, and speak from the heart. Here is an excerpt from his remarks: |

Good morning. As you know, for the last few months, there have been a lot of rumors, speculation—it has been a very difficult time for all of us . . . very stressful time . . . a lot of anxiety. Many events have occurred that raised the level of uncertainty about our future. I've been meeting with many of you to keep you informed about these events and the potential on all of us. I told you I would make every effort to get answers about our future—even if they are answers we don't want to hear—and I have those answers today. We have taken a long, hard, and very painful look at our operations. And, after a very extensive assessment of our manufacturing network, we have made the decision to phase out all activities. . . . I know this is a huge disappointment for everyone, and this is not what any of us wanted, including me.

This manager was as devastated as his employees and was not afraid to let it show. By putting himself in their shoes, he came across as a strong, compassionate leader who truly understood his audience and put their concerns first.

Here is another example. The director of a continuing medical education (CME) program who we'll call Susie was seeking $43 million in program funding and had to present her case in front of decision makers. I asked her what the story was, and she said even though her department's funding had been cut by 87 percent since 2005, they've continued to be successful and wanted to show management there is a science and art behind determining funding amounts and that the formula is valuable when it's done right. That's not the story or certainly not the story this audience needed to hear. If her department has been successful without the funding they need, why would management want to cough up the money?

So we brainstormed through a series of questions. As a former journalist, I am a firm believer that asking good questions will quickly lead you to important information necessary to better communicate with customers, colleagues, and other important audiences. These questions were aimed at helping Susie better address her audience to position her message.

> Question:   Who are you talking to?
> Susie:      The global management team.
> Question:   How many will be present?
> Susie:      About 15.
> Question:   Do all 15 people understand what medical education is?
> Susie:      They probably have different viewpoints.

Aha! Now we're getting somewhere. Because Susie knew the people she was talking to, she thought she understood her audience. However, she didn't fully consider that because the group consisted of different department heads of varying ages and tenure at the company, they had completely different perceptions of CME. Some thought it was a way for drug representatives to get into doctors' offices. Others considered it an important way to bring doctors up to date on the latest research. And a few didn't fully understand the purpose and probably didn't care. So it was up to Susie to lead this group to the results she was after. Next set of questions:

> Question:   What does management want to know?
> Susie:      Why CME is a good choice and how we'll spend the
>             money.
> Me:         What they really want to know what they'll get in re-
>             turn if they give you the money.
> Question:   What is your goal?

Susie:   To help them understand diffusion of innovation.

Me:   Do they truly care about the diffusion of innovation or understand what that means? They likely care about how innovation will increase performance and advance their business.

After brainstorming, it became clear that this audience really wanted to know how a greater investment in CME would drive performance and change. But until Susie cleared the field so everyone in the room had the same understanding of CME, she couldn't plant new seeds. When she reframed the story to tie her goals to what her audience cares about, she was in a much better position to get funding, which ultimately she did. Here is a paraphrased version of her opening remarks:

Good morning. I'm here to talk to you about the tremendous benefits of continuing medical education, but before I tell you what it is, I want to explain what it's not. The CME of today is not your grandfather's CME. It's not about gaining access to hospitals or a way to place your promotional materials. Today's CME is informal and lifelong training physicians receive throughout their careers to stay on top of the latest information in order to make decisions in the best interest of patients. Not only do doctors say they rely on CME, but in this survey released just last week doctors say next to articles in peer journals, these programs drive their decisions.

## COACHING NOTES

- It's important to remember that it's always about them, not about you. So when you said you were grateful to have extraordinary leaders, you could have mentioned traits or what these leaders did that made them extraordinary to help your audience learn from them so they might apply these things in their own circumstances.

- Look for ways to involve your audience on every level. How can you appeal to their senses? You understand the value of creating a modern-day multimillion-dollar database that can track sales, but what will a new database do for this specific group of listeners? Save time? Allow instant access to customers? Remember, think like them, not like you. What's in it for them?

- Audiences are not a one size fits all. Your theme of growth and expansion applies across the board, but that doesn't mean you give the same talk to every group. When you talk with employees, they care about job security, expectations, performance, and their role moving forward in these difficult times. You need to address that. Management has different concerns such as strategy, growth, trends, reputation, brand identity, sales, and competition, which you must address when speaking to them.

Audiences are a bit like football teams. The more you know about the opposition, the more likely you can score. When speaking, the more you know about your listeners, the easier it will be to address their concerns and achieve your goals.

To think like your audience, imagine you are away at college and call home to talk to your parents. What stories would you tell them? What would they want to know? What would you leave out that you don't want them to know? Now, picture yourself talking to a friend. What would you tell him? How might that conversation differ than the one you had with your parents? To better understand your audience, check off the following questions:

Who am I talking to?

What is the story I want to tell?

What do they care about?

If I sat in their seats, what would I care about?

What do I want people to take away from this presentation?

What should people think, do, know, or feel when I'm done speaking?

How does my message impact or affect them?

What are their biggest challenges or obstacles?

What real-life examples will help them better understand?

A senior strategist at a power management company was preparing to address a group of visiting French executives. I asked him three questions, and these were his answers.

Question: What is your goal?

Answer: To help them understand the issues that are important to *our* company.

Question: Why do they care what's important to your company?

Answer: Because *we* are the largest manager in the United States.

Question:   What do you want them to feel?

Answer:   An interest in *our* energy issues.

If you look closely at these answers, each one is about the company, not about the visitors. When we discussed why they would care about these answers, the responses were about the audience.

Question:   What is your goal?

Answer:   To help *them* understand how we are addressing critical issues that are also important to them so they can learn and perhaps apply the same strategies.

Question:   Why do they care what's important to *your* company?

Answer:   Because we are the largest manager in the United States, and we have extensive experience in areas they don't, which will be very valuable to *them*.

Question:   What do you want them to feel?

Answer:   Confidence that we would be an excellent example and potential partner for *them*.

## UNDERSTAND YOUR AUDIENCE FIXES

**Take a pulse check.** Just because you know the people you are speaking to doesn't mean you know what they're thinking. Prior to an important talk, e-mail a few key questions to a limited number of people to get their perspective.

Questions may include:

- If you could walk out with one key piece of information, what would that be?
- What are your greatest frustrations and challenges?
- What would make this meeting successful for you?
- What do you need that you're not getting?
- What issues or objectives are not being met?
- What keeps you up at night?
- What do you want to believe after this meeting that you don't believe now?

- If you had the power to do things differently, what would you do?
- How can we help you in a way we are not helping you now?

**Keep interest.** Involve your audience on as many levels as possible by including:

- Acronyms
- Analogies
- Anecdotes
- Case studies
- Comparisons and contrasts
- Examples
- Personal experiences
- Powerful numbers
- Problems versus consequences
- Questions
- Stories
- Then versus now
- Visual images

**Know your roadblocks and anticipate the potholes.** When you take time to think about who may object or challenge you, you can better prepare in advance to speak directly to their concerns.

No matter how sophisticated audiences may seem, they are people first.

Much like a television commercial that focuses on consumers, business communicators should remember that no matter how sophisticated audiences seem, they are people first. While it's important to speak to the business at hand, it's equally important to talk to mothers, fathers, sisters, brothers, sons, daughters, aunts, and uncles that are in each and every audience.

**It's not about you. It's about them.**

# CHAPTER 7
# Talk to Your Grandmother
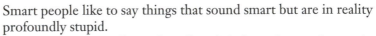

> Smart people like to say things that sound smart but are in reality
> profoundly stupid.
> —*James Carville, political consultant and strategist*

I miss my grandmother. I used to sit in her kitchen and talk to her while she cooked. From the time I was a little girl until I became a bigger one, she would ask me simple questions about school, friends, boyfriends, work, or whatever else was happening in my life at that moment. I never had to think about what words to use that might sound important, because my grandmother thought everything I said was important. I didn't try to impress her. She was impressed with anything I did. She just liked me for me.

Wouldn't it be great if every time we spoke at a meeting or met with superiors, we could talk like we talked to our grandmothers or mothers or best friends? Wouldn't it be terrific if we just spoke without analyzing and agonizing over our choice of words and instead just said what we had to say? When did we forget how to do that?

I am always amazed at people who are so full of personality when you just chat with them, but turn into someone you barely know and can hardly understand when they have to speak in more formal or important settings. This can be clearly illustrated through a request for help from a scientific group that arrived in my e-mail:

As a group we're not "punchy" or "crisp" enough in our spontaneous presentations or in situations where we're put on the spot. Can you provide coaching sessions to help us project the knowledge and grasp of the topic that we know we have but struggle at times to explain?

This particular group was used to talking to other physicians and scientists. They frequently used words like "protein therapeutics." When asked about progress in the area of Alzheimer's research, one of the researchers said that they were trying to "reduce the burden of amyloid plaques in the brain." Another explained that the "primary objective is to assess the compound's effect at the level of the target." Are you with me? I didn't think so. Even if you're talking to peers who do understand, it's still up to you to make sense of the information and help people understand what it means to them. Understanding your audience is critical, as discussed in the previous chapter. In this case, if the researcher was talking to his mother or grandmother, he probably would have explained it differently, perhaps like this:

We know that certain areas of the brains of Alzheimer's patients are filled with small, round deposits called plaques. By better understanding the effect on the brain, we hope to develop treatments that can improve mental functions by clearing or preventing plaques in people with Alzheimer's disease.

Consider another scenario. A pharmaceutical company has an opportunity to tell a *New York Times* reporter about a promising medication. Instead of helping the reporter understand the impact of the disease on families and patients and then sharing impressive results of a drug trial, the spokesperson bores the reporter with endless diagrams and medical flow charts. The story was never written. If the executive had stepped away from just the facts and talked as if he were explaining the story to his grandmother, he could have helped the reporter better understand the problem to appreciate the solution.

One of my favorite books written on the subject is called *Why Business People Speak Like Idiots* by Brian Fugere, Chelsea Hardaway, and Jon Warshawsky. It gives countless examples of business people using 50-cent words to make 5-cent points because they think using plain language makes them look less intelligent. The authors did a study that concluded just the opposite and summarized, "Your audiences, the kind of people who fuel up at Starbucks every day, don't like bull."

In our own sessions, we continually struggle with this dilemma. Here are some examples of biz-speak jargon contrasted with what Grandma might understand:

Jargon:    The elucidation of the entire human genome has made possible our current effort to develop a haplotype map of the human genome. The haplotype map, or HapMap, will be a tool that will allow researchers to find genes and genetic variations that affect health and disease.

Grandma:    The HapMap project promises to predict who is more likely to suffer from common ailments such as diabetes, arthritis, heart disease, and some cancers. By finding genes and genetic variations in individuals, eventually we will develop new therapies that can get to the root causes of these illnesses.

Jargon:    In June, an Israeli start-up company unveiled a 5.25-inch storage disk with a holographic coating that can hold a terabyte of data.

Grandma:    The entire Library of Congress is about 20 terabytes. You could put it all on 20 disks that could fit in a shoebox.

Jargon:    Act 1 includes 341 b states that no later than 60 days before each March 1, school districts shall notify, by first class mail, the owner of each parcel of residential property within the district of the existence of the school's district's homestead and farmstead exclusion program the need to file an application in accordance with 53 PA C.S. 8584 a in order to qualify for the program and the application deadline.

Grandma:    Homeowners could see a real estate tax reduction next year—either from slot money or from the mandatory referendum on tax shifting from real estate to earned income tax. This means that, for the first time, it is essential for homeowners to file a homestead exclusion application form by December 31.

Jargon:    Torisel is an enzyme inhibitor, a protein that regulates cell production, cell growth, and cell survival in patients with kidney cancer.

Grandma:    Torisel works by fooling cancer cells into thinking they're starving and then blocks their ability to sense they have enough nutrients to grow so they stop dividing.

> Ask yourself, is anyone really listening?

Now, I know what some of you are thinking; this won't work in your world because your colleagues are not Grandma and they expect more from you. But ask yourself, is anyone really listening? Let's take a look at impressive words that can be used in almost any business setting like integrated, functional, or responsive. In fact, these words are used so often that comedian Rodney Marks created the jargon generator, which allows you to apply three words (underlined below) on a chart to any situation to come up with business speak. For example:

- This system is *functional*, *transitional*, and has *flexibility*.
- By offering a *systemized* program with *organizational capability*.
- This initiative will provide *integrated logistical analysis*.

If you honestly believe you must establish your expertise by presenting yourself as someone who possesses great ability to verbalize complex ideas by talking in technical jargon and lingo, you can find several jargon generators online. Otherwise, take a page from William Shakespeare, who advised "speak comfortable words."

> Speak comfortable words.

## COACHING NOTES

- Don't assume that just because your audience is packed with managers and peers, you can talk technical jargon and lingo. You live and breathe your work. Your colleagues, though well versed, don't necessarily understand the complicated details you are laying out. Remember to explain technical facts in nontechnical terms, not ramble or lecture, and, whenever possible, use analogies, short phrases, and visual aids to increase understanding and retention.
- Look for ways to humanize the technology. Instead of focusing on multichannel sales automation, think about what this application means to your audience. How will it make their lives easier? Where is the need? What are the consequences of not adapting or having the new technology?

- You said safe commerce is more than a technology issue and open standards are critical to making commerce more secure. These are words. Think concept. If you explain that 21,000 cargo containers arrive in U.S. seaports each day and threaten the safety of the homeland, you can explain how your company can help protect the nation through tightening reporting requirements, entering data earlier, and extending data to customers, suppliers, and shippers.

- You have a great personality—you are charming and funny. Let that come through. It makes people like you, it makes them comfortable, and it puts you at ease as well. So many of us go into presentation mode when we stand up and talk—it's as if we forgot to bring our personality along.

- Instead of "change the treatment paradigm," keep it more conversational such as "change the way patients with this deadly disease are treated." It's much more impactful. Additionally, saying this is a disease caused by a deficiency of a certain enzyme is important, but when you added, "This is a scary disease because people don't know how fast it can hit and kill them. There are patients walking around every day wondering 'is today my day?'"—Wow! You had everyone's complete attention.

- Your ability to strike a balance between delivering facts and humanizing the information makes your message much easier to understand. For example, when discussing cancer, as you explained the risk was low, you balanced that with "but, even one is too many" or when discussing dementia, the balance was "concerning." As president of Fox News Roger Ailes appropriately titled his book, *You Are the Message*, and you were.

Just because someone understands the meaning of a word doesn't mean they understand what you're saying. If you tell someone you are in the communications business, do they really understand what you do? Do you sell telephones? Do you fix computers? Are you a journalist? Are you a printer? If you never knew your grandmother, then I give you permission to learn from mine.

## TALK TO YOUR GRANDMOTHER FIXES

- Use simple language that everyone in the room can understand.
- Eliminate slang and jargon. If necessary, give a brief explanation.

- Educate, don't pontificate.
- Be conversational. Don't lecture.
- Pay attention to people's reactions when you speak. If eyebrows are furrowed or someone appears skeptical, there is a good chance they don't get it.
- Look for opportunities to recap, paraphrase, and ask questions to make sure the other person understands what you are saying. Use phrases such as "So what you're saying is . . ." or "Let me make sure I understand . . ."
- Your listeners do not need to be the expert. That's why they have you. Tell them what they need to know to make decisions or to see things from your point of view.
- Practice with a friend. Ask him to help you eliminate buzzwords and gobbledygook.
- Adjust your words to reflect the listeners' concerns if you want to be heard and understood.
- Pretend your listener is your neighbor or someone you run into in the supermarket. She is educated and successful but not expert in your business. If she asked you about your work or a specific project, how would you explain it to her?
- If you are worried that people might not take you seriously or believe you to be credible, realize that the opposite is true. Your job is to help people make sense of information so it means something to them.

**There is a difference between dumbing it down and keeping it simple.**

# CHAPTER 8

# So What?

*I know you believe you understand what you think I said but I am not sure you realize that what you heard is not what I meant.*
—*Richard Nixon, former U.S. president*

Many believe the 2008 presidential election was the most important the world will know for a very long time because the stakes were so high. I, for one, will always remember being captivated by the analysts and pundits tripping all over each other as they scrutinized policy and tried to predict behavior of would-be voters. But the one lesson to be learned is not from policy, procedures, or where candidates stand on the issues. The lesson is simple. Listeners, like voters, want to be inspired and motivated. Even if people don't completely agree with what you say, if you move them, they will listen and perhaps even follow.

I recall a speech I gave at the International Association of Business Communicators conference in Los Angeles, California. It was held at the Century Plaza, a favorite of the late President Ronald Reagan, who coincidentally was being buried on that very day. I had my speech all planned out until I walked into the room and realized there was a great opportunity to share simple lessons taught by the 40th president of the United States. This was an audience of communicators. Reagan, whether you liked him or not, was dubbed "the great communicator." He had the unique ability to answer the "so what?" question. Instead of talking about the details of health care, he talked about why health care was important to people. He clearly understood how to use language to his benefit so what he said appeared to benefit others. Like any great communicator, Reagan spoke directly to his audience and rose above the fray, which made him appear very presidential. When once asked, "how can an actor be president?" he quipped, "How can you be president and not be an actor?"

I am not suggesting you need to take acting lessons or dish out one-liners to impress people when you speak, but I am suggesting it is important to answer the "so what?" if you want people to pay attention. If your customers or potential customers can't figure out who you are and how you can help them, that's a problem.

> If your customers can't figure out who you are and how you can help them, that's a problem.

A financial services company was getting ready to launch a new service that it hoped would generate millions in profits. To do this, they needed investors with big wallets, so we were called in to help them prepare for "the most important presentation in the company's history" to be delivered by the CEO, CFO, chief risk officer, director of marketing, and the company's analytics expert, who described himself as "responsible for development of risk strategies and analytical market segmentation."

Let me be painfully honest. I understand what those individual words mean, but I didn't really understand what he did for people, and if it wasn't clear to me, there's a good chance someone else wouldn't get it either. True, I'm one of those left-brain creative people as opposed to many of my right-brain technical-oriented associates, but you don't have to be a fiscal whiz to know the difference between exciting and who cares?

The mock presentation began with the CEO standing in front of a slide talking about the expertise of everyone on his team. This lasted approximately four long, painful minutes. An energetic and personable man during normal conversation, he flatly and monotonously said he's confident that his company will succeed because it has a lot of experience "recognizing securitization technology, which could change the landscape for nontraditional banks," to which I responded "so what?"

While he insisted the audiences he addresses would understand what he was talking about, I urged him to think about the so what instead of getting stuck in the actual words. So what problem is the company solving? So what makes this different from other banking solutions? So what will this do to penetrate the market, and how quickly will investors make money? That's what potential shareholders want to know. In much simpler terms, this is a company founded by veteran bankers who fully understand the frustrations of millions of small business owners tired of sitting in traffic, standing in bank lines, and waiting for needed loans. Once it answers the so what by stating the problem in relevant terms, it is better positioned to influence listeners by explaining how it will solve the banking problems of small businesses and how investors will profit.

In our performance sessions, we often utilize a three-step brainstorming approach dubbed H-A-P. It's short for happy, which is the end result everyone is after.

1. **H**eadline
2. **A**udience
3. **P**rove it

## STEP ONE

Step one is a bit of a commercial. By thinking through headlines the company would love to see in the morning paper, participants can brainstorm a broad range of so what statements that set them apart from competitors and promote their services to their target audience. Often, groups first come up with self-promotional headlines such as:

- We have experience in this space.
- Our people are great.
- We will act responsibly.

As a former reporter, I interviewed scores of people who did exactly the same thing. Instead of addressing how their experiences solve problems or what their people can provide that others can't, they wanted us to promote them. The reporter, just like a customer or audience, expects you to say your product is great, but that doesn't mean she believes you, which is why there is a little voice inside her head that keeps saying "so what?" or "prove it."

Brainstorming headlines you'd love to see in print about your product or service is a great way to address the so what for the listener. For example, if your headline says "Company X invested $150,000 in technology upgrades last year," that may be important to the company, but how did those technology upgrades solve problems? If you said "Technology investment reduces debt and spurs innovation, yielding new customers," you've answered the so what.

The financial services company discussed above provides an example of how this works. Every headline we brainstormed had to address the so what?

**Headline:** Different growth model that focuses on customer need

**Headline:** Wide open opportunity in small business banking that can save customers time and money

**Headline:** Experienced team—adapts to current challenging market conditions

**Headline:** Running a familiar play book in a more focused way to simplify the process

**Headline:** Using proven responsible methods to make money

**Headline:** Marketing and credit risk is conservative but effective

**Headline:** Current competitors have too many audiences versus our focused approach

**Headline:** Can help clients find the silver lining in the current credit situation

Once the headlines were exhausted, we combined the best of them to put together an overarching statement that read:

This is a terrific opportunity to invest in a company that is uniquely positioned to serve the banking needs of small business in a very challenging market.

While this may be what the company wanted to put out there, it isn't compelling or convincing by itself. It must be put into context with supporting evidence, facts, and examples so the company can address the so what for investors.

Enter step two which challenges the group to think through specific questions an audience of investors would likely ask. Addressing these concerns will help them back up key statements with proof.

## STEP TWO

**Audience:** How will you get customers to switch to you?

**Audience:** What is your plan for growth beyond launch?

**Audience:** These numbers seem high? Are your sales predictions unrealistic?

**Audience:** Realistically, how much market share can you achieve?

**Audience:** How can you stop others, especially bigger companies, from copying and taking away business?

**Audience:** Do you have any customers that have signed on?

**Audience:** How will you market and promote this?

**Audience:** What happens if you fail?

**Audience:** What is your biggest challenge or fear?

**Audience:** How important is this to the future success of this company?

**Audience:** How much cash do you have on hand?

**Audience:** What are your current investment plans, and what is the typical size of your investment?

Now they are ready to move onto step three which proves why this is a terrific opportunity to invest in the company and why they are uniquely positioned to serve customer needs in a challenging market.


## STEP THREE

**Prove it:** Recent data show that 25 to 30 million small businesses are being neglected, which means there is a huge untapped market.

**Prove it:** We focus exclusively on small businesses so we understand their very specific needs and how they want to do banking moving forward, and we are in a unique position to lead this initiative. The initiative includes . . .

**Prove it:** Extensive customer surveys show they are disenfranchised with poor service, high fees, mergers, and outsourcing. We provide faster access to money, no per-item transaction fees, and an entirely different growth model allowing customers to manage cash flow.

In our sessions, we also come up with real-life examples that have solved problems and can put real people into our proof points. For example, in this financial services brainstorming session, one of the executives told a story about a customer who was declined a loan after

45 years with the same local bank. He explained how his company was able to quickly and easily secure the loan, which allowed the client to grow his business.

Instead of sounding promotional or conceited, prove it examples answer the so what and offer important audiences concrete reasons to believe in what you're saying so they remain (H-A-P) happy.

One of the biggest mistakes we observe in these situations is the following misperceptions:

1. If I know it, everyone must know it.
2. If I understand it, everyone must understand it.

Just because your audience is packed with financial types doesn't mean they understand your business or know what you know. It is your job to answer the so what and tell them what you want them to know. If you assume everyone understands the problem and they don't, you've lost a huge opportunity to influence them.

> If you assume everyone understands the problem and they don't, you've lost a huge opportunity to influence them.

## COACHING NOTES

- Think about the so what? For example, when I asked you what this is about, you explained the old campaign wasn't working so you made a 180-degree shift to develop a clear, crisp campaign that provides greater control and more options for the customer. Say that! That answers the so what for your audience.

- Instead of just stating what you are doing, think about how you can tie what you are saying to benefits and how change means outcome—that is, delivery, innovation, collaboration. When you provide specifics, you help people understand what is different between how it is now and how it will be in the future.

- You consistently talked about outcomes and the importance of being a company that is not just about products, but what does that mean? It's important for you to answer the so what; when you say it goes beyond products and is focused on treatment regimens, that's a good opportunity to give specific examples, such as: "Bringing that range of products to other therapeutic areas allows health care providers and families to have a dialogue and focus on the outcomes they're after such as lowering costs and alleviating issues specific to them."

- You said that sales had increased by 8 percent in the first quarter. So what? That's what management is asking. Eight percent sounds like a lot and perhaps it is, but how can you put that in context? Eight percent compared to what? Is 8 percent significant in this down market? Did you beat your projections? How does this compare to the competition? Remember what we talked about—prove it, prove it, prove it. Just because you say it doesn't mean they'll believe you. Answer the question before it's asked.

- What is most apparent is you need to take a step back and think about the hotel guest. He doesn't care about your technology and how it works; he wants to know how you are going to make the process of getting online seamless and easy. In your surveys, guests told you that's a priority. If you can make that happen, you may give them a reason to choose you over the competition.

- If you are going to say "we have lots tools to help you," then mention some of those tools such as a professional online journal, but don't stop there. Tell them how that journal works and how it can help them. For example, "if you want to categorize prospects, section B is equipped with templates to do so."

- You lost me. Instead of saying "we will be accountable to members we serve" or "we provide leadership by example," give specific examples of how this organization has been accountable and has led the industry for decades. If you provide leadership by example, then give examples of how you've done that and how it produced results.

- Try to limit words like *multidisciplinary* and answer the so what. What are you really trying to say that they care about? If you say "our team is made up of lawyers, accountants, and analysts with expertise in bankruptcy, restructuring, and finance," not only is it simpler to understand, but you've showcased the expertise of your team.

- Don't leave people hanging. Marry them to the wants and needs of your listener. For example, when you say "best choice the company can make" and stop, it falls flat. But if you say "best choice the company can make to save money and better manage resources," it has more impact and reminds listeners why this is important.

- So what? You need to help them understand the problem and how it impacts them before you spout off the solution. Problem: People are getting stuck with incredibly high bills because claims are not being paid even though they are covered, and here's why. Solution: By changing the application of codes, we can fix this problem.
- Instead of "we have obvious challenges," which is about you and doesn't say much, remind them of the outcome everyone seeks: "While we have obvious challenges, if we do everything we can to bring compound X across the finish line, we can provide an entirely new option to more than 20 million people who have no option today."

More frequently than you might imagine, people contend that they are communicating this way on purpose. I once asked a company manager why his Web site seemed to be written in gibberish, to which he replied, "It's written this way on purpose because our Web site is directed to supply chain managers." That may be true, and he clearly knows his customers better than I do, but, like everyone, supply chain managers need to communicate to create awareness and understanding. If someone who comes to that Web site looking for information is even slightly confused, then the company has failed to communicate effectively and risks losing that customer.

## SO WHAT FIXES

- Go through every slide or every portion of your communication and ask so what? If you haven't answered those two words, fix it or get rid of it.
- Look for opportunities specifically at the end of segments, chapters, and summaries to remind people how what you're saying impacts them. Use phrases that answer those so what questions such as: "So, what this means is" or "to repeat" or "to remind you" so you are continually tying what you're saying to what they care about.
- Identify the audience's pain points in advance to help you address their so what.
- Role-play with a colleague. If you are talking to a customer, have that colleague pretend she is the customer and urge her to continually annoy you by interrupting and asking so what if you aren't addressing the customer's concerns.

- Don't try to impress. Using simple down-to-earth words that can help your neighbor better understand why something so complicated is easier than he realized is impressive enough and shows that you know your stuff.
- Ask how. If you answer the so what by saying it will improve time management, take it one step further by explaining how that will happen, which encourages you to provide relevant examples to your listener.

**In an age of complex communications, simplicity is more important than ever.**

# CHAPTER 9
# Reality Check

You people are telling me what you think I want to know. I want to
know what is actually happening.
    —*Creighton Abrams, U.S. commander of forces in Vietnam*

I was flipping through a business trade publication and saw an article
announcing the promotion of a colleague, so I sent him an e-mail con-
gratulating him on his accomplishment, only to receive the following
e-mail in return:

Thanks for the congrats! Nice to get into these industry magazines
but it is not the least bit impressive to my two teenage daughters.
One told me—"Dad, this looks like a magazine that only a geek
would read."

I can relate because I also have teenagers and then it struck me—if
you want a reality check, just talk to your kids. They will tell you what
they think even if you don't want to hear it. Why do we often forget to
get in touch with our real selves when we deal with colleagues and important listeners? Is it because we're afraid to say what we really think
for fear of saying the wrong thing? Or is it because it's safer to nod in
agreement than to rock the boat?

Perhaps we should borrow a page from the popular TV show *Seinfeld*. If you ask most people what *Seinfeld* was about, it's likely they
will tell you it was about nothing. In reality, *Seinfeld* was about everything. It was about everything you and I can relate to on a daily

basis: losing our car in a parking lot, being embarrassed at work, or brainstorming a get rich quick scheme such as selling muffin tops. I know you're asking yourself, what does this have to do with communicating in business?

As a television news reporter for two decades, I spent my fair share of days panicking people about the threat of bad weather, especially snow. Snow is a green light for fanatical reporters to blanket the region with live reports from highways that were not snow covered but might be soon or from supermarkets packed with customers who feared the potential forecast would leave them stranded indefinitely and unable to get necessities such as milk and eggs. Most reporters typically despise this obsessive approach to attracting viewers, but you have no choice— you are the worker bee and you go where you're told. So one winter at ABC-TV in Philadelphia, I decided to voice my dissent and complained that we were unfairly scaring people to get ratings. I was quickly corrected and told that when bad weather is forecast, our HUT levels (homes using television) go up, which proves that people want this information. Arguing, I insisted the only reason more people tune in is because the station is scaring the you-know-what out of them. In this case, what I said really didn't matter and certainly didn't change behavior, but I felt better about stating what I believed to be true.

I have dubbed it the *Seinfeld* approach because in a comical way, the *Seinfeld* show was about being true to yourself even if it meant rubbing someone else the wrong way. Yet, on a broader scale, that authenticity is missing in meeting rooms, offices, and in front of listeners who really count. Instead of strongly stating a point or advocating a position that might offer an idea or potential solution, too often we worry about presenting a dissenting opinion, offending a boss or client, not being perceived as a team player, or offering an opinion that we're not certain those in authority will respect. It's the dodgeball approach. Instead of getting in the center of the ring and taking a hit, we hug the outside of the circle and no one knows what we really stand for.

Ask any CEO and she'll tell you she's surrounded by cubicles of yes-men (and women), which is why many hire outside consultants who aren't afraid to tell them what they might not want to hear. I was sharing this advice at a luncheon one day when a manager interrupted me and said, "Let me get this straight. If I listen to you, I can go home and tell my wife something she doesn't want to hear?" Well, I wouldn't count on that one, but I have to imagine a direct, honest conversation in any relationship—personal or business—is a reality check worth thinking about.

> Don't tell me what I want to hear. Tell me what I need to know.

**Case and point.** A big-time New York public relations agency was working on a national awareness campaign that was tied to a sensitive and highly controversial issue. At a somewhat tense message brainstorming session designed to develop consumer-friendly messages and tackle tough questions, I raised several unwanted questions that I was certain would be asked by mainstream media. The public relations expert was visibly annoyed and made it clear that lawyers representing the client did not want these questions asked and they were off limits. I explained that, in this context, it didn't really matter what lawyers wanted or didn't want because the media doesn't work for them and reporters will ask questions that their readers want answered. Therefore, if I did not raise these issues and prepare company spokespeople to address them, our firm would be doing an incredible disservice to the client and we should be fired. Needless to say, the public relations firm did not take kindly to that remark but was ultimately scolded by the client, who warned, "Don't tell me what I want to hear. Tell me what I need to know."

It's always easier to bury your head in the sand than disagree with someone who can affect your career. However, when you fail to put it on the line, you undermine your own credibility. If you find yourself in a similar situation and you're not sure what to do, ask yourself these questions:

- What do I want people to feel about my organization?
- Am I telling them what they need to know to make informed decisions or covering my butt?
- Are the real problems and issues on the table?
- Am I being painfully transparent?
- Do I understand my listeners and their specific concern?

For example, we worked with a family whose jailed husband was about to be released. The community was outraged because he had been convicted of a sex offense and neighbors did not want him moving back home. The family drafted a statement talking about his commitment to treatment, his pledge to being a better man, pending protective legislation, and monitoring, none of which addresses the real concerns as posed by the question above. In this case, neighbors couldn't care less about treatment. Their only concern was for the safety of their children and community. Here is an edited version of an e-mail excerpt from one or our crisis consultants who worked with the family:

> Please try to understand that this statement is NOT ABOUT YOU but is ABOUT THEM. For that reason, it must address their fears and concerns rather than how YOU feel about the situation.
>
> No one cares that he is playing an active part in his recovery. No one trusts him or believes anything he says anyway—or anything you say in his defense. He has no credibility with the neighbors, media or the public despite how you feel about his personal progress. I understand how difficult this must be for you and your family, but you want to ask for THEIR patience.

**Case and point.** A big-city utility company received a call from an Associated Press reporter who was writing a story about contaminants in drinking water and had identified this water department as one of the biggest offenders in the country. He wanted to interview the top brass. Initially, there were naysayers who claimed nothing good would come of participating in an interview.

However, for years, this same utility had complained that it wanted citizens to know it was a great steward of the drinking supply and was tired of drowning in silence. After much disagreement and debate, we decided to address the problem head on, offer perspective to address concerns, and communicate why we were providing a reality check even if the truth was hard to swallow.

| | |
|---|---|
| **Head on:** | Drinking water is contaminated with pharmaceuticals. |
| **Head on:** | This is a problem nationally and internationally. |
| **Head on:** | We take this seriously and want to be proactive. |
| **Perspective:** | The water is absolutely safe to drink. To put it in perspective, these contaminants are so infinitesimal that you would have to drink eight eight-ounce glasses every day for almost 800 years just to reach the caffeine equivalent of one cup of coffee. |
| **Reality:** | We choose to look for problems so we can control them. |

**Reality:**   We're vigilant about safety and want to be at the fore-
                front.

**Reality:**   We want to proactively communicate to keep you in-
                formed.

---

To handle yourself, use your head; to handle others, use your heart.

---

Former first lady Eleanor Roosevelt once wrote, "To handle yourself, use your head; to handle others, use your heart." Yet, because our first instinct is to defend, spin, or cover our butts, we forget to let our compassionate selves shine through. While surveys show that trust in government and big business is steadily increasing, they also indicate Americans are still very skeptical and it's no wonder. As this book was being written, the governor of Illinois was thrown out of office for influence peddling. Former NASDAQ chairman Bernard Madoff was jailed for 150 years for the largest Ponzi scheme ever reported. Banks and automakers were bailed out by taxpayers, and drug companies are being fined for illegal marketing practices. Through it all, there is a missing reality check when people try to explain themselves.

**Get real:**   As the 2010 largest oil spill in U.S. history continued with no end in sight, BP CEO Tony Hayward was spotted on a fancy yacht in England not too long after he publicly stated he wanted his life back. If the poor choice of words wasn't bad enough, that came on the heels of BP Chairman Carl-Henric Svanberg's apology for referring to victims of the Gulf of Mexico disaster as "the small people." Seemingly unable to come down from their ivory tower and understand that the situation was not about them, BP honchos would have fared far better in the court of public opinion if they had been seen talking to the so-called small people, and cleaning off oil-slicked animals on murky beaches instead of sailing on pristine waters.

**Get real:**   When gasoline prices neared $4 per gallon in 2009, causing anxious Americans to cut back spending amid fears of not being able to afford to drive to work, ExxonMobil CEO Rex Tillerson went on national TV to justify his company's record profits. It's unlikely that people on tight budgets could relate to his explanation that because his business is one of large numbers, a profit of $40 billion isn't really as big as it sounds.

**Get real:**   After Enron CEO Kenneth Lay was charged with corporate fraud in a 2001 accounting scandal that took his company down, cost shareholders tens of billions of dollars, and emptied the life savings of thousands of employees, his wife Linda appeared on the *Today Show* to defend her husband. It's doubtful too many viewers were sympathetic when she tearfully mourned her own losses, including the family vacation home.

Perhaps, as Eleanor Roosevelt suggested, when speaking, we really should have heart. People want spokespeople to be human, to be real. Whether you are doing an interview with the media, delivering negative financial news, talking with employees, or trying to land that new job, if you're not authentic, then it's doubtful listeners will relate to you. If they can't relate to you, it's not likely they'll trust you. If they don't trust you, nothing you say will really matter.

---

If they don't trust you, nothing you say will really matter.

---

## COACHING NOTES

- It's okay to be human. How you say something is just as important as what you say. In difficult situations, we sometimes forget to be human beings. We forget to empathize. We forget to show concern, afraid that if we show emotion we might be perceived as weak. While you don't want to fall to pieces in front of your audience, showing an appropriate level of emotion during difficult circumstances can make you and your message much more believable. The fact is, you're relaying sad news, and it's okay to be sad.

- It's your job to consistently convey your purpose and mission. Maybe you won't get the contract, but at least they'll know you're the real deal. So let's cut to the chase: don't just tell them what you think they want to hear, give them your expert opinion; that's why they are considering hiring you to begin with.

- I understand your policy that when "something happens" you prefer to wait until the matter is resolved, but you could really shoot yourself in the foot if we don't do a reality check. The reality is someone could and probably will find out before you resolve this. My advice is to be as forthcoming, honest, and proactive as possible. Develop a standby statement that briefly addresses what happened and what actions you are taking to quickly remedy the situation. If someone calls, you are prepared, can control your message, and do not come off as evasive.

- You did nothing wrong, but to hide from these accusations is wrong. The fact of the matter is as soon as you learned that the health of your employees could be in jeopardy, you didn't sit around and wait for authorities to find out. You contacted the FDA. You launched the investigation. You called an employee meeting. You have much to be proud of, and I strongly advise you to put it out there. But we're not going to do this without preparing appropriately. People feel first and think second. You must communicate real feelings with real words, not just the facts.

Shortly after 9/11, we worked with a small medical device company that found itself in a unique position to manufacture millions of vaccination needles, which at the time were believed might be needed in the event of another attack. The company anticipated competing against a much larger and very politically connected company that could potentially produce and package products faster. Our company immediately went into "poor me" mode, focusing on why it probably wouldn't get the business instead of concentrating on how to craft messages to help it win the lucrative contract. We put together a reality check session that focused on what it wanted decision makers to know and why it was more qualified than the competition even though it was a much smaller company. Below are some message-based notes used to pitch the business.

**Reality check.** Our company is the original developer and remains the only company that has continued to manufacture this product even when this disease was not a threat.

**Reality check.** We have been manufacturing and supplying this product worldwide for nearly 40 years and plan to double our workforce if awarded the contract to offer high volume at lower cost.

**Reality check.** We are financially stable and have invested significant resources over the past several months to upgrade technology and create sufficient manufacturing capacity to meet 100 percent of the current demand and forecast over the foreseeable future.

**Reality check.** From purchasing the raw material to manufacturing the needle to design, packaging, and distribution, we can take the product from start to finish.

**Reality check.** We are experienced at national emergencies and have worked 24/7 to supply NATO soldiers with millions of devices enabling them to combat chemical warfare. We are willing to partner with the competition and share this know-how because what matters most is the safety of the American public.


The company won the business and continues to enjoy substantial growth and expansion today.

Reality checks are often difficult because it's tough to assess ourselves or admit we don't know what we don't know, especially in front of other people. This occurred during a crisis training we developed for an organization. We worked closely with the client to design a real-life scenario about a sexual assault that would escalate throughout the day, forcing participants to think on their feet; speak to various stakeholders, including the media and community; make split-second decisions; and learn from their successes and mistakes. Following the program, the safety director complained to his bosses and to us that he felt like he was the guy on the hot seat all day and that the "bad news" in the fake scenario was a reflection on him. He also did not like the outcome, which was based on the reality of many unfortunate stories we had covered as journalists.

I try to take comments seriously so we can improve in the future, but I wanted to do my own reality check to make sure I wasn't missing the mark. After consultation with the other crisis coaches, these are notes we shared with the client.


- While we would never intentionally make anyone look bad and we try to be as open as possible to constructive criticism, we feel there was a missed opportunity by the safety director, who could have taken charge but didn't. As the director, he has knowledge that others don't and could have offered important safety facts to put the story in perspective, talked about security presence, stellar record, what is done 24/7 to protect people, partnering with other law enforcement agencies, and put an emphasis on safety programs. There was an urgent need to quickly communicate and control the information as the incident escalated. Everyone in the room learned from it, which was the purpose of the program.

- It is so important to take a reality check and realize that not only was this designed as a learning experience, but it is essential not to take what happens in these situations personally. While I know he is very committed and passionate, and I saw what an asset he was at the last planning meeting, it concerns me that if something really bad were to occur, this type of emotional and very personal reaction would not be conducive to navigating the problem effectively and portraying the organization in the best possible light.

## REALITY CHECK FIXES

To take your own reality check, ask the following questions:

- What do I want people to know?
- What are the facts as opposed to rumors or perceived facts?
- What do people think they know that they aren't discussing?
- Would the health, safety, or well-being of anyone be jeopardized if I don't communicate what I know?
- What do we know or feel that we're not discussing?
- Are the real issues on the table?
- Why am I afraid to say what I really think?
- Am I taking this too personally?
- What is the possible outcome if I don't reveal certain information?
- Am I just being polite because I don't want to offend or look foolish?
- What's the worst that can happen if I have this difficult conversation?
- Could my real feelings change the course of action?
- Will my actions compromise trust, credibility, or my reputation?
- Am I able to take responsibility without blaming others?
- Am I hiding anything?
- What is the right thing to do?
- If I were my listener, what would I want to see happen?

Being straight with people is probably more important than it's ever been. Thanks to an insatiable demand for information and the ease of instantly sharing that information with people across the globe, I believe the average citizen has forced big business to change. Information such as compensation that was once private is now public. For many companies, the days of lavish golf outings and pricey gifts to prospects are over. People can spot spin almost as quickly as Philadelphia Phillies shortstop Jimmy Rollins can steal a base. The inability to recognize and accept this can spell the difference between success and failure.

**Be honest with yourself if you want to tell the truth to others.**

# CHAPTER 10

# Queasy Times

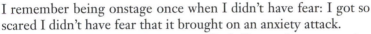

I remember being onstage once when I didn't have fear: I got so
scared I didn't have fear that it brought on an anxiety attack.
                                            —*Carly Simon, singer-songwriter*

My youngest son didn't speak until he was nearly four and a half years
old, which was followed by many years of speech therapy to help him
overcome fluency and auditory processing struggles. So you can imagine
our incredible pride when, at 12 years old, Alec took the stage in a lead
role in his camp production of the Greek comedy *Lysistrata*. We were
amazed at the number of lines he had to memorize and deliver, which
he did with grace and ease. About three-quarters of the way through the
play, which was attended by more than 200 people at a local theater, he
forgot one of his lines. My eyes darted nervously to my husband's, when,
suddenly, the prompter who was off to the side of the stage loudly yelled
out the line to Alec. The spectators were silent. For my husband and
me, the seconds that followed ticked endlessly. What if Alec panicked?
My stomach felt a little queasy. Finally, he stopped, smiled, looked out
into the audience, and then, pointing offstage, quipped, "Whatever she
said!" The crowd roared, and the aspiring actor took an unscripted bow.
Ironically, even though *Lysistrata* is a comedy, in this version, he got
the only real laugh of the night, but they were laughing with him, not
at him.

   It could have gone much differently. Appearing on stage or at a company event is nerve-wracking. Some clients confide they don't sleep for
days before a big presentation. When I shared the story about my son
with a client, she said, "I would have just died; I would have been too
paralyzed to continue." Yet continue he did and received a standing

ovation. What's the worst that can happen if you forget your line or don't remember the next slide you intend to talk about? Will you die? Not likely. Will you be fired? Probably not. Will you make people nervous and uncomfortable? If you act nervous and uncomfortable, others will be nervous and uncomfortable for you.

---

If you act nervous and uncomfortable, others will be nervous and uncomfortable for you.

---

Losing your place, forgetting what you want to say, being interrupted, and fear of failure are more common than you may realize. It feels terribly uncomfortable at the moment, but, as my dad would say, the world will not come to an end. This chapter is devoted to helping you apply strategies to overcome common fears business communicators tell us make them queasiest. This includes blanking out and being judged by others, especially management. Just as intimidating in today's workplace are cell phone interruptions. Beyond.com polled its members and asked, "What behavior do you find bothersome when attending a business meeting?" Out of 2,300 responses, business professionals ranked cell phones most bothersome, followed by domineering personalities, people who never contribute to the conversation, and Blackberry checkers.

A huge problem for business professionals also includes competing conversations, also known as sidebars, and that's queasy number one.

## QUEASY 1: SIDEBAR DISCUSSIONS

I received the following e-mail from a client who had to facilitate an important meeting being attended by all of his superiors.

The day went quite well; however, one issue arose on which I'm hoping you could share some insight. What do you do when a sidebar discussion breaks out and you're standing there at the front of the room, not necessarily even involved in their conversation—how do you regain control of the room and your presentation?

That's a tough one, especially because the people in that room were superiors who controlled his fate, but here are a few strategies you can apply to better manage sidebar conversations:

- Stop talking. Look directly at them, even if one of them is the CEO. You will clearly get their attention, which positions you to ask a question related to the discussion you want to have. A few examples:

  "Gentlemen, excuse me, but it would be really helpful if you could provide your thoughts on this issue."

  "I want to be very sensitive to everyone's busy schedules and time constraints, so I'd like to keep this moving as quickly as possible."

  "I'm sorry to interrupt but I want to make sure that everyone participates together, so if you can pick up the conversation a bit later, I'd really appreciate it"

- Return to the group. Ask them to rejoin the group conversation. For example:

  "I want to make sure we're not missing good ideas or important information when everyone is talking at the same time and I'd like to try to keep track of everyone's ideas so we can all benefit."

- State the rules. Set up guidelines or expectations in advance such as asking people to silence their electronic devices or telling them you will leave ample room for discussion following the presentation. Explain that you want to be respectful of their schedules so you can minimize distractions and be as productive as possible in the shortest amount of time required.

- Use signals. Sometimes nonverbal visual signals such as holding up one finger, waving at the talkers, or gently putting the palm of your hand forward in a hello gesture is effective. They will look at you and you can say:

  "If I can have your attention, please; thanks so much."

While you might feel a bit uncomfortable interrupting a superior, you may actually score a few points. By being respectful but direct, you are exhibiting leadership communication skills and showing you are not afraid to speak up and take charge. Sure, they could be surprised for a moment, but they will respect you for being assertive, and you will feel good about involving everyone and keeping your agenda on track.

## QUEASY 2: BLANKING OUT

There was a cougar on the loose in a suburban community when I was a local television reporter, and I was sent to cover the story. As the anchor read the lead in, I stood in a field where the animal was last spotted while the cameraperson kept telling me to move back so he could get a wider shot for the broadcast. As I backed up, the anchor said, "let's go live to Karen," and I blanked. I had stepped on what I thought was a huge snake. Just in case you're wondering, according to the *Book of Lists*, the fear of snakes ranks number two among most people, second only to the fear of speaking in public. Not only did I completely forget what I wanted to say, but I was so freaked out that I rambled for nearly four minutes while the show producer screamed at me through my earpiece to shut up.

Not everyone steps on a snake on live television, but when you blank out in front of an important audience, you feel just as queasy. The adrenaline kicks in, you start to stammer, clear your throat, say "um" a lot, and turn a few shades of red. What can you do?

- Stop talking. Take a deep breath and pause. It will feel like lightyears to you, but your audience will hardly notice. You can repeat your main point or last point to help you get back on track.
- Rehearse out loud. Broadcasters almost always rehearse out loud to help them quickly recall key points they want to make. In this case, there was no time because we were out looking for the cougar right up to air time. Thankfully, we didn't find it!
- Helpful notes. Like slides, your notes should be bullet pointed and easy to see so you can glance at them for recall.

## QUEASY 3: SAYING NO

The customer is not always right. Ironically, as I write this chapter, I was reminded of this while helping a company prepare experts to talk about a new therapeutic option approved by the FDA. I scheduled a planning call with my main contact, who invited nine other people from assorted business units to participate. Not a good move. Too many people mean too many opinions and too many competing agendas, which is precisely what happened. The team leader had a very different idea of how the program should be structured, and, like a bull in a china shop, she let me know who was in charge, insisting we run our program her way. Not having a communications background, she didn't understand what was required to help her colleagues learn most effectively, and she asked us to counsel in areas slightly beyond our expertise. Inadvertently, she was setting us and the participants up to fail.

I had a bad feeling about this, and, after sleeping on it, I called a superior to help sort it out. I wanted to complain about her but knew I had a greater chance of seeking the outcome I was after if I asked the right questions to give the boss an opportunity to talk and give myself an opportunity to listen. This way, I would be better positioned to redefine our area of expertise and address his objectives. Otherwise, I was prepared to tell him the company was wasting its money and should cancel the program. I was willing to risk losing my client as opposed to losing my credibility. It was a gamble. Not only did it pay off, but the boss bent over backward to do everything possible to make the day a success. He also had some stern words for the bull and told her she was to immediately cease and desist. Upset and ego bruised at first, she ignored me, but then had a change of heart and called to iron out the wrinkles so together we could deliver a smooth session.

In the end, the program proved better than first imagined because we both backed off and tried to understand how to accomplish each other's goals by leveraging our individual expertise in a way that would best benefit the participants.

To do the same, try this 3-S approach:

- **Stop talking.** The secret to getting what you want is getting other people to talk about what they want. If you listen carefully, you will be able to ask questions and seek input that facilitate conversation and make them feel they are a valued partner.

- **Suggest alternatives.** After you understand their limitations, suggest alternatives that accomplish their goals and show you are willing to compromise to meet competing agendas. But they must clearly understand how your plan will generate results.

- **Structure properly.** Think about the takeaway you want to leave them with, and briefly outline your main points of discussion in advance. It's not always about doing it your way. In this case, saying no led to saying yes to collaborative ideas that provided participants with a fresh, innovative approach to learning.

## QUEASY 4: REPAIRING RELATIONSHIPS

Have you ever had a disagreement with a colleague or client? Perhaps you said something you shouldn't have or wish you had said something differently. How do you repair that relationship so you still have the other person's respect? In Queasy 3, the bull made the first move by calling me directly. She said she wanted me to know there were no issues between us and that I had her complete cooperation. Whether she meant it or was instructed to call is almost irrelevant. What's important is that she changed the game and put us both back on a level playing field.

- Stop talking. Don't be afraid to admit a mistake or misjudgment. Honesty always remains the best policy. Even if you don't fully agree, show the other person you value the relationship and want to work together to fix whatever ails.

- Act quickly. If you sense there is a problem, don't wait. Communicate honestly and directly to show your concern and interest in maintaining a good relationship.

- Face to face. If possible, meet in person or telephone the individual, because there is too much room for misinterpretation and rambling when communicating by e-mail.

- Get over it. Even if you aren't at fault, don't stand on ceremony. Tell the person that there is an obvious miscommunication and if you are at fault or partially at fault, apologize. Relationships, whether personal or professional, are based on trust and respect. Others want to know that you are human and not afraid to admit mistakes.

## QUEASY 5: BATTLING BUTTERFLIES

Being nervous can work to your advantage if you use it to energize your talk or presentation. Learning to do this will help your butterflies fly in formation so you can control them instead of letting them control you.

Rich, the chief controller at his company, was given a first-time opportunity to present at an important investor meeting. He was fully prepared, but really nervous. Instead of ignoring his anxiety, he began by telling his audience he was really excited to have this opportunity to talk to them but this was a first time for him and he was really nervous.

Listeners chuckled and smiled, which he said put him at ease and made him feel like he was talking to friends.

- Stop talking. Before game day, identify what makes you nervous. In Rich's case, he feared talking to strangers. When he figured out a way to see them as friends, his butterflies settled down.

- Arrive early. When you introduce yourself and say hello in advance, audience members will no longer feel like total strangers, which helps alleviate anxiety.

- Start strong. Developing meaningful opening remarks and rehearsing them over and over so you really know them will help you get off to a strong start and increase your comfort and confidence. By doing the same at the end, you are less likely to ramble.

- Movement matters. People frequently ask if they should move when they are in the front of the room. The short answer is yes, because, for most people, even a little movement is natural, which prevents you from looking stiff and uncomfortable. Instead of holding onto a podium or locking your feet to the floor, come out from behind, gesture, and take a few steps here and there. Be careful not to block the slides.

- Practice out loud. The more you say it, the better you know it. The better you know it, the more relaxed you will feel. Too often, colleagues tell me they don't have time to practice. If you spent all this time preparing, why would you quit when you're almost at the finish line?

## QUEASY 6: BAD BOSS

If you've worked long enough, you've probably encountered a difficult boss. Studies suggest the most common reason for unhappy employees and low morale is bad bosses. In fact, people typically don't leave bad jobs; they leave bad bosses. So, how do you best communicate with someone who likes chocolate when you like vanilla?

- Stop talking. Even if your boss is the jerk of the year, you need to listen before you erupt. Think of talking to her as if you were speaking to a child. If you become emotional with the child, the child will probably keep pushing your buttons. If you remain calm, focused, and speak in measured tones, you will project confidence and the child will eventually back off.

- Action plan. Schedule a formal meeting instead of barging into his office. Before speaking, create an action plan. Come up with two or three points you want to discuss, such as obstacles that are preventing you from doing your job. Instead of complaining, offer alternatives or solutions and explain how these will make you more productive.

- Over their head. If all else fails and your boss is abusive, write down the problems and keep a running list that you can eventually take to HR or a superior. Instead of saying "my boss yells at me," give specific examples of what made that yelling inappropriate or offensive. For example, years ago, an editor in my newsroom yelled obscenities all the time. The screaming didn't get him in trouble, but the use of foul language eventually did.

Remember, it's important to act professionally to maintain trust and credibility even during queasy times.

## QUEASY 7: LOSING LISTENERS

The only thing worse than looking out into your audience and seeing the chap in the front row sleeping is when you hear him snore and fear everyone else can hear him too. It is foolish to think everyone will hang onto our every word every time we speak, but there are ways to maximize attention when you fear people may be tuning out.

- Stop talking. Sometimes pausing for a long moment will grab attention, because listeners wonder why you've stopped and what might be coming next. The silence can build anticipation and strengthen the importance of a point you're trying to make.

- Perk up. Drawing people back with phrases such as, "If you take nothing away from this talk today, remember this" or "The reason this is incredibly important to you" can help perk them up. Asking questions or seeking feedback will also help listeners stay involved by participating in the presentation instead of simply observing.

- Vocal variety. Changing your pace and pitch, punching or emphasizing important words by speaking a little louder will help wake people up. You may feel like you're talking too loud, but you will come across as more animated and energetic.

- In their face. Moving closer to your listeners so you can make eye contact or walking around an audience is permissible as long as you are not crowding them or making them feel uncomfortable. Sometimes, the sleeper will open her eyes out of sheer embarrassment. If you're sitting at table, get up for a few seconds and walk to the board or easel to write down a point to help refocus attention.

## QUEASY 8: HOSTILE AUDIENCES

Robert is an architect for a residential homebuilder and has to make presentations at community meetings frequently packed with angry people who don't want another housing development going up in their backyard. He says he often feels queasy because neighbors often have the wrong facts but won't listen; they interrupt, argue, and make him feel very uncomfortable and unwelcome. As we worked through Robert's concerns, what became apparent was that Robert prepared for these meetings by focusing on how to explain the development plan instead of thinking through how to address community concerns. Here is an excerpt from our communications.

> You've got an audience full of people who have a mindset before you even open your mouth. You must correct negative information or misperceptions at the onset, speak frankly about their concerns, show them you understand or you will not be able to establish credibility and sincerity. If you don't clear the field, you can't plant the seed.

---

> If you don't clear the field, you can't plant the seed.

---

- Speak to their concerns. Until you address what they came to hear about, they will be preoccupied and will not fully listen to you. Instead of ignoring their problems and going right to your own agenda, speak to their fears to clear the elephant from the room.
- Remain calm. If you fire back, you will only escalate their fire and get sucked into a cycle of negativity. Avoid criticizing, blaming, or putting someone on the spot in front of others even though they're doing it to you.
- Stay focused. Stick to the facts you wish to convey instead of offering more information that might prompt additional arguments.

- Point of view. Acknowledge their perspective even if you don't agree and offer facts and information to address their issues.

Some years back, Patrick desperately struggled to hold people's attention when he had to speak at internal meetings. Yet, when not at the front of a room, he was magnetic, personable, and hilarious. Nothing seemed to help, until he told me he was a diehard Yankees fan. Being from Philadelphia, I couldn't share his passion for the Yankees, but what struck me was how his entire demeanor, from voice to body language to the red in his cheeks, lit up when he spoke about his team. So I gave him some homework. Patrick had to come prepared to win this Phillies fan to his New York way of thinking. Fat chance!

The next morning, someone I hardly recognized showed up in full Yankee garb, carrying a baseball bat, glove, and props with a Yankee logo painted on his face. He delivered one of the most informative yet engaging business presentations I can remember. When I asked him why he couldn't impart this same enthusiasm at company meetings, he said, "Because I'm not talking about the Yankees at business meetings."

Without realizing it, Patrick did more than talk about the Yankees. He had passion for his subject and thought about how to fervently convey his message to this doubting Philadelphia fan. He prepared in advance and showed up early to plaster the room in Yankee paraphernalia and stand at the door with a huge smile to greet me when I walked in. He knew my doubts and objections and spoke right to them. He dumped most of his slides and prepared note cards to prompt his memory. He brought his story to life with big gestures and movement such as swinging a bat or faking a throw out at home plate. These are techniques he could apply when talking about his business, which he also passionately believed in.

Although Patrick did not convert me to a Yankee fan, once he got going, he did forget he was nervous. Like the quote from singer-songwriter Carly Simon at the top of this chapter, if he had stopped to think about his fear, he would have felt queasy instead of just being in the moment and creating an experience for his audience.

**When you please your audience, you'll be pleased with yourself.**

# CHAPTER 11

# Political Lessons

George Washington is the only president who didn't blame the previous administration for his troubles.

*—Author unknown*

In the year 2000, I ran for political office. I could write a whole book on that experience alone, but the significance of trying to secure a seat in the Pennsylvania state house isn't about my experience, it's about what political campaigns can teach business.

At the time, I was hard at work building my own business, which included coaching and training for the Pennsylvania Democratic caucus. The Republican state representative in my home district had received a lot of negative press for allegedly smacking his girlfriend in public so Democratic leadership saw a good opportunity to reclaim the seat and thought tapping a former television reporter with name recognition was a great strategy. When I was first approached, I laughed out loud as the conversation went something like this.

| | |
|---|---|
| Leadership: | How would you like to run for PA House? |
| Me: | Not a chance. |
| Leadership: | Why not? |
| Me: | Should I tell you the truth or tell you what you want to hear? |
| Leadership: | Oh please, we want the truth. |
| Me: | For starters, I've interviewed hundreds of politicians and never liked any all that much and, no offense, but I have no real desire to be like any of you. |

Then I signed up.

Like many naïve first-timers, I believed I could do what *I* thought was right but quickly learned there were way too many people trying to maneuver my invisible puppet strings. There were the phone calls in the middle of the night from an intoxicated house leader confiding of his wife's infidelity, then asking for my help on issues. There was pressure from labor threatening to pull campaign funding if I didn't commit to voting their way on state liquor regulations. Then, after wearing out four pairs of shoes from knocking on 25,000 voter doors and running one of the closest state races in history, there was the verbal public whipping from a high-powered legislator scared of losing his clout if I didn't win the seat, which would have secured a Democratic house majority. I lost by less than 3 percent, most of it in absentee ballots.

There were great people too: Hundreds of people, many whom I never met, who volunteered and gave money and thousands who actually switched their voter registration to vote for me during the primary. There was also tireless and terrific guidance from incredibly savvy advisors from whom I learned so much and still call on today.

Like any product, promise, service, or idea, the key is to inspire and motivate so people believe in what you're selling. As an example, politicians have to sell themselves every time they speak. Let's say a candidate appears warm, friendly, and sincere, but when you meet them in person, they are scowling, not as happy as they appeared on TV, offer a droopy handshake, and seem distracted as you speak to them. You would probably rethink your decision to vote for that person.

Political campaigns can teach professionals a great deal. The rise of social networks has significantly impacted the way politicians communicate with their constituents, and business leaders can learn valuable communication lessons from Millennials who have grown up on LinkedIn, Facebook, My Space, and YouTube. While these channels were not as prominent when I ran for office, they were already forcing people to talk *with* instead of *at* the listener by having more personal conversations. Learning how to keep the conversation real is just the start.

---

Business leaders can learn valuable communication lessons from Millennials who have grown up on social networks.

## LESSON 1: KEEP THE CONVERSATION REAL

When you read a blog, you can almost hear the writer speaking, see him smiling, and feel the intensity of his thoughts. It's unscripted and unrehearsed, much like a conversation you would have with a friend. The writer is typically passionate and talks to people in her own language.

As a high-profile television personality, I had name recognition that most unknown politicians can't buy. But I ran against a worthy opponent with experience I lacked. Urban sprawl was a much-debated issue and garnered a large amount of media attention. Every time we were both questioned about it, she talked from experience as a member of the township planning commission and was usually quoted. I was not. Then it dawned on me that I needed to keep the conversation real and speak people's language, so I changed my approach. The next time I was interviewed, I said, "Traffic has gotten so bad out here in Montgomery County that I could balance my checkbook on the way home from work." Granted, you don't need a college education to come up with that one, but it resonated with readers, and every time I said it, I got quoted, so, of course, I said it all the time.

Politicians, like newscasters, understand the importance of using real-life examples and storytelling to impact listeners, but business professionals lag behind, fearing they will not be taken seriously or that what's appropriate in other settings is not appropriate in business. Quite the opposite is true. In medicine, it's the stories of sick patients that inspire researchers to search for cures. In families, we pass stories through generations to inspire loved ones never to give up. In wartime, we cling to stories that offer hope about people who have overcome insurmountable odds. The stories of grief, hope, and optimism that followed the horrific events of September 11, 2001, are forever etched into our personal and national psyche. Stories are real and create rapport communicators need to bring the message home.

## LESSON 2: ADJUST ON THE FLY

Most political candidates surround themselves with a core group of advisors who metaphorically represent a family sitting around the kitchen table discussing issues of the day. As a team, they listen to each other, provide support, tackle challenges, and strategize to achieve goals. Good kitchen tables also have a gift of being able to recognize pivotal moments and adjust communications on the fly.

When President Obama campaigned in 2008, his original campaign slogan was "Change You Can Believe In." His opponent, John McCain, latched onto the phrase and also started talking about change. Instead of repositioning or letting McCain be perceived as the agent of change, Obama quickly switched to "Change We Need," keeping his core message optimistic but tweaking it for voters.

In business settings, executives have often said to me, "I don't want to say that because it might be too optimistic" or "Yes, we are on track with our goals, but I don't want to over promise." While these are valid concerns, business professionals who are quick to dwell on the negative risk turning off investors, customers, colleagues, and other important audiences who are looking to them for inspiration and motivation. This is not to say an executive should paint a rosy picture when things are not so rosy. But adjusting remarks that provide guidance and insight to help people climb the hurdles is far more optimistic than someone who continually talks gloom and doom.

For example, in 2008 and 2009, when housing and stock prices plunged to historic lows, crippling the economy, it was difficult for anyone to deliver positive news. Yet newly elected President Obama maintained a steady calm when repeatedly reminding people that, while recovery would be long and painful, he was confident his controversial stimulus package would eventually put America back on the right track, making the country even stronger in the future.

Inspirational business leaders understand the importance of strategizing with others to consistently communicate upbeat messages that provide hope by telling people here's what's happening, here's what we're doing about it, and this is what it will look like when we get through it.

## LESSON 3: EVERYONE DOES NOT HAVE TO LIKE YOU

Celebrities realize that popularity is subjective. Some people might be attracted to dark, handsome, chiseled features, while others prefer a blonde, slender, softer look. It's almost like being a stockbroker. When the market is good, your stockbroker is a beloved genius, but when the market tanks, the broker isn't so lovable or smart.

Politicians recognize this as they recognize not everyone is on the same side of an issue. While some may try to please everyone, many do take a stand and stick to their position. Businesses, however, typically loathe criticism and often want to "set the record straight" or respond when someone writes or says something negative about them. Too often, this can backfire.

I worked with an off-campus college housing organization that found itself in a predicament. College students, being college students, had a loud, raucous party at one of their properties, and, thanks to modern technology, cell phones captured images of topless coeds, which were posted on YouTube. You can imagine the outrage of college officials who wanted to react by publicly responding through the media. What they failed to consider was whether a response would actually call more attention to what happened and fuel a story that was contained and viewed by a limited audience on YouTube. Additionally, would they give the impression that they monitor students' online behavior and then sanction based on that behavior? They did craft a statement to be delivered should someone call. No one did, and the furor quickly quieted down.

## LESSON 4: BE ACCOUNTABLE

In my campaign office, we had a young woman in charge of our door-to-door walking campaign. It was up to her to determine what neighborhoods we canvassed and how many times we returned. There was a big map in the office with colored pins stuck on streets that illustrated where we had trudged. Shortly before the election, I noticed we missed an entire section of the district. When I questioned her, she became very defensive and claimed her strategy never included campaigning in this area. As it turned out, she made a mistake and was embarrassed to admit it. If she had taken responsibility, we could have changed course and potentially secured additional votes.

> When people are unaccountable, they often make excuses, blame others, or play dumb, which can create an atmosphere of mistrust.

When people are unaccountable, they often make excuses, blame others, or play dumb, which can create an atmosphere of mistrust. In campaigns as well as business, accepting responsibility and not being afraid to say you erred or judged a situation inappropriately earns people respect and creates confidence in your ability to lead.

My older son was only nine during my short-lived political career, but he taught me a lesson I will never forget. It was a very competitive race, in which many people said they would only vote their party regardless of personal beliefs. On election night, my son and husband were assigned to hand out literature at a polling place. Every time someone would walk in the door, Brett would run up to them, hand out my flyer, and scream "vote for my mom!" On the way out of the voting booth, an older man grabbed my husband's arm and said, "I've never voted for another party in my life until tonight, and I did it because of your son."

Without knowing it, this nine-year-old instinctually knew that politicians can't win races without good grassroots organizations, but, more importantly, he cut through the politics and grabbed at their hearts.

> He cut through the politics and grabbed at their hearts.

According to an article published in the *Wall Street Journal* (September 30, 2008), the top five executive skills sought by organizations are strategic thinking, ability to work across many functional areas, ability to drive results, general leadership, and a core financial understanding. While political campaigns teach all of these skills, they can also teach executives how to build stronger organizations by being authentic communicators who empower others to spread their message.

## EXECUTIVE TAKEAWAYS FROM POLITICAL CAMPAIGNS

**Takeaway 1:**  Tell people how you will get them where they want to go.

**Takeaway 2:**  Clearly and consistently communicate actions.

**Takeaway 3:**  Seek input and work as a team.

**Takeaway 4:**  Understand the constituent's viewpoint.

**Takeaway 5:**  Have purpose and passion.

**Takeaway 6:**  Adjust messages on the fly.

**Takeaway 7:**  Show empathy and compassion.

**Takeaway 8:**  Maintain an optimistic attitude and approach.

**Takeaway 9:**  Be accountable.

**Takeaway 10:**  Engage others to spread your word.

Political strategy, like business strategy, is driven by daily conversations that take place with a few trusted advisors or with crowds of thousands. Though what you say may be different for each group, how you say it is who you are and what will endear people to you.

As President Ronald Reagan was entering the operating room after being wounded in a 1981 assassination attempt, he joked to the surgeons, "Please tell me you're Republicans," to which one doctor responded, "today, Mr. President, we are all Republicans."

Like the 40th president of the United States, my young son understood how to make politics personal.

**Lead with your heart to win the respect of others.**

# CHAPTER 12

# Owning Media Interviews

*Our job is only to hold up the mirror—to tell and show the public what has happened.*

—*Walter Cronkite, broadcast journalist*

There is a comic strip that hangs in my office. The punch line says, "If at first you don't succeed, blame the media!" I chuckle every time I read it, because blaming the media is almost as all-American as Monday Night Football and probably with good reason, right? After all, reporters dig and interfere. They've been accused of rarely getting the facts straight and exhibit a vulture mentality that sucks the life out of people. Others claim they're only interested in ratings, allow sales departments to drive story content, and don't seem to care about ruining reputations. After all, if it bleeds, it leads, as the saying goes.

I cannot defend every accusation. After all, as a veteran reporter, I shoved many microphones in faces of grief and have overstayed my welcome in numerous neighborhoods. However, I will tell you from experience that reporters aren't thinking about ratings or sales when they cover stories, and most are not out to get you. I realize that's a hard pill for some to swallow, but reporters are storytellers who are trying to gather accurate information they can condense, explain, and present in the most interesting and engaging way possible. They will ask the tough questions they think their readers, listeners, and viewers would want answered, and they will edit long-winded responses into attention-grabbing sound bites that best fit restricted formats.

It's important to realize reporters don't always determine what gets covered or how it's covered. Even if there is nothing happening or nothing new to report, editors and producers will often insist on coverage and force the reporter to look for new angles to keep the story alive.

I recall being sent to the scene of a pothole that neighbors described to our newsroom hotline as a "crater." They said it was so large that a car had been swallowed up in it. I was scheduled to do a live report at the top of the 5:00 P.M. news. When I got there, there was no crater; just a big pothole with a car's front tire dangling over the edge. I called the newsroom to say "no story here," and they said, "do it anyway." Incredulous, I argued but was informed that the helicopter had already been dispatched over the scene, and there was not much happening that day, so if we didn't broadcast the story, there was nothing else to replace it. I did the live shot.

I remember a similar scenario in Limerick, Pennsylvania, following a devastating tornado that killed two people. Ironically, the movie *Twister* was playing at a Limerick theater that week, so it was determined that all proceeds would be donated to help the tornado victims. I was scheduled to cover the fundraiser and broadcast live at 11:00 P.M. However, when we tried to set up our live truck, we couldn't get a signal anywhere in the area, so I suggested we return to the station and put the story together there. I was overruled. The producer said we were to find a place to broadcast live, which we ended up doing almost 20 miles away in the middle of highway that had absolutely no connection to the story. Yet I had to explain to viewers why I was standing in the middle of traffic on a busy highway and couldn't tell them the producer was irrational. So I said something ridiculous like, "It was on a night like this without a star in the sky that Limerick residents would be shaken from their beds just a stone's throw away."

I share these stories because it's necessary to understand that a lot of what happens in media land is completely out of your control. You can't control what's covered and how it's covered or influence decisions that are made. But you can control the words that come out of your mouth, and you can recognize opportunities to partner with the press so they become your mouthpiece to the public. While blaming the media may be a popular pastime, business professionals would benefit far more if they better understood the needs of reporters who cover them in order to advocate their position to make a difference to a reporter's audience.

To do this, it's helpful to understand the reporter's job:

1. It is not her job to protect your reputation.
2. It is not his job to advance your career.
3. It is not her job to ask questions to trigger what you want to say.

4. It is not his job to write the story you think should be told.

5. It is not her job to include everything you told them.

6. It is not his job to provide you with a copy of the story in advance.

It is your job to understand the rules of the game so you can play offense instead of defense.

Corporate executives are often terribly wordy and sometimes defensive when explaining what they do or why they're doing it and incorrectly assume the reporter knows or should know more than they really know. They can get visibly annoyed and take questions personally instead of realizing the journalist doesn't fully understand their business, and they have a great opportunity to spread their message.

> The key to your success is to think like the reporter and not like you.

The key to your success is to think like the reporter and not like you to better connect with readers, listeners, and viewers whom you can't see or hear. Let's say you're a doctor who is offering advice to a consumer publication about how people who suffer from depression can get through the holidays. It is natural for you to want to discuss years of research, data, and safety profiles before discussing solutions. While that information may be relevant to certain audiences, it is far more compelling to put the facts into perspective by explaining the magnitude of the problem and how the problem affects families, the workplace, and relationships. If people don't understand the problem, they can't appreciate the potential solution.

I work with a company that is repositioning the way it manages its business. The CEO is warm, passionate, and loves to talk about his vision for the future. That's the problem. He keeps talking. He had an opportunity to interest the *New York Times* in a business story about how and why the company's new direction could potentially benefit millions of people, but every time we role-played the potential interview, he kept talking about outcomes without providing any real context. I suggested that before he tried to explain why his company is part of the solution, it would be helpful to explain the difference between how things work now compared to how things will work differently in the future to help the reporter put the information in context. He said he didn't want to spend his time educating the reporter, who should "do their own homework."

If you want to influence outcomes and have greater control over your message, you should picture yourself as a helpful teacher who is happy to educate the reporter so she can understand the value of what you do and share it with others. If you make the assumption that most will read up on you and be fairly well versed in advance, you are being overly optimistic and risk missing opportunities to tell your story.

When reporters cover stories, they ask the following three questions. (1) Who cares? (2) Why do they care? (3) How is my reader, listener, or viewer affected? They do not want volumes of information or a history lesson. They want you to give them the bottom line and back it up with relevant facts. Every day, thousands of people speak out on behalf of the companies and organizations they work for. They talk about what they want people to know instead of addressing what people really care about. It's important to understand that you are not talking to the reporter. You are talking to the reporter's audience.

For example, if a reporter is assigned to cover a story on a multimillion-dollar highway project, unless she is talking to a very technical highway trade magazine, she isn't interested in all of the technical

> It's important to understand that you are not talking to the reporter. You are talking to the reporter's audience.

details of the project, but she does want to know how the project will affect people in the area. Spokespeople need to talk in concepts and put information in perspective so they can prepare messages that speak to the wants and needs of the reader.

By helping audiences hear what they heard, feel what they felt, and see what they saw, spokespeople can bring the story to life for them. Like a good book or television series, when you appeal to people's emotions, you have a better chance of keeping them engaged. That's what sells advertising, which keeps media outlets in business.

So what can you do to better prepare for media encounters when you're not always sure where a reporter is headed and what he might ask? Let's begin by understanding media mentality. For starters, there is no such thing as an objective reporter. While most reporters strive to be fair and accurate, they come equipped with their own set of biases and are frequently assigned stories based on a newsroom's preconceived notion of the truth. They also rely on other media reports for facts, which are not always correct or confirmed and inadvertently find their way into reported stories.

That's why preparing for a media interview is similar to preparing for a football game. You need a game plan. You must first determine where you're headed, how you're getting there, and how you're going to stay one step ahead of the opponent's plays. Like kickoff, you need to come out strong and take control of the field, because first impressions score big.

By mapping out what you want to say in advance, you are better poised to control information and communicate positive messages. To do so, think of a media encounter as a simple five-step process using the word *media* as an acronym that I will describe in more detail.

1. **M**essage platform
2. **E**xamples
3. **D**elivery
4. **I**ngratiate yourself
5. **A**nticipate questions

## MESSAGE PLATFORM

Develop and limit what you want to say to three key messages that tell the reporter's audience what you want them to know, such as what is happening and what actions are being taken to solve a problem. Less is always more when trying to focus attention. If you deliver nine points, you're leaving it to the reporter to decide which two or three points she finds most interesting because she doesn't have time to report it all. When you focus and prepare in advance, you can say what you have to say and shut up, which keeps you on track and helps the reporter narrow the story into the limited space that defines her medium.

As an example, draw a triangle. In the center of the triangle, write the question what's the story I want to tell? Then answer that question in brief sentence. Label each point of the triangle with the numbers 1, 2 and 3. These are three key messages you that support the story you want to tell. Each point will ultimately include supporting points. As an example, these are abbreviated messages put together prior to the closing of an east coast supermarket chain.

Point 1   *What is happening:* ABC supermarket chain is closing after seven decades in business in order to remain competitive.

Point 2   *Store status and action steps:* ABC chain is selling stores to XX chain, and here's the time line.

Point 3   *Future opportunity for improved service and growth:* XX chain
          is better positioned to provide a competitive edge against
          much larger operations.

## EXAMPLES

Under each message point, we developed several supporting points
and examples to offer more detail as abbreviated below.

Point 1   *What is happening:* ABC supermarket chain is closing after
          seven decades in business in order to remain competitive.

## Supporting Points

- We've taken specific actions to help the communities and families we serve and to protect the employees who built our company, which include:

  - No job losses for associate managers.
  - XX stores will make every effort to assimilate our personnel
    into their operations.
  - The XX Foundation will receive a portion of the proceeds
    resulting from this transaction, which will be used to support
    the communities it serves.

Point 2   *Store status and action steps* ABC chain is selling stores to
          XX chain and here's the timeline

## Supporting points

- Give new hours of operation and changes.
- Changeover will occur in seven stores on the following dates.
- Additional dates that affect shoppers.

Point 3   *Future opportunity for improved service and growth:* XX chain
          is better positioned to provide a competitive edge against
          much larger operations.

## Supporting points

- XX chain is part of a conglomerate of more than 200 food stores
  with thousands of associates and has the necessary resources to
  remain competitive in today's market.
- Anticipate new job creation and programs.
- Long-term stability.

Instead of simply answering questions and hoping for questions to trigger your message, plotting this type of a roadmap in advance puts you in the driver's seat to direct you to the points you want to deliver. This doesn't mean you won't get surprised by some twists and turns, but planning in advance helps you stay on track and better control the message.

## DELIVERY

Media coaches teach you how to use phrases called bridges (additional examples offered in chapter 21) that help you incorporate messages into your answers and more easily transition from point to point. Bridging also enables you to deflect attacks and turn negative statements into positive messages. In our sessions, we call this the A-B-C approach. That means Acknowledge what they asked you and address it, then Bridge to Communicate your message. Here are some A-B-C examples:

Question:   How come your plants continually have such terrible performance ratings and are being called the poster child for air pollution?

A:   There is nothing is more important than the safety of our employees and this community. Our priority is to maintain a safe and healthy environment while providing reliable energy at affordable costs.

B:   However, it is important to understand . . .

C:   This is a 60-year-old facility that is continually being upgraded, and the most recent $500 million repowering initiative included . . .

Question:   Isn't it true you are paying people to talk about your product online?

A:   It is not our policy to pay people to talk about our products. We understand the need to provide unbiased information, and we take that very seriously.

B:   It's important to point out that . . .

C:   Well-respected third-party experts have been offering their own opinions on the excellent safety profile of our product and the significant improvement they've noticed.

If you want to watch people do this, all you have to do is turn on the Sunday morning political talk shows, where newsmakers often ignore the question and say whatever they want. I don't want you to ignore the question, because it sounds phony and makes you appear as if you have something to hide, and seasoned reporters can usually see right through you, which doesn't bode well for additional coverage and future relationships. Additionally, when you prepare media messages in advance, if it feels like you're drowning, think of those messages as islands of safety and use bridging phrases such as "it's important to understand," "what we do know," "that's not my area of expertise but what I can tell you," or "I appreciate your concern, but the facts are as follows" to pull you back onto dry land.

While style is important, it does not trump content. When asked a question, answer it. If you don't know the answer, then say so and, if appropriate, offer to find out. If you don't want to answer a question, explain why by saying something like, "This matter is in litigation so it would be inappropriate for me to discuss it" so the reporter doesn't think you have something to hide.

It's also important to look and sound confident when speaking in person, by phone, or by e-mail. On camera, smile when possible to appear warm, friendly, and open. When talking to a reporter by phone, try standing up, which will help you come across as energetic and engaging. By e-mail, be as succinct as possible to minimize misquotes. If the reporter wants more information, he'll ask for it. If you are excited about something, then sound excited. By the same token, if you are discussing a difficult situation, make sure the tone of your e-mail or voice reflects your concern.

## INGRATIATE YOURSELF

There is nothing worse than a corporate spokesperson that puts themselves or their company before the needs of people affected by the story. Ingratiating yourself doesn't mean sucking up to a reporter, which will completely turn them off. It means showing concern and compassion for others, which should be expressed with the first words out of your mouth. Instead of launching into facts first or being disagreeable, briefly address those affected. For example, during a role-playing session, I asked a spokesperson about insinuations that his company was continually cited for violations. He replied, "We're not continually cited for violations and if you had checked your facts, you would know that."

Not only did he repeat my negative words, which could then be attributed to him, but he sounded defensive, smug, and a bit arrogant. He could have said, "Safety is our top priority and we have completely corrected the problems that were called to our attention. However, I would like to clear up some misperceptions . . . "

Not only would this have sounded different, but he would have ingratiated himself to reporters by appearing thoughtful and caring. It would have also been an opportunity to reframe the situation and deliver the most important point first, which should be done whenever possible.

Not only does this help a spokesperson begin, which is often the toughest part of an interview, but what you say prompts follow-up questions, which is what gets the interview going.

## ANTICIPATE QUESTIONS

We advise people to develop two lists when preparing for media and other interviews. The first list is easy. It's all the questions you will likely be asked with succinct, corresponding answers you will provide. The second list is the tough one and even more important than the first. It's the questions you don't want asked, can't answer, or hope they don't ask. These are the questions that keep you up at night. Preparing doesn't guarantee you won't get blindsided, but it sure helps minimize the risk.

It's also essential to get good media training, which can be applied in so many aspects of communication. A lot of people, including disc jockeys, public relations experts, and even psychologists, offer this service, but think of it this way: If you were going on trial for tax evasion, would you hire a tax attorney or a divorce attorney? The answer is obvious. This is no different especially when your reputation is on the line, which it always is. You want to select a media coach who has extensive real-life deadline-packed news experience who can help you understand how reporters think, what questions they will ask, how they might use your responses, and how the story will be covered so you can do your very best to own that interview and shine in the spotlight.

## COACHING NOTES

- State your most important message immediately—frame the story as soon as you speak. Example: "Let me make it perfectly clear

that this is not our product. Someone has copied our product."
You were able to quickly and clearly make the reporter understand
what had happened, as opposed to assuming she knew what you
knew or had seen the news.

- Be careful of using too much jargon, such as "hazard trees," "15-foot
ceiling," and "best management practices." Just keep it simple—
the trees are touching the power lines, which is what causes these
outages.

- Think about context and perspective. For example, explain that
in the past five years, there have been 32 blackouts and then state
that you've pinpointed the problem so they understand why this
is important. You can't just say that you want reliability, which
alone doesn't mean anything. To them, reliability is lights on and
air conditioning working on a hot day.

- Instead of starting with "yes, it's a chemical," start with the message you want to deliver. The first thing out of your mouth is key.
Avoid words like *chemical*—people are scared, so reframe it using
words like *element* or *compound* and then offer examples so people
understand how it relates to their lives.

- Deliver what you want to say. If you want them to know something, say it as opposed to waiting for the question. If they don't
ask the question, you may miss an opportunity to deliver your message. Do not assume they know what you know or understand the
problem, no matter how simple you think it is.

- Put yourself in their shoes. If you lived in their neighborhood,
what would you care about? You would care about property values, the safety of your children, open space, and taxes. They don't
care about your problems! They care about themselves, so help
them understand how your work can help solve their problems.

- All of you kept talking about consistency and control they would
have logging on from their hotel room, but those words don't
mean much to the guest. You are assuming that the guest thinks or
knows there is a problem. Explain what the problem is so you can
tell them how your solution will make the world of difference to
them. They care about hassle-free connections—speed, efficiency,
and ease of use. They care that it works and they don't care about
what you have to do to make it work.

- Be more definite. Instead of, "We believe we are doing a good
job," tell us what you are doing, so the reader can decide you're

doing a good job. We sort of expect you to say that, but if you say you provide for 1.5 million people per day and this is what they get, you've given it some teeth.

- No matter who you are talking to, you must speak from their vantage point. Put yourself in their shoes to make your words mean something to them. They don't need all the details. They don't need an education. You will dilute your message. This is not about what you need. It's about what they want.

- Look for opportunities to turn negatives around. For example, instead of "when not used appropriately, it can be toxic," say "when used appropriately and monitored continuously as we do, it is safe, effective, and extremely important to preventing disease."

I would be remiss if I left you believing that reporters only think about getting the story and meeting deadlines. Like you, many are sons, daughters, parents, husbands, and wives who deeply care about others. I'd like to put myself in that category and share an experience I had while working at WPVI-TV in Philadelphia. We received a phone call from a viewer whose son had allegedly been sexually abused by a youth group leader. She was pressing charges, which we confirmed with police, and wanted to talk to a reporter so people knew what was happening and could protect their children from this person who had not been arrested.

I set up the interview and was scheduled to be the lead story on the 11:00 news that evening. As we finished the interview, the mother had a change of heart about letting us air her interview. She had other young children at home and feared retaliation from this man, even if we didn't show her face. I called the station and explained the situation to the producer, who urged me to convince her to let us show the story. He said it was already 10:00 P.M. and he had nothing else to lead the show. I said I would, but I didn't. When the woman asked me what I would do if this was my family, I said I would do everything I could to protect my children and would not go on TV to talk about this. I called the producer back and said I tried my hardest but couldn't talk her into it. Simply put, I lied to protect the woman I had interviewed.

## OWNING MEDIA INTERVIEW FIXES

**Ask questions.** The reporter is not the only one who can ask questions. You or your representative should find out who the reporter works for, what the story is about, what their deadline is, who else they may be speaking to, and what information they would like you to provide so you can offer specifics that would be helpful.

**Off the record.** There is no such thing as off the record. If you don't say it, they can't quote you. Even though reporters gather information for background purposes, everything you say can be attributed to you, including before and after chit-chat that turned out to be more interesting than the actual interview.

**No lies.** A lie will haunt you forever. Every time you or your company is in the news, media organizations will reprint or rerun your lies. There is nothing more important than open, honest communication. If you make a mistake, admit it and talk about what you're doing to correct the problem and prevent it from happening again.

**Know their needs.** Television needs visuals. Radio needs interviews. Print needs quotes. Think in those terms. If you're talking to a television reporter about the summer corn crop, conduct the interview in front of that corn field, where they can see it, rather than in an office, where they can only imagine it.

**It's not about you.** Reporters are not here to promote you. They don't care how great your legislative bill is. They want to know how that bill benefits or affects the lives of their listeners, readers, and viewers. Will it save them time, improve schools, or reduce taxes, and how much will it cost?

**It's okay to be real.** People want to relate to you. No one wants to hear from a robot that is so on message that he or she never smiles or shows emotion. Enthusiasm is contagious. If you want to engage a reporter, then be passionate and energetic so he can feel how you feel.

**Worry about what you can control.** You can't control technical difficulties, where your story is placed, or the way your picture came out. You can control how you act, what you say, and your attitude.

**Don't produce the story.** Try not to tell the reporter how to do her job. You should provide information to guide her, but, ultimately, she will write the story. The reporter does not work for you and is not interested in promoting you or advancing your career.

**Never wing it.** Spokespeople who appear natural probably rehearsed a long time to sound like they're speaking off the cuff. Just because you have the gift of gab in the boardroom doesn't mean you're ready for the front page. Practice and rehearse over and over again. You can't do it often enough.

**Speak their language.** Speak simply and conversationally. If the reporter doesn't understand you, then he can't explain it to the reader. Don't talk down to him, but think about how you might explain a difficult subject to a high school class or your own bright children.

Understand that being quoted doesn't equal credibility. In this new age of 24-hour news coverage, reporters have more time than ever to fill and more places to go to gather information ranging from traditional to social media. Reporters have always chased the competition, following up on other media and reporting those facts as their own.

In today's climate of blogs, podcasts, and social networks, fact and fiction frequently blur as the media try to cut through the clutter and attention-seekers clamor for press. The other day, a high-level executive asked me, "How can I be the sound bite?" It's not about the sound bite. Sure, the one-liner might get you on CNN, but is that what you really want? Before you silently answer yes, ask the real question: "Do I want a one-shot deal, or do I want to position myself or my client as an ethical and credible source who the media will repeatedly call for insight and perspective?" If the latter is true—and I hope it is—you are on your way to owning media interviews, which will help you gain a reliable and competitive edge.

**Help the reporter help you tell the story you want told.**

# CHAPTER 13

# No Presence

Sometimes you can't see yourself clearly until you see yourself through the eyes of others.

—*Ellen DeGeneres, comedian*

When Sam called, he wasn't exactly sure what he wanted or needed. He told me his boss said he should get some "presentation coaching," and he wanted to take advantage of the offer because his company was in the midst of a somewhat hostile takeover so he wasn't sure how long he'd have a job. He said learning how to present better might help him if he had to interview for a new position. It sounded easy enough.

To learn a bit more about how others perceived Sam, we decided I would call some past and present colleagues who could weigh in on his style. Without exception, people raved about Sam, calling him a "go-to guy" and "someone you want on your team." Everyone said he was "off the charts" in substance, and they also said he was a very good presenter. "So, help me out," I almost pleaded with one former boss, "what's the problem?"

After a long pause, the man said, "Sam needs to be more of an asshole." Slightly surprised, I asked why anyone would want a coworker to be a jerk. He said that while Sam was everyone's buddy, he didn't come across as "executive material" and needed to be seen by others as an assertive, take-charge person who had presence and purpose.

I don't believe you have to be an asshole to convey presence, but I do believe how you are seen by others directly translates to career growth. While Sam's colleagues saw him as someone they could rely on, they said he was too accommodating when communicating and did not exude executive presence. So, what exactly is executive presence and how do you get it?

If you asked 10 people to provide an explanation, you'd probably get 10 different answers. Executive presence isn't easy to define, because it means different things to different people. But when you have it, people seem to take notice. They'll say things like, "he controls the room" or "she commands attention as soon as she speaks" or they have "it." From years of work with hundreds of executives on four continents, I think it's important to explain what "it" is not before we talk about what "it" is and how to get "it." Executive presence is not about first impressions. It's not about ability, and it's not necessarily about content, though knowledge and expertise are important. Executive presence is about consistent, long-lasting impressions created over time by the way someone continually expresses herself and engages with others.

Think about people you might consider great communicators. Names like President Ronald Reagan, Martin Luther King Jr., Apple co-founder and CEO Steve Jobs, Oprah, President Bill Clinton, or former General Electric CEO Jack Welch likely come to mind. They command attention and speak with conviction. You don't have to be well known to stand out. All of the communicators I mentioned and others whom you may admire take time to understand how their listeners feel so they can clearly and compassionately speak to audience concerns even if they can't immediately address issues or solve problems. By being direct and speaking from the other person's point of view, they come across as real human beings who put others first.

In Sam's case, he did care about his listener, but he was so consumed with being liked and accepted that he continually deferred to others in an effort to please and accommodate instead of taking ownership and standing behind his remarks. Instead of projecting confidence, his body language unintentionally conveyed uncertainty and lacked commitment when he spoke.

Often, when someone is said to have executive presence, he is perceived as a person who can walk into a room and immediately command attention by the way he stands, speaks, and makes steady eye contact. Some say those with presence have a "wow factor" and are typically not afraid to voice their ideas even if those beliefs are contrary to other opinions. Former President Ronald Reagan, who was nicknamed "the great communicator," said "I wasn't a great communicator, but I communicated great things."

In our work, we've consistently observed that people who exude executive presence understand that their ability to impact or influence is judged by how they say something, not just what they say. While presence varies from person to person, they understand that executive presence is how you use your personal style to empower and connect with others.

---

Executive presence is how you use your personal style to empower and connect with others.

---

The following 10-step behavior approach shows what you can do right now to strengthen your personal style.

1. **Speak up.** Be a regular contributor at the table. Don't wait for others to ask questions. To provide valuable input, prepare three or four points you want to deliver in advance of a meeting or important conversation.

2. **State your beliefs.** Articulate your ideas even if others don't agree. Leaders stand up and voice their opinions without apologizing or making excuses. State what is correct, not what you think others want to hear.

3. **Use strong words.** Avoid disclaimers and tentative phrases such as "It seems I get results" or "I hope to have the plan by August" or "In my humble opinion" or "To be honest with you." Replace these evasive words with stronger, more assertive language such as "I firmly believe" or "It is clear that" or "The facts are as follows."

4. **Exhibit passion.** Speak with passion, energy, conviction, and commitment. High energy and emotional content appeal to people on a very human level. If you don't believe in what you are saying, no one else will.

5. **Take credit.** You need to be your own cheerleader. Self-promotion is not bragging. It's taking ownership and credit for your hard work so people notice you. Certainly give credit to others where credit is due, but it's not necessary to overly compliment or repeatedly recognize others, especially when you have contributed to the project's success.

6. **Pause.** Don't feel a need to fill the silence. Give people a chance to think for a second about what you've said before you move

on. This will position you as a more thoughtful speaker and help you come across as comfortable and confident in your delivery of information.

7. **Ask challenging questions.** Show that you will not take things at face value and ask questions to help you gain as much information as possible to understand issues in order to reframe the conversation and help others make informed decisions.

8. **Delegate.** There is a difference between delegating and doing. It's always important to help people, but that doesn't mean doing their work for them. Instead of always offering to "put something together for you" or "give it to me and I'll see what I can do," it's important to take charge. Offer to help, but don't be timid to suggest: "why don't you put it together and then I'll take a look at it."

9. **Get to the point.** Instead of backing into conversations or delivering details first, state your main point up front so you deliver a clear, concise message that goes to the heart of their concerns so they are interested in your viewpoint.

10. **Have a heart.** Being firm and definite doesn't mean you have to be rude or nasty. If you aren't true to yourself, people will likely see right through you. Always be polite and use tact when questioning or challenging the opinions of others. It will help you foster conversation and put people at ease so you can create an atmosphere of trust and open dialogue.

To talk about creating a more powerful presence without discussing body language and nonverbal communication in greater detail would be like learning to drive without learning to park. They go hand in hand. Consider how you feel during your own conversations when someone won't look you in the eye or appears to be backing away from you instead of leaning into the discussion. What about that great date you had with no kiss goodnight? Did you give off the wrong signals or did he?

Joe Navarro, author of *What Every Body Is Saying: An Ex-FBI Agent's Guide to Speed-Reading People*, writes that, as an eight-year-old exile from Cuba living in Miami, he first started studying what people were saying with their bodies because he didn't understand English. An expert in nonverbal behavior, he says the subtle movements of hands, feet, eyebrows, and facial expressions can betray one's thoughts and feelings.

I recall interviewing the owner of a pharmacy accused of selling a deadly combination of drugs. When my photographer and I approached him as he entered work early one morning and asked him whether he was sorry, he quickly said yes while pushing his way past the camera into his store and slamming the door in our faces. Clearly, his body language did not match his words.

So much of what we communicate is spoken without words. From posture to facial expressions, gestures, eye contact, clothing, personal space, and touch, we constantly send silent messages that give off loud signals. Learning how to manage these signals will help you project presence and help listeners truly hear what you have to say. Some years back, I took my mother and her friend to hear President Bill Clinton speak at a local high school. When we were leaving, my mother said, "He was looking right at me," to which her friend replied, "no he wasn't, he was looking at me." A moment later, a woman tapped them on the shoulder and said, "excuse me ladies, I couldn't help but overhearing you and must correct you; the president wasn't looking at either of you, he was looking at me."

That small story is a huge example of how masterful communicators like the former president use eye contact to engage audiences of one or one thousand. In small groups, they will deliver one complete thought to one person before looking at someone else. In larger groups, where it's not possible to make eye contact with every person, connective communicators look at people in each section of the room, again, delivering their thought to one corner before moving on to the next. They also use their space purposefully by standing still when making a significant point and pausing before moving to make another point.

Some people have confided that making direct eye contact makes them incredibly nervous, so here's a tip. Look at the other person's forehead right in between the eyebrows. It will look like you're looking her in the eye and she won't know the difference.

To better understand how nonverbal behavior can affect perceptions of someone and how you might overcome this, I'll paraphrase a conversation I had with a human resources manager about her observations of a company director's style, and his remarks regarding his challenges. I will then add notes I sent to help him with presence points, called PP for short.

> HR person:   He's awkward in front of our executives and will just charge into his talk while everyone is standing around.

Director: It's very challenging to get things started when they're talking.

PP: Think of yourself as leading the discussion instead of participating.

Begin by saying good morning. If they don't stop, say it again slightly louder and tell them to take their seats so we can all get started. You can even say you know how busy everyone is, so you want to be respectful of their time.

HR person: He needs to better set the stage and be direct about what he wants to discuss.

Director: Due to the amount of projects, I have to give a lot of information in short time periods, and I get stuck in the details.

PP: That doesn't mean you should speed up, start with the details, or overwhelm them with minutia they don't need to know. Think about the story and what it means to them. For example, when you were through, you told me "they are leaving millions of dollars of revenue on the table." Start there to get their attention.

HR person: He looks down a lot and seems unsure of himself.

Director: I need to use my notes, and I have a lot of them.

PP: Instead of writing out your notes, put them in bullet points so you can glance at the notes but explain the information in more conversational terms. When we did that, you were far more animated and engaging.

HR person: He comes across as jerky and uncomfortable.

Director: I never know what to do with my hands.

PP: When you talk naturally, you talk with your hands, and that's exactly what you should do because you come across as more energetic and interesting. Use gestures to illustrate your points.

You are likely familiar with the phrase "perception is reality." If you approach others with arms folded across your chest, hands shoved in your pockets, and eyes focused on the floor, you will probably be perceived as unapproachable and perhaps not very executive-like even if the perception is not accurate. Projecting presence doesn't mean you should be something you're not, but it does mean learning to use your authentic self to communicate with impact.

## COACHING NOTES

- It's not necessary for you to qualify what you believe with "to be honest with you." Does that mean you're not usually honest? Of course not. Just say what you have to say directly.

- You are not a motivational speaker so it's not necessary to start scripting your hand gestures. What's important is to make sure your body language says "I'm approachable!" That means open hands, palms up using your fingers and hands to illustrate points or show listeners the charts. Keep your hands out of your pockets, and do not hold the lectern. Put your hands behind your back, in a praying position, or crossed in front of you, which creates a barrier between you and the audience.

- Here's an old TV trick. Sit with your butt up toward the front of the chair as if you have a small pillow behind your back. This will help you lean into your message and appear engaged.

- To prevent from swaying or rocking, think of your wedding photos. The photographer probably had you put most of your weight on one foot to hold you in place. You can do the same.

- There is a fine line between coming across as confident or conceited. Being upbeat, definite, excited, and passionate certainly expresses confidence. But if your body language conveys arrogance and your mouth appears to be smirking, you risk coming across as phony and perhaps full of yourself.

- I know it's relaxed dress at your office, but if you are in the driver's seat that day, you need to step it up a notch. That doesn't mean jacket and tie when everyone else is in khakis and shirtsleeves, but it does mean business attire such as nice pants and a button-down-collar shirt. Remember when you asked me why I never show up in jeans? I'm the hired gun, the so-called expert, so it's important to look the part.

- When you are in front of a group, you are in a position of authority. You are the professional who is there to share information, so you need to remain a step above. Even if you're going out for a beer with these people when the meeting is over, this is not the role you are in now. If you want to have presence, then be present.

> If you want to have presence, then be present.

## NO PRESENCE FIXES

**Videotape yourself.** Watching yourself on video or working with a professional coach will show you how others see you. A professional coach can give you feedback, suggestions, and techniques to improve. By practicing the techniques on video and playing them back again, you will start to notice changes and improvement.

**Super Bowl mentality.** If you were a football player and this was Super Bowl day, you might be a bundle of nerves, but you'd be in high gear. Put that energy into full drive when selling and presenting ideas. Even if there is a microphone, project to the back of the room so you are seen as strong, confident, and in charge.

**Impressions matter.** It only takes a glance for someone to form a first impression. You don't have to spend a mint, but it's important to dress the part for interviews, appearances, and to convey your image in the workplace. That includes wearing clothes that fit properly, shoes that are shined, and colors that compliment you. Good grooming goes a long way, too.

**Smile frequently.** If you are delivering sad news, smiling may be inappropriate, but look for every opportunity to turn up those corners. People who smile are perceived as warm, friendly, approachable, and happy.

**Give them space.** Different people have different spatial requirements. Some want to stand close while others prefer more distance, so if someone appears to be backing up a step or two, give him the space he needs.

**Positive posture.** People with presence stand straight and lean slightly into the conversation or room, giving the impression that they are having a personal and even intimate conversation with just you.

Years ago, I was sent to interview Governor William Jefferson Clinton of Arkansas shortly after he announced he was running for president. It was rather silly as there were hundreds of reporters milling around to get a glimpse of him getting off the train at Philadelphia's 30th Street Station, and my newsroom told me to get an interview with him. Yeah, right. So after the sniffing dogs checked us out, we waited and waited until the magnetic Clinton was spotted coming up the stairs. Everyone started yelling at once, all clamoring for a few words, so, even though I couldn't see a thing, I figured I could yell as loud as anyone. I stuck my microphone high above my head and started yelling.

"Governor Clinton, Karen Friedman here from ABC in Philadelphia, can I speak to you?" I felt ridiculous, when suddenly the charismatic candidate walked up to me, extended his hand, looked me directly in the eye, and said, "Bill Clinton, and you are?" I froze. Seriously, I forgot my name. So he prompted me by asking, "What can I do for you?" To this day, I can't recall what I asked him, but I clearly remember how his eyes never left mine, making me feel as if I was the only person in that room.

This was probably the finest example of presence I've personally experienced. It was a win for the reporter who scored the interview, a win for local viewers who saw the interview, and a win for the station that spent the next 24 hours promoting its exclusive interview with the man who was to become the 42nd president of the United States.

**People with presence are like magnets that pull others in.**

## REFERENCE

Joe Navarro, *What Every Body Is Saying: An Ex-FBI Agent's Guide to Speed-Reading People* (New York: Harper Paperbacks, 2008).

# CHAPTER 14

# Managing Messages

*You Are the Message.*

—*Roger Ailes, president of Fox News*

I recently attended a workshop at a women's leadership conference titled *How Leaders Inspire: What We Can Learn from Aristotle*. Given the title, I looked forward to an inspirational session packed with lessons from great leaders. Instead, the presenter was anything but inspirational. She spent the first part of the workshop flashing the definition of the word *leader* on a slide and imparting statements such as "leaders need followers or they won't have anyone to lead." She then showed a clip from the movie *Gettysburg*, where an actor portraying General Robert E. Lee delivered a lengthy, impassioned plea urging his troops to follow him. Then she turned to the group and asked what we learned from the movie clip.

If you are going to talk about being inspirational, then you must be inspirational. You must be your message. It is also critical to make sure examples you use to support your message resonate with your audience. While General Robert E. Lee played by Benjamin Black in the 2004 adaptation of *Gettysburg* was passionate about his mission, the workshop presenter failed to deliver her own message with passion and could have offered role models more relevant to this specific audience. For example, the conference was held in Chicago the day after President Barack Obama was elected. There are few people who inspire as he does. Oprah calls Chicago home and is an example of a savvy businesswoman this mostly female audience would likely admire.

Roger Ailes, quoted at the top of this chapter, wrote a book titled *You Are the Message* in which he says, "when you communicate with someone, it's not just the words you choose to send the other person that make up the message. You're also sending signals about what kind of person *you* are" (1988). In other words, if you want to energize, you want to ooze energy. If you want to motivate, you have to be motivational.

As someone who has interviewed tens of thousands of newsmakers and has also counseled thousands of people to better control messages and communicate those messages successfully, I have observed that people who communicate most effectively have something in common which I have dubbed the C-P-R™ approach to messaging. Commonly known as cardiopulmonary resuscitation, an emergency medical procedure, my acronym is about breathing life into messages to make people interested in what you have to say. In my version of CPR, *C* stands for compelling, *P* means personal, and *R* is for relevant. To make a message compelling, you must make it personal. When you personalize a message, that message becomes more relevant. Or, look at it backward. To make a message relevant, you have to make someone care. To do that, it's essential to personalize that message so it is more compelling. This is the only way you can move a listener to action.

> To make a message compelling, you must make it personal.

In the early years of business, I had this incredible opportunity to provide media and political training at then First Lady Hillary Rodham Clinton's Vital Voices conference in Uruguay. Women from 34 countries across South and Central America participated in the conference, which was spearheaded by Clinton and Secretary of State Madeline Albright. Being married to the president of the United States at the time and a rock star in her own right, on the day Mrs. Clinton was scheduled to deliver the conference keynote, thousands of people began lining up outside the meeting hall in the wee hours of the morning to try to get a seat inside for the lunchtime speech. Because I was a trainer on the project, I had access to Clinton's prepared remarks, which I read in advance. Even so, I could never have anticipated what followed.

Prior to the speech, there was a three-hour plenary session where high profile political and business leaders from across the region discussed the issues. During the session, Clinton jotted down occasional notes as people were speaking. When it was her turn to address the packed house, she expertly weaved their comments into her prewritten remarks, which made her message more compelling, personal, and highly relevant. People felt that she had been listening, that she understood their problems, and that she truly cared about what they had to say.

Regardless of education or status, people are more likely to listen if they can relate to what you're saying. They will care if the message affects them. However, in our own sessions, we find there is often confusion as to what a message is, what it isn't, and how to develop one that will resonate with specific listeners. First, let's start by debunking a few myths:

Myth: A message is a slogan.

Myth: A message is a tag line.

Myth: A message is an advertisement.

Myth: A message is a mission statement.

Myth: A message is a marketing statement.

What is a message? Messages should communicate what you do and how it benefits, impacts, or affects the listener.

The most important question to ask when developing a message is "who am I speaking to?" so you can tailor the message specifically to their concerns if you hope to achieve results. Let's say you're a scientist who has to present study results to management. As a scientist, you are most comfortable talking to peers about the specifics of your research. Yet management may be more concerned about a time line hiccup to determine whether they should keep funding the project. You must know the results you seek in advance to tailor your message to the specific listener. Often, messages are too broad and approach audiences as a one size fits all. This is a huge mistake, because one person's candy is another's toothache.

---

One person's candy is another's toothache.

---

Communicating is not about talking. It's about connecting. To make your message connect, think of it as a triangle described in chapter 12 or a three-legged stool, which is the same idea. Label each leg of the stool with the numbers 1, 2, and 3, which will ultimately represent your three key message points. But before we brainstorm messages, on the seat of the stool, write down what you want your listener to feel when you're done talking. Do you want them to feel you are in control of a situation? Perhaps you want them to feel that your company can provide greater services than the competition. If they feel, they'll care. If they care, they'll listen. Once you clearly know what you want someone to feel, you can start to organize your central message or theme and deliver it in a clear, compelling manner.

We worked with an international religious organization that wanted to establish visibility in order to attract new supporters and funding from the community but struggled with message clarity. When we first got together, the organization's leadership was very determined to deliver the same internal messages they had used for decades. They were talking about religious priorities and policy that mattered to them but did not align with their goal of raising money from outsiders. Additionally, they could not clearly articulate what their society did or how they planned to move forward. Even among themselves, they weren't sure why people outside of their schools and ministries would give them money.

Through a series of questions, much like I would ask if I were still covering news stories, we prioritized and identified goals so the organization could address the concerns of external audiences. Once they agreed on message headlines, we identified key facts and example to support the messages and looked for ways to compress information.

Here is an abbreviated outline of the exercise that helped the society organize its thoughts into one statement.

Question: What do you want the audience to feel?

Answer: That we are good people with a good mission.

Question: What is that mission?

Answer: To help others.

Question: How do you help others in the outside world?

Answer: We provide tools for women and children in communities across the world.

Question: What kinds of tools?

The questions continued until we came up with a simple, short, compelling headline that told the outside world what they do and why it's important. The overarching message statement was:

Through education and social programs, we provide tools and skills to help women and children around the world overcome obstacles such as poverty, illiteracy, and abuse—so they can lead productive lives and make a difference in their communities.

From there, we made a list of all the points they wanted to make, and then whittled that list into three main messages, our three-legged stool. The remaining points were used to support the bigger messages. This is an abbreviated example of what it looked like:

### Leg 1: Who we are and what we do

Organization X is a 160-year-old organization of women across four continents whose expanding mission is to improve the lives of women and children around the world through education, social programs, and partnerships that give them tools and skills to overcome obstacles such as poverty, illiteracy, and abuses so they can lead productive lives and make a difference.

- Partnering with religious and nonprofit organizations to help people find good jobs and provide for their families. Specifics include:
  - After-school and summer programs, sports, reading
  - Inner-city volunteer programs
  - Parenting programs

### Leg 2: Future plans and impact
### Leg 3: Financials and how you can help

When messages are organized around a central point and then backed up with specifics, they provide more context and meaning for listeners. Think of it as a wow factor. A good example or analogy will wow a listener and increase retention. Just the facts without context are yawners. Look at the difference between a wow and a yawn.

Yawn:   Debris from Hurricane Katrina totals 55 million cubic yards across southeast Louisiana

Wow:    Debris from Hurricane Katrina could fill 3.5 million large dump trucks. That's enough to reach all the way around the Earth at the equator and you'd still have enough trucks left to stretch from New York to Denver.

Yawn:   China's trade surplus surged to $101.9 billion last year, more than triple the $32 billion gap recorded the year before.

Exports rose 28.4 percent in the same year to $762 billion, while imports rose 17.6 percent to $660 billion.

Wow: With total global trade of $1.42 trillion, China is now the world's third-biggest trading nation. China has now overtaken Japan in merchandise trade and remained just behind the United States and Germany.

Yawn: This was a massive spill that has dumped more than a billion gallons of coal waste in central Tennessee.

Wow: The spill unleashed more than a billion gallons of sludge—enough to fill 1,660 Olympic-size swimming pools.

Looking for different and interesting ways to make points to keep the attention of your listeners is important, but it's equally important to make sure these points are consistently connected to your core message and not just delivered to be catchy or cute.

## COACHING NOTES

- I think you need to provide more context when comparing managers and leaders. Make sure they understand the difference. Perhaps: leading is about direction and vision, while managers carry out the tasks to make that happen. Then you can better transition to why you want to be a better leader by remembering (or never forgetting) how you got here. Keep it simple. The key question you want them to answer is would you want to be your boss?

- Until you talk about something that affects them, they won't pay attention. To do this, think about your goals and how to frame what you want to say from their perspective. Your story about Sam was so real that your natural energy and passion came through. You also became more animated and projected in a greater way because you pulled them into the experience, which was your message.

- Once you've narrowed your theme, pick out the key message points that support that theme and will be relevant to them. For example:

  - A specific animal that you studied could lend useful information for fighting Alzheimer's and Parkinson's. Start there, then show them the data. Then you can explain the data but put it in context by speaking to the mystery of these cells so they relate to how what's being done with animals might eventually translate to humans. It's much more compelling and meaningful, and when you practiced it that way, you were far more engaging.

- I'm encouraging you to personalize even more. If you are going to mention other products, don't assume they know what Product A is for or what Product B does—tell them. This way, every single person is taking away the same information and will know what's in it for them and why they should care.

- As you move through your talk, think about ways to marry value, benefit to the message. How does this benefit Suzie's baby? Be the problem solver. The message isn't the product. It's the problem the product will solve. If you present the problem in terms relevant to their work and life, then the solution or recommendations have much more impact. In a sense, you are looking for opportunities to interject moments they will remember so your message is memorable.

## MANAGING MESSAGES QUESTIONS TO ASK

Who am I speaking to?

What do I want them to feel?

What is their biggest challenge or problem that I can solve?

How does what I'm saying impact, benefit, or affect them?

What are my goals?

How does my message tie to my strategy, growth, vision, or direction?

What everyday, real-life examples would make this message more relevant?

If I only had 10 seconds to speak, how would I explain this?

## MANAGING MESSAGES FIXES

Your job is to deliver your message regardless of what others think they know or want to hear. You are your own advocate or cheerleader. Your job is to inform, persuade, educate, motivate, and help people understand how your words affect them.

**Identify your audience.** Speak to your listeners' specific concerns, questions, fears, and challenges.

**Ask the right questions.** By asking questions your listeners will ask, you can marry your goals to their concerns by including the information in your message points.

**Create the takeaway.** Determine the single most important message you want your listeners to remember so your message resonates with them.

**Use the three-legged stool.** Limit your key headlines to three major points and organize subpoints around them. For example: 1. Problem. 2. Action steps. 3. Results.

**Use people pleasers.** Use real-life examples and experiences about people who mean something to your listener and make your message more relevant.

It's important to note that sometimes you'll have to fine-tune your message as circumstances and audience concerns change. As long as you constantly keep your listeners concerns in mind, you will have a better chance of developing people-centered messages that speak to hearts as well as minds.

**Good communication is not about talking. It's about connecting.**

## REFERENCE

Roger Ailes, *You Are the Message* (New York: Doubleday, 1988).

# CHAPTER 15

# Likeable Leadership Lessons

—⊷

> Your friendliness, combined with your empathy and relevance, will make you a likeable person—but it's your ability to be real that will make you absolutely shine.
> —*Tim Sanders*, The Likeability Factor

You don't have to be a barracuda to be a likeable leader. When a long-time client who we'll call Tony was promoted to CEO of a publicly traded biotechnology company, it was critical for him to make a great impression as he addressed company employees for the first time. When he rehearsed, he clearly knew his stuff, but the talk seemed flat as if the real Tony—the guy with personality that everyone was excited about—went missing.

I asked him what kind of a feeling he wanted to convey—what kind of a company atmosphere he hoped to continue or create. He thought about it and said, "I want this company to feel like the chili cook-off we had the other day—fun, interactive, competitive with feelings of camaraderie and teamwork." He said he wanted employees to know he had heart and would always put people first as his compass to help guide the company in the right direction.

Saying so and making people believe so are quite different. Tony needed to be himself so his enthusiasm and optimism could inspire employees, who were a tad anxious about the changing of the guard yet eager to follow his lead. Instead of talking about where he wanted to take the company, he needed to show people what the company would look like under his direction.

So we threw out the planned script, dumped the slides, and started over by showing a picture of a very sick patient. A genuine and heartfelt

Tony told the patient's story; explaining what her days were like before the people who worked for his company developed a new medication that provided quality of life she had not known for years. Tony explained that that was the kind of company he wanted to continue to grow. His words motivated and captivated the hundreds of people in the room, who remain committed to helping him move forward. His continual desire to let others see him as a human being has endeared him to colleagues, investors, and the community at large. If that's not enough, under Tony's lead, the company was one of the best performers on Wall Street during the crash of 2008.

In that year, a poll conducted by the Pew Foundation asked the public to give one-word descriptions of political candidates. The words used to describe then New York Senator Hillary Clinton were experienced, strong, untrustworthy, intelligent, smart, determined, and another word that rhymes with rich. On the television show *Meet the Press*, the late Tim Russert asked political strategist James Carville what this means, to which Carville replied that he knows Clinton and finds her to be very likeable, but people who do not know her may think she's smart, experienced, and tough but "not a particularly likeable person."

Likeability goes a long way toward getting elected, promoted, motivating people, and closing deals. While it's not required to succeed, people want to like you, but they will have difficulty liking you if they can't relate to you. For example, Washington Redskins quarterback Donovan McNabb is a very likeable fellow. He smiles, looks you in the eye, publicly admits mistakes, accepts feedback, and plays well, which doesn't hurt. His positive attitude is contagious. Contrast him to Terrell Owens, a talented wide receiver for the Cincinnati Bengals, who is widely criticized for his arrogant, egotistical behavior, making him not very likeable to many. Both men are hugely successful, but it could be argued that McNabb's likeability makes him a leader that Owens is not.

In business, like sports, leadership doesn't mean people will follow you. It doesn't come with a big title like CEO or quarterback. The leaders and sports celebrities I know have a lot of qualities in common, such as purpose, passion, and confidence. But the real leaders like Tony have home field advantage because they practice people skills and communication skills that strengthen relationships, which make them likeable. I firmly believe if you want to become more successful, you need to make people your number-one priority. In my experience, these are the leaders others want to follow.

> If you want to become more successful, you need to make people
> your number-one priority.

In an article titled "How To Become More Likeable" by Michael
Lovas, author and cofounder of AboutPeople, Lovas says likeability is
not the result of luck and lists what researchers say happens to people
who develop likeability skills:

1. They're more successful in business and in life.
2. They get elected, promoted, and rewarded more often than those
   who are less likable.
3. They close more sales and make more money.
4. They get better service from all types of service providers.

As this book was being written, I stumbled on that lesson as I at-
tempted to lease a new car. After doing my homework, I knew exactly
what car I wanted and where I wanted to buy it. I had actually referred
several friends to a specific salesman at this dealership, who was rec-
ommended to me, but I had never met him. This should have been a
done deal. Yet what happened when I walked into the dealership astounded me and is a leadership likeability lesson. I introduced myself
to the salesman, told him about the customers I had sent him, and requested a test ride, committing to signing on the dotted line if he gave
me a good price.

He began the test drive by peeling out of the lot at full speed to impress me, which backfired because I was gripping the door handle in
surprised fear. When I asked him to slow down, he told me it was important for him to let me experience the car. When we returned to the
lot following our joyride, I explained that my current car had a very
simple navigation system and given I could get lost in a bathtub, an
easy-to-use navigation program was a priority for me. Instead of taking
the time to walk me through the GPS system, which he insisted was
much easier than my current vehicle, he pressed every knob, button, and
touch screen he could locate, which succeeded in overwhelming and
confusing me. Clearly, this was about what he cared about. Offering
little in terms of price, I left and when I called a few days later to negotiate a better deal, he said there wasn't room to negotiate.

Here's the kicker. When we spoke and I shared my concerns about
my experience with him, instead of seizing an opportunity to save the

deal, he sent me a defensive and hostile e-mail accusing me of not really wanting to buy a car from him. Needless to say, I leased the car from another dealership. The dealership was further away and less convenient, but I didn't mind because I liked the salesperson, which led me to believe I would have a better long-term experience with the dealership.

How your message is received can directly impact how your vision and direction is embraced.

---

How your message is received can directly impact how your vision and direction is embraced.

---

In Tony's case, he empowered his employees by echoing and reinforcing their values and continued quest for an organization dedicated to finding new ways to benefit patients. They saw the same down-to-earth, likeable coworker they admired and trusted before he was promoted, which inspired them to give him a chance.

As a television reporter some years back, I received a phone call from my son's daycare center as I was about to leave for work. They said he was running a high fever and I needed to come get him. But on that day, I had no one to take care of him, which is what I explained to the producer when I called. Expecting her to understand, she said they were very short-staffed that day and if I didn't come to work, I would leave them in a real bind. Terribly upset, I apologized and said there was nothing I could do. After a tense silence, she said, "Well, there is something you can do. You can hang up and call back. Tell whoever answers the phone that you're running a fever and can't get out of bed, and don't mention that we spoke." Then she hung up.

When I first shared this story in a published article on leadership communications, I wrote, "It was at that moment I clearly understood the difference between a boss and a leader. A boss is simply a superior who exercises control. A leader understands the importance of relationships and making people feel valued through what is or isn't said." I received several e-mails and phone calls blasting this producer for asking me to lie and saying these are not leadership traits.

While being dishonest is not acceptable, this producer understood the unfortunate "that's not my problem" attitude under not-so-effective leadership that had created a myriad of problems in that newsroom. Granted, it would have been better if she had said, "I hope your child is feeling better and we understand," but unfortunately office politics aren't always that black and white. By telling me to bend the truth, she was a human being who silently communicated that she understood.

## COACHING NOTES

- You should look at the entire DVD of your broadcast. You went on tangents that were completely off message, brought up points you weren't asked about, and laughed inappropriately. I realize your laugh was because you were uncomfortable, but the listener doesn't know that, and you could give an entirely incorrect impression as to the seriousness of these events and whether you put your customer or profits first.

- You are a really nice guy, and that's why people like you. You come across as genuine, sincere, and as someone who would do anything for anyone, which works in your favor. Unfortunately, it also works against you. It's great to help people, but that doesn't mean you have to say yes to everyone or do it for them. Try delegating a bit more by saying, "Here's a suggestion." You can even show them how to do it, and then *let them do it!* It's sort of like parenting; we want to protect our kids, but if we do everything for them, they'll never learn.

- As a leader, it is your job to talk to the entire group, not just a select few or an important few. Otherwise, you could alienate some of the team. Even if the higher level people get caught up in discussions they find most interesting, this is about all of them. You can talk with the people you want to impress later or call another meeting.

- This is about your goal as a manager. In this case, your data were blasted and took the wind out of people's sails. It's leading a lot of experts to question the hypothesis. Based on what you know and believe, you want to rebuild their confidence, so stick to your guns. Not everyone will like it or agree, and they don't have to. Given that you say you want their feedback, whether it's good or bad, tell them that right up front.

- As you know, I am not big on cramming something down someone's throat and sounding like PR 101 or flak delivering the company line. I think in this case, it's critical to appear opaque and come across as genuine, honest, and someone who values what others think and is open to having a real discussion with them—a discussion from our vantage point that is focused. They might not agree with you, and that's okay, but your attitude and demeanor will convey that you are genuine and truly believe in what you are saying and the company's strategy.

- You need to explain that this was a strategic business decision that had to be made in order to best serve the customer. Each and every one of you *must* deliver that message with empathy and compassion. These people must be told they are appreciated and valued so they feel you are being honest, straightforward, and are not stringing them along.

## LIKEABILITY LEADERSHIP FIXES

**Eye contact.** Look people directly in the eye when you speak, and stop to listen to what they have to say. When you acknowledge other people's feelings and permit their opinions, they know you value their input.

**Mirror magic.** When people smile real smiles, their whole face lights up. If you have trouble smiling, look in the mirror and practice your facial expressions so you can see what looks real and what looks phony. Think of someone you love, like a child or pet, and put on that face when you communicate with others.

**Seek feedback.** Survey or question others to see how you are perceived, so you can assess personal communication areas that may need improvement. Self-awareness is the best step toward change, growth, and continued development.

**Say it, don't spray it.** If you have something to say to someone, say it directly to the person instead of talking behind her back. When you gossip about or criticize someone to others, you create distrust and contribute to poor morale. Make it clear to your subordinates that you will not tolerate this kind of behavior.

**Make it easy.** Put systems in place to foster an atmosphere of open communication where people are not embarrassed to ask questions, speak their minds, raise issues, and challenge other's opinions to create dialogue and talk through problems.

Being likeable as a communicator doesn't mean you have to agree with or attempt to please listeners to get results or to get ahead, but if you want people to follow you, they have to believe in what you say. As

Margaret Thatcher, former British prime minister, said, "If you set out to be liked, you would be prepared to compromise on anything at any time, and you would achieve nothing."

> If you set out to be liked, you would be prepared to compromise on anything at any time, and you would achieve nothing.

Being likeable is about being authentic to what you believe when speaking to others. Martin Luther King, Jr. articulated fairness and faith, while modern-day President Barack Obama communicates change. Both understand the power of staying positive even when navigating difficult times, and people relate to them because they come across as believable and real.

I recall when the CEO of a technology solutions company I worked with did an interview with a local business paper. It was a great opportunity for him to publicly redefine his company's mission as it was going through significant changes. When I saw the article, I could barely believe it, because it was full of big words and devoid of any human messages, so I called the corporate communications person who had prepared him for the interview and expressed my opinion. She said she told him the same thing, but he insisted this was a "business-to-business" interview, not a human interview. Honestly, I couldn't make this stuff up. Who did he think ran businesses, developed technology, and read publications? If you want to be a likeable leader, start with being human.

**Likeable communicators stay true to themselves when speaking to others.**

# CHAPTER 16

# Keepers and Catchy Phrases

I often quote myself. It adds spice to my conversation.
—*George Bernard Shaw, British author*

In 1987, I covered one of the most horrific stories ever reported. A man named Gary Michael Heidnik was arrested for kidnapping, torturing, and raping six women, who he kept imprisoned in a hole that he dug in his Philadelphia basement. It was later learned that Heidnik killed two of the women and dismembered one of their bodies. Not surprisingly, the media attention generated by this gruesome story was somewhat of a circus. Reporters from all over the country descended on Philadelphia, angling for the latest news and wondering who would defend such an animal.

The defense attorney that stepped to the plate was a charismatic up-and-coming young man by the name of Charles Peruto, Jr., whose father was already a local lawyer superstar. Like father, like son, the young Charlie loved the attention, especially the television cameras, and we loved him right back. Charlie got it. He understood that great quotes made headlines, and he wanted to be in those headlines. So on the day the news broke, I shoved a microphone in his face and asked, "Mr. Peruto, why would you take this case?" to which he responded, "I'll give you one million reasons why." One million dollars was the sum Peruto was allegedly paid. For our report, that was a keeper.

Keepers are short, crisp, and catchy snippets that drive home a point in an interesting and attention-grabbing manner. Peruto could have said that everyone is entitled to a defense or that he was being paid handsomely, but he knew he only had a few seconds to make the point. The more memorable he could be, the more likely he would get into the story.

> Keepers are short, crisp, and catchy snippets that drive home a point in an interesting and attention-grabbing manner.

Keepers are not limited to media but are an effective way to cut through the clutter and spice up business communications as well. It's important to recognize I am not suggesting turning your business communications into pithy sound bites. However, by animating your message with an analogy or visual example, not only will you increase retention, but you will help your listener understand the concept. For example, an oncology team I worked with had to present the results of a clinical trial in patients with advanced kidney cancer to a group of their peers. Most people in the room were familiar with the disease state and the promising anticancer agent, but not everyone had a medical background, and some were seeing the trial results for the first time. The goal of the presentation was to show listeners that this was a very promising therapy, because it targeted cancer cells differently than other therapies and could keep patients alive longer. Part of the challenge was to briefly explain how it worked; what scientists call the mechanism of action.

The presenter explained that by "inhibiting a protein the therapy blocks the processes through which both normal cells and cancerous kidney cells grow and divide." That sounds simple enough for this audience to understand, but it's not a real keeper that people can visualize or remember when they leave the room.

Another presenter said the same thing, but explained it differently. He said the therapy works by "fooling cancer cells into thinking they're starving." He went on to explain that, because the cells can no longer sense they have enough nutrients to grow, they stop dividing. That's a keeper.

UCLA professor Albert Mehrabian studies how we receive meaning when people speak to each other. He suggests that 7 percent of the message we receive is from the words, 38 percent is from tone and voice, and visuals account for the remaining 55 percent. While that means body language such as eye contact and posture can impact listeners both positively and negatively, creating visual images with your words can also boost retention and understanding. Here are some other examples:

Dull:   Conservatives have looked at this seat and decided that he would not be a relevant candidate against a five-term senator.

Keeper:   "Running against Arlen Specter is like having your teeth pulled without Novocain."
—Larry Ceisler, political consultant

Dull:   This is more than the standard downturn where unemployment rises for a while and income tax and sales tax revenues are weak, and there are a number of reasons this is happening, including weak consumer spending, high energy prices, and dropping housing values.

Keeper:   "Think of the economy as an overweight, middle-aged man with a mild heart attack who is now on rehabilitation . . . a man who has had too much to eat, too much to drink, stayed out too late, and is forced to take a breather. He is at risk of a more severe heart attack if he doesn't get back in shape."
—Mark Zandi, *Moody's Economy.com*

Dull:   The sex addicts who use the Internet undergo a speedy progression of their addiction.

Keeper:   "The Internet is the crack cocaine of sex addiction."
—Unknown

Dull:   Intussusception is a medical condition in which a part of the small intestine has invaded another section of the intestine.

Keeper:   "Intussusception is triggered when the bowel folds over on itself like a collapsible telescope."
—*Bloomberg News*

Dull:   At stake is the future of what has been Obama's signature domestic initiative.

Keeper:   "They've pushed all the chips into the middle of the table on this."
—Ed Gillespie, advisor to President George W. Bush

Just as important as keepers are the words and phrases we use when delivering presentations, leading meetings, or trying to convince a boss why more resources are necessary to keep a project moving forward. Often, presenters fall flat, because, instead of using language that is catchy and convincing, they sound as if they are trying to convince themselves.

> Often presenters fall flat, because, instead of using language that is catchy and convincing, they sound as if they are trying to convince themselves.

Not convincing:   We believe the airport is safe.

Convincing:   Safety is our top priority.

Not convincing:   I don't think the two incidents are related.

Convincing:   The two incidents are completely unrelated.

Not convincing:   It is not our policy to discriminate.

Convincing:   We do not tolerate discrimination of any kind.

These examples illustrate using an active or passive voice. The active voice is more direct and comes across as more convincing. The passive voice typically uses more words, and the words are not as crisp or energetic. Active words can help you motivate, inspire, and sell your vision.

I have spent a lot of time with the director of investor relations for a worldwide pharmaceutical company. He is incredibly bright and personable but tends to use phrases such as "pretty sure," "maybe," "could be," and "might"—words that can be showstoppers. His boss says he comes across as unsure of himself, unconvincing, and lacking confidence, which will ultimately affect his ability to rise in the organization. Here are some notes from one of our sessions designed to help him use stronger words and deliver them with more conviction when speaking to the financial community.

Question:   How does Product X grow beyond generic entry?

Lacks confidence:   It should continue to grow.

Conviction:   We strongly believe or we are firmly committed.

Question:   You're probably not going to switch that many patients from Drug X to Drug Y this quarter. How will that affect earnings?

Lacks confidence:   It could affect earnings a little.

Conviction:   We fully expect Product X to continue to grow. Not only does it currently have the highest share in the marketplace, but we have launched

|                     | five products in the past two years, which has meant a large amount revenue growth. |
|---------------------|-------------------------------------------------------------------------------------|
| Question:           | How will you get them to switch?                                                     |
| Lacks confidence:   | It will be tough at first.                                                           |
| Conviction:         | Product X is the next-generation treatment.                                         |
| Question:           | What are your thoughts on Product X based on the latest failed trial?               |
| Lacks confidence:   | Yes, we were disappointed.                                                           |
| Conviction:         | We're firmly committed to our partnership—7seven of the nine Phase 2 trials have produced very good results. Four additional trials are planned. |
| Question:           | R and D spending is off the charts. Can you explain?                                |
| Lacks confidence:   | It takes a lot of money to bring a drug to market.                                  |
| Conviction:         | Six launches in two years have meant a significant investment. Now we are able to talk to doctors and provide additional clinical data that are extremely important to patients. |
| Question:           | Earnings will likely dip next year. Are you confident?                              |
| Lacks confidence:   | We're pretty confident.                                                             |
| Conviction:         | We are extremely confident.                                                         |

This is not what some people might refer to as spin. This is about coming across as direct and confident. By defending, overexplaining, or trying to justify, you can inadvertently rob your words of power. It is also important to own what you say. For example, if you publish scientific data about a breakthrough therapy, it can be reported without speaking to you. But if you are interviewed or asked to discuss your research, you have an opportunity to say what only you can say by using this kind of wording:

- What we discovered
- What we did
- What we found
- What we learned

- What we saw
- What we observed
- What we looked at

Explaining what you saw or did gives you ownership and highlights your expertise. Additionally, powerful words such as *significant, critical, important,* and *key* help call attention to what you are saying and can bring back people who may have tuned out.

## CATCHY PHRASES

This is key

This is significant because

What's critical to understand

What's important to understand

I'd like to call your attention to

What we can't lose sight of

The reason we are so encouraged

What makes this unique

Unlike any other product

What we do know

What this means is

What's so rewarding (or exciting)

If you only remember one thing

When a journalist interviews someone, she can't always report what that person said word for word, so she edits out words to make the quote more succinct while still communicating the tone and message to readers. Successful communicators do the same thing in order to keep people focused and capture their attention.

A client of mine was recently promoted to head the marketing efforts for a new product. He's going to address his colleagues at an upcoming meeting and wants to come across as clear, crisp, and as direct as possible, which is not his style or strong point. He admittedly says he uses too many words, takes too long to get to the point, and is not "catchy." To get ready for this presentation, he sent out an e-mail asking colleagues for input so he can tailor his remarks to their concerns. Below is a sample of his initial e-mail and the changes we made to punch it up.

## INITIAL E-MAIL (EDITED FOR PUBLICATION)

Many of you may not have heard, but I will now be heading up the XX Global Team. I will be working closely with our team of Sam and Julie and have worked with many of you over the last few years and have truly valued that partnership. With both Product A and Product B, what I can promise you is that the team and I will bring passion and energy to the mission of helping you maximize brand growth in XX.

Why I am writing this e-mail is that we are preparing for a meeting in October. As we prepare for this meeting and work on an agenda for the session, I would love to get your perspective on a few questions. This will allow us to craft a session that truly meets your needs. So, if you can respond to me by September 28, that would be great.

## REVISED E-MAIL

As some of you know, I am now leading the XX Global Team and am really excited about it as I have worked with many of you over the last few years and have truly valued these partnerships. I commit to you that with both Product A and Product B, our strong team of Sam and Julie will bring passion and energy to the mission of helping you maximize brand growth in XX.

As we prepare for the October meeting, I would like your input on a few questions to help us craft a session that truly meets your needs. I'd appreciate your response no later than September 28.

### E-mail to Client

- Eliminating excess words when you write and speak helps you focus the reader or listener's attention and get your message across as quickly and succinctly as possible and prevent misunderstandings. Additionally, present tense as noted in the e-mail example is stronger and clearer. For example, "We provide financial guidance each quarter" is stronger than "We will provide financial guidance in a couple of months."

As a television reporter, it seemed there was never enough time to report what I learned in less than two minutes' time. Reporters are notorious for pleading for more column space and air time, but you quickly learn that, when you are forced to cut and edit, your stories actually become better. I call it the GPS of good communication. In this case, GPS stands for good communicators plot the shortest route.

Good communicators plot the shortest route.

## COACHING NOTES

- You need to practice losing those ums and uhs and words you use to fill the silence. It's far more effective to be silent, because these filler words detract from your credibility and make you tough to listen to.
- You said, "We have some, um, aspirational goals." That's not really a keeper and not very motivating for listeners. Think about analogies and strong words such as, "We're excited about the direction we're headed because it will offer a full menu of options for people who are hungry for more."
- Great example about long-term data when, instead of offering just the numbers, you said, "this equals one million patient years."
- Analogies are great. Your "hybrid" example to illustrate a crossover vehicle is a perfect example of an analogy that helps the listener get it.
- Try to eliminate words so you can deliver in a more definite manner. For example, instead of, "So, thanks for listening to me today," which is almost apologetic, how about "Good morning. I want to talk to you about a devastating disease that has no cure."
- Your comparison to developing a new business model that represents a silo is good and visual, but then what? You can't just say it; you have to describe what it means and how it will be used to benefit people.
- Be careful of those passive disclaimers: "It seems I get results" versus "I get results," or "I crave the plan by August" versus "I would like the plans on my desk by August 5," or "In my humble opinion" versus "In my opinion," or "I firmly believe," etc. Think in terms of I believe, this is what I think, I saw xyz and this is why.

## KEEPERS AND CATCHY WORD FIXES

**Be your own editor.** Go through every segment and ask yourself whether it adds to what you are writing or saying. Try paraphrasing to see if you can say the same thing using fewer words.

*USA Today* **approach.** Pretend you're speaking to *USA Today* readers in order to help you put concepts in the simplest terms possible to make it understandable for others.

**Apply analogies.** Simple analogies that create visual impressions that are catchy and memorable such as "fingernails on a chalkboard," "it was so hot you could fry an egg on the pavement," or "has a mind like a steel trap." When explaining a complicated concept, think of an everyday example you can compare it to. For example, if you are explaining a questionable political initiative that might fail, you could liken it to a poker game by saying, "they've pushed all the chips to the middle of the table."

**Ad copy approach.** Ads are written to address people's wants and needs. The words appeal to our emotions and stress the benefits of a product or service. Create a list of catchy words with benefits that would appeal to you if you were your listener. For example, if you are selling washing machines, benefits might include energy efficient, quiet, leak-proof, high performance, good value, and long lasting.

**Tweet it.** If you only had 140 characters to make your words matter, how would you say it? That's a good exercise for trimming the fat.

**You can quote me on that!**

## REFERENCE

Albert Mehrabian. *Silent Messages—A Wealth of Information About Nonverbal Communication* (Los Angeles, CA: self-published), http://www.kaaj.com/psych/smorder.html.

# CHAPTER 17

# Just a Meeting

> The best way to sound like you know what you're talking about is to know what you're talking about.
>
> —*Author unknown*

Several years ago, *Fast Company* magazine published one of the funniest articles I've ever read, titled *How To Stay Awake in Boring Meetings*. On their blog, *Fast Company* staff said it had popped up in their inbox, so they posted it to offer readers ways to stay awake in meetings, seminars, and on conference calls. I'll paraphrase it for you.

1. Before your next meeting, prepare by drawing a 5" × 5" square card. Divide it into columns—5 across and 5 down to give you 25 one-inch blocks.
2. Write one of the following words in each block: synergy, strategic fit, core competencies, best practice, win-win, bottom line, to tell you the truth, paradigm, value-added, leverage, game plan—there were many more. Every time you hear one of those words, check off the appropriate box.
3. When you get five blocks horizontally, vertically, or diagonally, stand up and shout "BULLSHIT!"

What made this business bingo post even funnier were the comments people posted, such as:

"I had been in the meeting for only five minutes when I won."
"My attention span at meetings has improved dramatically."

"The speaker was stunned as eight of us screamed 'BULLSHIT!' for the third time in two hours."

I don't want to add to your boredom by writing a chapter on how to make your own meetings more interesting. I want to help you change your approach and mindset to meetings you attend so you are noisy when necessary to advocate your position and develop visibility, so when you speak, people know it's because you really do have something to say.

For starters, there is no such thing as just a meeting. Every meeting poses opportunities for discussion, generating ideas, producing outcomes, and positioning yourself with your peers. Whether it's a quick update or weekly requirement, the impression you make on peers can indirectly affect your raises and promotions. That means you have to prepare.

Take the case of a senior executive I'll call Robert. He's brilliant, which is why he heads up a multimillion-dollar business division at his company, but his boss says he doesn't offer much at meetings, that he "talks to simply talk," and he "needs to understand the right time to speak and the right time to shut up." Additionally, the boss says Robert doesn't fully engage people below him, so he appears snobbish and aloof.

Robert had a completely different take on this. He told me he doesn't want to "show off," so most of the time he remains quiet but then feels as if he should have said something so he tries to come up with remarks on the spot, which typically don't add much to the conversation. He also said that most of the people at these meetings don't understand the high-level information he deals with, so it's easier to just sit back as opposed to trying to "dumb it down" for them. The unintended result is that Robert comes across as someone who doesn't have a strong plan and is not very interested in what others have to say. Privately, his boss told me if he doesn't step up to the plate, his future at this company is at risk.

> If he doesn't step up to the plate, his future at this company is at risk.

As Robert and I started to tackle his dilemma, something else emerged. Robert confided that he was a bit intimidated to speak up for fear of not measuring up to his boss, a charismatic, impressive speaker who had the ability to deliver a "pithy" message on the spot. This was a tough one.

We began by identifying Robert's goals, which we would tackle over a period of time:

1. Develop more visibility and influence.
2. Execute views in meetings and presentations.
3. Engage better with people to advocate position.
4. Improve leadership skills to present vision and strategy.

In our own meetings, we role-played some of his meetings and came up with the following strategies to help him develop a more dominant and influential voice.

## COACHING NOTES

- Don't treat your meetings as just another meeting. Before every meeting, recognize the opportunity in advance. Will a greater understanding of the information prompt management to make a greater investment? Can you put research in perspective for those who don't have your level of knowledge so they are engaged in your work and the conversation at hand?

- To avoid feeling like you have to come up with remarks on the spot, identify two or three things you may want to talk about in advance. This way, if someone heads in that direction, you are prepared to add to the conversation or to bring up an idea that has not been discussed.

- Use open-ended and clarifying questions to draw others out and help facilitate the conversation. Questions such as, "so what you are saying is" or "if I understand you correctly, you are suggesting." Sometimes, repeating what someone says in a different manner and raising a question is also helpful. Example: "So, Jeff, if we continue with the current schedule you've outlined, does that mean we will hit our goal before the end of the year?"

- If you are expected to provide an update or status report, prepare a simple one-pager that you can distribute to people at the meeting to keep you on track and help them digest the concepts. Practice your delivery out loud before the meeting.

- Instead of comparing yourself to others or fearing you may not impress people, think of meetings as an opportunity to share information that is important for others to understand and that may help your boss and others make decisions.
- If you think of something to add while someone else is speaking, jot it down so you can add to the conversation at the appropriate time or when the person is done speaking.

In another situation, a colleague called and invited me to her meeting. I thought she wanted me to facilitate a message development session surrounding the launch of an important product, so I was surprised and a bit disappointed to learn that another agency was running the meeting. I asked her why she wanted me to attend, to which she replied, "I want you to be the bullshit meter." Knowing she probably had not read *Fast Company*'s blog, I didn't quite get it until I sat through the meeting.

The agency had two short hours to tap the collective brainpower of two leading subject experts. They seemed well prepared and began by showing these respected thought leaders the results of what they had researched regarding brand differentiation, communication challenges, and phrases that might be used to capture the essence of the product. Based on this information, they presented wording and messages they thought worked and asked for the experts' opinions. The experts gave wonderful feedback on wording they considered to be misleading or confusing and even suggested a more compelling message than one of the messages that had been developed for the meeting.

What happened next was astounding, and it's when I clearly understood my role. The woman leading the meeting was so stuck in her own agenda that, instead of recognizing an opportunity to capture concepts, correct information, and gain valuable insight, she kept bringing the meeting back to her prescribed messages in an effort to move the room toward the agency's vision and language. Not a good plan.

I was caught between that so-called rock and a hard place; actually, I think was under the rock. The agency wasn't very happy to have me in the room to begin with, because they viewed me as competition. So if I spoke up, I would make them look bad in front of everyone, which could affect other business opportunities down the road. Yet

I owed my no-bullshit, unedited opinion to my colleague, whom I called when the meeting was over. It went something like this:

Colleague:   What did you think?
       Me:   I think if they were going to lock the door and throw away the key before they even stepped inside, you could have saved a ton on flying those guys in and wasting everyone's time.
             [Silence.]
       Me:   I know their messages sound a lot sexier, but their job is to facilitate so we can eventually get to the right words, not push their own agenda.

The role of a facilitator is to ask open-ended questions that will stimulate discussion, generate ideas, and produce outcomes. It's often tougher than it appears. To do it well requires premeeting homework so you are familiar with the issues and can ask the right questions, as the agency did. It also means listening. When you listen, you are better poised to accept opinions, ideas, and even suggestions that may appear peculiar at first but turn out to be great. By being flexible, you can guide people through ideas so they reach those aha moments and answers by themselves. That makes it their meeting, not yours.

> Guide people through ideas so they reach those aha moments and answers by themselves. That makes it their meeting, not yours.

Why, then, do situations like I described seem to happen all too frequently in the workplace? Effective moderation and facilitation is a learned skill that takes time and practice. It requires good listening skills so you can navigate and change course when needed. When I first started my business, I received a great piece of advice from my brother, Jordan Friedman, who, at the time, was a health educator at Columbia University. He said to always remember that this is their meeting, not yours. He advised me not to get so stuck in what I wanted to accomplish so I wouldn't miss opportunities to let others discuss what was important to them. The strategy he advised is balance.

Sometimes we walk into meetings with unfair assumptions or preconceived notions, thinking we already know what people are going to say. If we tune them out or shut them down because they say something differently or don't say what we want them to say, we can rob ourselves of opportunities to clarify, learn, and receive information differently because we failed to listen.

As a professional speaker, I have also been guilty of talking too much. When you talk, you can't listen. We should probably borrow a line from our congressional representatives, who are often heard saying, "yield the floor," which means when you are done speaking, yield the floor to someone else. True, our representatives are as guilty as the rest of us when it comes to actually shutting up and saying something, which is why it may sometimes be necessary for all of us to occasionally turn our bullshit meters on.

## JUST A MEETING FIXES

**Have a plan and plan to speak up.** Prepare talking points and potential questions in advance.

**Talk to everyone, not just a select few.** Otherwise information can be too detailed and you risk tuning people out.

**Remember to use helpful phrases.** Having a couple of lines to ease you into the conversation will also ease your nerves—phrases such as "I'd like to point out," "I'd like to bring up," "It's important to call your attention to," "In addition to what has been discussed," and "There may be another way to look at this."

**Express, not impress.** Look for opportunities to add to the conversation by conveying information that can provide context, create understanding, and help people make informed decisions. There is no need to show off. If someone disagrees with you, look at it as an opportunity to prompt a productive discussion using some of the questions below.

**Encourage feedback.** Using the following open-ended questions and words to elicit information and encourage discussion:

- Tell me about . . .
- What do you think of . . .?
- How does this make you feel?
- What's your opinion?
- Why do you think this happened?
- What do you think we should do about it?

- What if we did this?
- What did you notice about . . .?
- What if we did . . .?
- What would happen if we did . . .?
- In your experience, . . .
- Tell me about . . .
- So, you've suggested . . ., but what do you think about . . .?
- What ideas do you have about . . .?

Rephrasing and clarifying questions encourages listeners to agree, verify, or correct information and further the discussion.

- So, what you are saying is . . .
- What do you mean when you say . . .?
- So, I think what you are implying is . . .
- So, if we hear you correctly . . .
- Help me understand.
- So, you are saying if we do this or that . . .?

Closed questions are shorter and more pointed to limit discussion.

- Does anyone have any additional questions?
- What is the exact number?
- Do you understand what I've stated?

Additional facilitation tips and techniques can be found in the resource section at the back of this book.

**Anyone can show up. Not everyone can stand out.**

## REFERENCE

"How to Stay Awake in Boring Meetings." *Fast Company Staff Blog*, April 25, 2006, http://www.fastcompany.com/blog/fast-company-staff/fast-company-blog/how-stay-awake-boring-meetings.

# CHAPTER 18

# Internationally Speaking

Music is the greatest communication in the world. Even if people don't understand the language that you're singing in, they still know good music when they hear it.

*—Lou Rawls, musician*

There was a boom box perched on a rickety wooden chair. It was playing some sort of Latin tune, but you could barely hear the music above the voices of some 400 women chattering at tables set up in the massive tent on the plantation in Montevideo, Uruguay. They were from South and Central America—Bolivia, Chili, Argentina, Venezuela, and Peru—and only spoke their native tongue so it was difficult to communicate. We would lean across the table and try to talk.

"Where are you from?" asked one, speaking in a different language than the other.

"I do not understand," she yelled back.

Have you ever noticed that when people try to communicate in different languages, they start to yell at each other, hoping that if they speak loudly, it will help the other understand?

"I SAID, WHERE ARE YOU FROM?"

They were women from emerging democracies who had just spent the past four days in a variety of workshops learning how to communicate more effectively so they could find their public voices; women who had suffered years of persecution and abuse but came together because they wanted to know how to be like American women and make a difference in their homelands. Former first lady Hillary Rodham Clinton spearheaded the event. I was a media trainer on the project.

So, this little lady from Bolivia saunters to the center of the tent, puts one hand on her belly and slowly starts moving her hips back and forth to the boom box beat, the rhythm emanating from the very center of her. Then, without a word, another woman moved onto the dirt floor, swaying from side to side, her head moving ever so slightly, eyes closed, hearing the same beat. And another and another, and another, all coming forward, swaying from side to side, their fingers now entwined, their footsteps choreographed in a language even the best Hollywood producer could not re-create. Within minutes, 400 women and a few men who were present crowded together, their feet shuffling back and forth, their hands warm from each other's touch. No one said a word, yet their voices were so loud. The sound in the tent on that chilly night in Montevideo was almost deafening, as hundreds of people from worlds so far apart suddenly understood each other, for they were all speaking the same language.

> Hundreds of people from worlds so far apart suddenly understood each other, for they were all speaking the same language.

You don't have to talk to say something. Every time I travel, I learn that lesson again and again. I also learn that most people are eager to teach and not necessarily judge when those who don't communicate in the same tongue make embarrassing mistakes. I had the pleasure of listening to an English-speaking presenter in Argentina, where the primary language is Spanish. Wanting to endear himself to his audience, in advance he asked someone how he could say "I'm happy to be here with you today" in Spanish. When he stood up and introduced himself, he said; "*Prefiero no estar aquí hoy con ustedes,*" which, when translated, actually means "I would rather not be here with you today." Everyone started laughing as they realized his goof, but he had no idea why they were laughing and later told me he panicked, thinking maybe his fly was open.

I've done it too in a country where English is the language. As a student attending a foreign studies program in Manchester, England, I ordered an ice cream cone and asked the server if he could put jimmies on top, which, in my hometown, means chocolate sprinkles. He was visibly offended, and I didn't know why until someone told me that, in England, at least at the time, jimmies was slang for the word *piss*.

President Richard M. Nixon once said, "I know you believe you understand what you think I said, but I'm not sure you realize that what you heard is not what I meant." While this happens in everyday communication when people do converse in the same dialect, getting lost in translation can lead to an even bigger minefield of missteps in today's multinational business environment. That's why understanding and appreciating different communication cultures can help prevent embarrassing and sometimes offensive faux pas that unintentionally affect your ability to build productive relationships.

My friend Steve Crowe, the executive director of commercial operations in Latin America for Pfizer, says it's important to understand that language isn't always about words or slides. In his experience, welcoming body language such as eye contact and open gestures is critical to creating a warm, friendly environment that facilitates communication and drives understanding. He also advises a little humility goes a long way.

"I personally have given speeches in the worst Japanese, Chinese, Portuguese, French, and Spanish that was tough for people to understand, but the response was welcoming and overwhelming," Crowe confided. "It bonded me with them because they saw me as real and appreciated that I tried to speak their language."

Nothing could be truer than what happened in Cartagena, Colombia, when dining with three colleagues one evening. Two of us only spoke English, a third (Carlos) only spoke Spanish, and the fourth, who spoke many languages, offered to translate so Carlos could participate in the conversation. At first, it seemed staccato-like. Carlos would say something, she would translate, and then I would ask her to ask him something else, and so on. After dinner, we remained at the table talking when it dawned on me that Carlos and I had been communicating without translation help. What was more astounding was that we actually understood each other. It wasn't the words; it was expressions, gestures, animation, and laughter that created bonding and comprehension.

It's equally important to understand subtleties, customs, and etiquette and realize that what people say in another country might not mean the same thing in your environment. In Asia, for example, I found that people rarely said no because it was considered impolite. Instead, they would offer "that might be possible" or "we would consider it" even if they actually meant no. In Beijing, I found that strong eye contact, which is important in the United States, can be seen as disrespectful. Not understanding this at first, when ordering breakfast at my hotel, I found it discourteous when the waiter wouldn't look at me until someone explained, "a waiter is not considered equal to a guest," so it would actually be disrespectful for him to make eye contact.

In Japan, people often laugh when unexpectedly confronted by a different viewpoint. First impressions may be that the person is laughing at you when most likely the laughter is an expression of surprise. Japanese also value silence, so it's important not to negatively interpret silence while communicating in that country. Similarly, handshakes, lack of spatial awareness, and facial expressions in different cultures can offend without intention. If you are communicating to multicultural audiences, there are a number of fixes to increase understanding regardless of the language barrier.

## COACHING NOTES

- Expect the process to take longer than it would in your culture and to involve more communication, meetings, and correspondence. Choose examples from your client's workplace to help him understand how you might help him.
- They will likely ask you for a lot of detailed information, so you should prepare it in advance to supply if requested. Be careful of words and references to your work here in the States they might not understand. Check with your people to make sure of wording that might need to be changed and adjusted.
- I would urge you to ask for a translator from the region who has expertise and understanding of your products and industry. This way she can use the same language and explain data in a way that is appropriate for this audience.
- In Japan, it's important to make sure your team is in agreement and not show any kind of disagreement publicly or among yourselves in front of them as they will be offended and it is considered impolite.
- In some cultures, people want to stand up and voice their opinions, which we would consider grandstanding. But these people have very few opportunities to get together in a very public forum, so this is the first chance they have to be heard. Give them rope and listen, but look for opportunities to pull them back in and keep the meeting moving without embarrassing or offending.
- Your feelings can be communicated through nonverbal facial expressions and body language, which can cause problems when

communicating with people in some countries who consider long-winded speeches to be poetic, so be careful of your actions and be observant of theirs as well.

If you grew up before computers, cell phones, and cable TV were the norm, then you likely remember how expensive it was to call another city, much less another country. Unless you traveled, your impressions of people from other countries were formed from movies and books. I'm not quite that old, but I marvel at my children, who benefit from the culturally diverse society that is today's norm.

I conducted a two-day media and crisis communications program in Singapore attended by an organization's representatives from 16 countries, including Malaysia, Pakistan, Thailand, Saudi Arabia, Australia, and Indonesia. The program was very successful, but even greater learning took place after hours, when a group of us went to the famous Raffles hotel. With assistance from sips of the authentic Singapore sling, the open discussion of controversial world events and sharing of different beliefs made the world seem that much smaller and it's people that much closer.

> Sharing of different beliefs made the world seem that much smaller and its people that much closer.

The night was topped off at a dance club, where language, opposing viewpoints, and cultural differences were drowned out by wide smiles and the beat of the music, a universal language that spoke louder than all of us.

## INTERNATIONALLY SPEAKING FIXES

**Advance advice.** Speak to colleagues who have gone before you. Find out as much as you can about the venue, attendees, likes and dislikes, and accepted communication practices.

**Word choice.** Be as specific as possible to avoid misinterpretation and misunderstanding. That means eliminating excess words and phrases such as "What I'm trying to say" or "If you will" or "To be candid with you" or "What I want to explain." Additionally, try to avoid jargon, acronyms, and idiomatic expressions such as "dime a dozen," "bang for your buck," "by the skin of your teeth," "mountain out of a molehill," or "early-bird special," which don't always translate well across borders.

**Slow down.** It takes listeners longer to process words when they are not spoken in their native language and when a translator is providing interpretation. It is essential to speak slower and pause between thoughts. The slow-down-and-pause rule is appropriate for all public speaking, so you pronounce words clearly and give people a chance to digest what you are saying.

**Pictures not words.** If you are using slides, try to eliminate as much text as possible, especially if the words are not their first language. Even if the slides have been translated for your audience, pictures are far more powerful to drive your message.

**Examples.** Use examples from the audience's hometown or business environment to help foster understanding. When I speak to a foreign audience, I will ask someone to explain key stories in the daily newspaper to see if I can use what's in the news there as a way to illustrate points and make it relevant to the listener.

**Mix it up.** When there are people from numerous countries who speak many languages, people who speak the same language will often try to sit together at meals and events. If possible, break up the groups so they have to work at communicating with each other.

**Handouts.** Create simple handouts in their language to help them follow along and remember what they've learned.

**Translators and translation.** There is a frequent misperception that words are translated individually from one language to another, which is not so. In South America, for example, a translator told me she uses 20 to 21 more Spanish words for every English word spoken, so context and meaning is often lost. Whenever possible, meet with your translator in advance to give him a sense of your style, timing, and wording. When using video clips or slides, I always show them to the translator so she can ask questions and do her best to deliver it in my tone and style.

**Educate your own people.** Help your people be their best by coaching, training, or providing tools to share best communication practices and pitfalls.

**Allow picture time.** I have found that audiences—especially in South, Central, and Latin America, where I've spent a lot of time— love to have their picture taken with presenters. Build in some extra time for photos and for people who want to ask you a question but were shy to do it in front of others or for those who just want to share a few extra words.

At a communications training program I conducted in former communist Romania just 12 years after the fall of the Iron Curtain, I was interviewed by a local reporter who repeatedly asked me, "are you telling the truth?" She wasn't accusing me of lying, but her readers had different definitions of truth because, for decades, Romanians did not enjoy freedom of speech. Program participants quietly confided that, even though they now lived in a democracy, they believed they would still be punished if the government didn't approve of what they said. Even today where censorship is prohibited, there have been some reported attempts by the government to influence the editorial content of media.

It's important to remember that the way people communicate and interact with each other is different from culture to culture and can be affected by historic events. I've learned that their truth may not be my truth, making it more important than ever to look for common ground.

**All communication is equal when you don't let words get in the way.**

# CHAPTER 19

# Hug Me

⌒

Everyone has an invisible sign hanging from their neck saying, "Make me feel important." Never forget this message when working with people.

—*Mary Kay Ash, founder of Mary Kay Cosmetics*

I was sitting in a coffee shop in Lenox, Massachusetts, quietly reading the newspaper and sipping my latte when a total stranger with flaming red hair and a big, toothy smile breezed in and plopped down at my table.

"Hi," she said. "Okay if I join you?"

I looked around the place at all the empty seats but thought better of pointing that out to her.

"Sure," I said. "No problem."

I don't remember her name and I don't remember much about her, but I do remember our conversation because it's stayed with me all these years.

"You have kids?" she asked.

"Yes, two boys," I replied.

"I have one girl and I'll tell you something every parent needs to know. If your son walks into a room to talk to you and you're busy, you better put down what you're doing and listen when he wants to talk. Make sure he knows that he's more important than anything you have going on. Get up and give him a hug."

I'm not sure why that woman chose my table on that spring morning, but perhaps it was fate. Maybe it was a message I needed to hear because, like many busy parents, I'm guilty of listening to my children with half an ear and sometimes not listening closely enough. While that doesn't make me or any of us bad parents, it does address how we can inadvertently make people feel that what they have to say is not all that important.

It's a problem that haunts the workplace. A 2008 BNET (bnet.com) survey asked more than 1,500 senior managers and executives around the country what they really think of the top boss. When given a list of a dozen words to describe their CEO, only one in five employees picked "caring" or "warm," suggesting that, when it comes to people skills, big bosses aren't getting great marks.

In an article on the BNET Web site, Rafael Pastor, CEO of Vistage International, a networking organization for CEOs, called it a real problem. "CEOs do not do a good enough job of inspiring their employees and making them feel important and valuable. Their soft skills are not as finely honed as their other business skills."

Gallup's research turned up similar results, suggesting engaged employees are more likely to contribute if they work in an environment that makes them feel valued.

That's not to suggest we have to run around the office hugging people to show our appreciation, but there must be ways to embrace people by the way we communicate. That's why I decided to conduct my own unofficial survey of colleagues, associates, and clients to find out what they value in a boss that would inspire, motivate, and make them more likely to follow the leader. I sent out select e-mails and posted discussion links on Twitter and LinkedIn directing people to a three-question survey. Here are the questions:

1. Can you share an example of a boss or coworker who made you feel valued and important? What did they do or say and what can others learn from them?

2. Can you provide an example of someone you've worked with who is a terrible communicator and explain how what he or she does negatively impacts the workplace?

3. In your personal opinion, if you could name one thing that makes someone an effective business communicator, what would that be and why?

I received nearly 30 responses, and no one mentioned words frequently associated with leaders, such as *smart, vision,* or *powerful.* Instead, the two words that repeatedly showed up in people's responses were *communication* and *respect.*

> The two words that repeatedly showed up in people's responses were *communication* and *respect*.

Responders said they felt most inspired and empowered when bosses clearly and frequently communicated what they wanted and respected the opinions of employees. They said they felt valued and recognized. Pretty simple? Well, not really.

Christopher Florentz, manager of corporate communications at CSL Behring, shares a story about his experience as an employee at a nuclear facility. A new chief operations officer instituted Saturday-morning meetings for middle-level managers. When they objected, Florentz says the COO made it clear that every manager was expendable, that the company owed them nothing but a day's wage, and that, in today's times, company loyalty to employees is a thing of the past.

"When I told him trying to put the fear of God into his managers would not get results, he beamed as if I had just paid him the highest compliment in the world," Florentz said. Florentz says what followed in the next year was an exodus of the most talented managers and that it took years after that for the business to fully recover.

If that story makes you say, "well it's obvious that guy was just a jerk and most people don't act like that," you might be surprised at how many jerks are lurking behind office doors. As a television news reporter, I learned early on that I was only as good as my last story. Most of my bosses didn't care about the great job I did yesterday; they wanted to know what I was going to do for them tomorrow.

While at ABC TV in Philadelphia, I was eight months pregnant with my second child. Being slightly high risk, my doctor told me to take an early maternity leave, but I decided to tough it out. The news director was agreeable to whatever was best for me, so we compromised and I agreed to work three days a week with the understanding that I'd get easy assignments and not be put in any dangerous situations.

One night a fire broke out at a chemical company, and the assignment manager told me to go. I refused, explaining it wasn't safe for a pregnant woman to be exposed to potentially toxic materials and I had an agreement with the boss that I would not cover these types of stories while pregnant. What followed was hard to believe. The manager unleashed a tirade of four-letter words, told me there was no one else around to cover the story, and said if I couldn't do my job, I shouldn't come to work. He then called his boss, who told me she didn't see any reason why I couldn't cover this chemical fire and if I wouldn't go, she wanted to talk to my doctor. I was upset and appalled, and the next day I told the news director I would not work three days a week, but would take my doctor's advice and return after my full maternity leave. No one ever apologized, and the event left a bad taste in my mouth that remains to this day.

Yet for every jerk there are great managers who seem to have that human touch that makes people feel valued and recognized. Judy Hoffman, former chemical company executive and author of *Keeping Cool on the Hot Seat*, says when she was an administrative assistant, she had a boss who made her feel valued because he encouraged her to share ideas even if she wasn't part of the inner circle. Instead of shutting her down when he disagreed, he would listen. "I guess what it all boiled down to was that he respected me," said Hoffman. "By listening to me, taking some of my suggestions and explaining why he couldn't go along with something, he made me feel important."

Marsha Egan, CEO of The Egan Group, describes a similar experience. "The boss who motivated me the most did a great job of describing the end result he expected and didn't constantly second-guess me." Egan says she was willing to work harder for this person because he was not afraid to admit mistakes and ask for help. "This humanized my boss for me and made me think he was a better person for not trying to cover things up."

One of the oldest and best business lessons learned about communicating positively, openly, and honestly is the infamous 1982 Tylenol case that is still a model of how corporate America should communicate. Widespread panic ensued when seven Chicago-area residents died after someone poisoned Tylenol capsules with cyanide. Instead of burying his head in the sand, Johnson & Johnson chairman James Burke, who built his reputation on putting the customer first, made himself available to every news outlet possible. The company immediately withdrew Tylenol from the shelves, costing an estimated $100 million. When Burke was asked to explain company decisions, he said things like, "Somebody has chosen a product from our corporation as a murder weapon" and "one of the ways to make these decisions is to ask how you would feel if it was your own child."

Burke won the hearts of listeners and viewers because he spoke from the heart. Lost sales never entered the conversation. Diane Peck, vice president of human resources at Stanford University, believes the things that are really important to people in many situations are not monetary. "Everyone wants to make money and earn enough to produce whatever standard of living they want to have, but more important to people is, How am I treated? Am I valued and respected? Am I proud of the place where I work?" Peck advises thinking about how you can inspire and motivate by recognizing people and putting them first, as Burke did. She says leaders need to make people feel that their contributions are important, because they are.

---

Leaders need to make people feel that their contributions are important, because they are.

---

Shortly after my second son was born and I had already left my television career, he had his tonsils and adenoids removed. Yet a few years later, he appeared to have the same symptoms that ultimately resulted in the tonsillectomy. We took him to multiple doctors, who scoped, prodded, smiled, and said, "don't worry, Mom, nothing is wrong." At the time, I had flown to Stanford University to do some media training with Jed Black, the director of the Stanford Sleep Disorders Center. As we role-played, I couldn't help thinking he sounded like he was talking about my son. So when I returned home, I called him and explained the situation. He immediately advised a sleep test, but when I made the request to doctors at home, they insisted it wasn't necessary and that I was overreacting. I called Black again, and, even though he had never met my son, he personally called the Children's Hospital of Philadelphia and ordered the sleep test, which concluded that not only did my child have severe obstructive sleep apnea but his oxygen levels were dangerously low.

Black was not my boss, but he made me feel that my opinion and observations mattered. Even though I wasn't a doctor, he treated me as an equal. If I could have reached through the phone, I would have hugged him.

Superior attitudes that group people into important and not-as-important buckets are frequently communicated in ways that don't involve words. Some companies show how they value visitors by putting visitor parking spaces close to the front door, while other businesses make the visitors walk so the executives can have a front-row spot. There are companies that provide concert and sporting event tickets to bigwigs only and other companies, like PMA Insurance Group in Blue Bell,

Pennsylvania, that hold lotteries so all employees have an equal shot at getting the hottest ticket in town.

Charlotte Sibley is the senior vice president of leadership development at the Shire Pharmaceutical Group. She gave a great speech on the responsibilities of leadership when she was awarded woman of the year by the Healthcare Businesswomen's Association. She told a story about her first job in the corporate world of Wall Street, where she saw senior management as powerful, unapproachable, and all-knowing gods (she says there were no goddesses at the time!) until she met Charlie Buek, the president of the U.S. Trust Company. Sibley said he was the exact opposite.

"He insisted that everyone call him Charlie, not 'Mr. Buek,' explains Sibley. "That made such an impression on me and I vowed that if—and it seemed like a remote possibility at the time—if I was ever in a senior position, I would do the same, so I wouldn't intimidate junior people."

Ask people at Shire and they will tell you Sibley is well respected, admired, and liked because that is the way she leads today. She told me she always tries to think in terms of being a servant/leader, not a superior. "We don't always have to be out in front as leaders," says Sibley. "Think of a stage manager—you never see him on stage, but the play can't go on without him—oh, excuse me, without her! Sometimes, we need to be alongside people, encouraging them, and sometimes behind them, pushing them to excel." Or, as Abraham Lincoln said, "There go my people; I must follow them, for I am their leader."

It's always effective to look for ways to speak from the perspective of your listeners. For example, if you are an airport director, it's about the passenger. If you manage a supermarket, it's about the shopper. If you work for a pharmaceutical company, it's about the patient. If you are talking to employees about the future of a company, bring it back to what's in it for them.

## HUG ME FIXES

**Treat everyone the same.** When you make people feel equal, they are motivated to contribute and respect everyone's opinions and differences.

**Encourage communication.** Seek feedback at all levels and help people understand their suggestions are important even if they aren't implemented.

**Be clear.** If you are going to provide feedback, be specific so people understand your expectations, what they need to work on, and if there are certain things you want them to do.

**Hear it from you.** Talk *to* people, not *about* them. If you have a problem with someone or want them to do something differently, let him hear it from you to avoid second-guessing and misinterpretation.

**Remind people they are important.** It's easy to make someone feel important when she is the new kid on the block, but don't forget to thank people for a job well done throughout the years.

**Care and concern.** We all have off days and sometimes they get in the way of our work or cause us to be short-tempered. Try to find out what's going on if someone seems out of sorts and how you or the company might be able to help him.

**Teach, don't tell.** Think about mentors you've had in your life. They lead by showing and helping, not by intimidation and fear.

**Admit mistakes.** It's natural to make corrections and point out mistakes, but don't be afraid to admit your own mistakes as well. It makes you human.

**Communicate often.** Without communication, people are left to their own interpretations. Sometimes what isn't said is more harmful than what is said.

**Be approachable.** Don't forget where you came from and what it was like when you were climbing the ladder. Be real and approachable to motivate others.

---

> Sometimes what isn't said is more harmful than what is said.

---

Mary Kay Ash, founder of Mary Kay Cosmetics, who is quoted at the beginning of this chapter, was committed to making people feel important by rewarding hard work. She embraced top performers with vacations, jewelry, and pink Cadillacs, and they, in turn, helped her build an empire that was listed as among the 100 best companies in the United States to work for. Ash, like the people who answered my short survey, put a great emphasis on people skills or what former General Electric CEO Jack Welch called soft skills. Welch said it took him more than 20 years to recognize that the hard stuff was the soft stuff, which is emotional intelligence and authenticity.

Our mini survey bears the same opinion. When we asked contributors to name one thing that makes someone an effective business communicator, this is what they said:

Be honest, clear and complete; trust your people to use the information wisely. If there is something you cannot say/divulge, then just say so.

— Charlotte Sibley, Shire Pharmaceutical Group

When a person considers the "what ifs" ahead of time and communicates them to those involved in the process, it allows for smoother and more effective communication.

— Paulette Ensign, Tips Products International

Clearly articulate expectations and communicate them to ensure they have been received and are understood.

— Christopher Florentz, Public Relations Specialist

Communicate positively and often. A leader who has a positive attitude can positively infect an entire organization with frequent consistent messages.

— Marsha Egan, The Egan Group

Trust. It is hard to gain but if you care about something deeply in business and communicate that to others, trust is gained.

— Kimberly Jungkind, Pfizer

Last summer, my younger son who was mentioned earlier in this chapter went to overnight camp. There was a boy in his bunk who was very homesick and wouldn't leave the bunk to participate in activities or socialize with other children. On visiting day, the camp counselor called me aside to tell me about something that happened with this boy involving my son. He said that while all the other children went their own way, my son came back to the bunk and sat with that homesick boy for hours. He played cards with him, drew pictures with him, and reassured him that everything would be okay until the boy finally joined the others. The counselor said "your son made that kid's summer a happy one." I was so proud that I almost cried on the spot. If a 13-year-old boy, who isn't as learned, coached, or experienced as most professionals, can be such a mensch, which means "a good person" in Yiddish, then I have to imagine if people want to work at it, that lesson can transfer to any workplace that hopes to foster an atmosphere of open communication and trust.

**Be a mensch to make others feel valued and important.**

# CHAPTER 20

# Gut Check

The most important thing in communication is to hear what isn't being said.

—*Peter Drucker, management guru*

Some might call the late Peter Drucker one of the greatest management minds of all time. His beliefs and strategies for managing complex businesses problems outlined in his 38 books are still followed by some of the most recognized and respected leaders today.

I chose his quote for this chapter because Peter Drucker believed in putting people first and telling it like it is—or at least like he saw it. He taught generations of managers to lead forward by speaking the truth and to look back for lessons learned.

Technology has dramatically changed the way we communicate since Peter Drucker's day. Whether at the office, in our communities, or at home, it's all about efficiency. I'm embarrassed to admit that my husband and I are sometimes guilty of texting and instant messaging each other in between the floors of our home instead of getting up off our butts to speak face to face. Yet, as Drucker also said, "efficiency is doing things right; effectiveness is doing the right things." There is clearly a difference, especially when you are trying to talk your way out of trouble.

From cave paintings to mail service to telephones to e-mail, the evolution of communication is increasingly remarkable because we can instantly communicate with people all over the globe, making the world seem smaller. In a post-9/11 era, companies have been forced to become more sophisticated at developing plans to anticipate and manage crises worldwide, because there is no longer lag time in a 24/7 online environment. When there is even a hint of scandal, the online conversation often begins before anyone can call a meeting to figure out what to say or do.

In summer of 2009, a small plane carrying two brothers and one of their teenage sons crashed in the Hudson River, killing all three. Before the story even broke, my brother, a friend of the Altman family, received a text message from his daughter informing him of the tragedy. Similarly, when US Airways Flight 1549, piloted by Captain Sullenberger, went down in the Hudson, a ferry passenger broke the story on Twitter from his iPhone, reminding all of us of the importance of communicating quickly and efficiently.

But taking a lesson from Drucker, there are some aspects of communicating during tough times that have not changed and probably never will. That includes being humble, apologetic, empathetic, and sincere if you hope to build credibility and trust.

Easier said than discovered, I believe most of us have an internal gauge that allows us to check our guts on the most basic level in an effort to help us do the right thing. If we pull into a parking lot and someone is waiting for a spot with her blinker on, most of us will move on to another space, because our gut tells us this is the correct thing to do. These types of occurrences happen on a regular basis, and we give them little thought. We just do what's right or what is socially acceptable. On a simple level, we let common sense guide us. We instinctively understand how our actions will affect the outcome. We are our own crisis managers.

In both our personal and professional lives, we can't always predict the unexpected, because so many things happen without warning, but that's not to say we can't learn from other situations in an effort to check our guts and better manage mistakes. For starters, the fear of not communicating should be greater than the fear of communicating.

> The fear of not communicating should be greater than the fear of communicating.

Tiger Woods is a perfect example of how *not* communicating almost always makes things worse. With the exception of an online statement, the golf superstar stayed silent for three months following a Thanksgiving car accident that unveiled a sordid tale of multiple marital affairs. By not speaking quickly, he fueled resentment and speculation and kept the story alive. When he finally apologized at a widely televised news conference, he did so by reading a scripted statement and then refused to take questions, which implied that he may have something to hide. Additionally, the longer you wait to apologize, the guiltier you appear.

**Gut check 1.** When I penned a column about this and advised Woods to take questions, some of my readers said they disagreed and thought the golfer didn't need to explain himself to anyone other than his wife. Let's take a gut check on this. Woods is a public figure. He has benefited from years of positive coverage, sponsorships, adoring fans, and endorsements so he can't have his cake and eat it too. As a public figure or company or community leader, you are accountable for your actions, and the longer you wait to address them, the more interest and coverage you will generate.

**Gut check 2.** Many of these same readers said if Woods had opened up to questions, people would have wanted intimate details about his sex life, including the number of indiscretions. Let's take a gut check on this, too. No matter who you are, you get to control the information. Just because someone asks you something doesn't mean you have to provide specifics. You can say the details are personal and you won't discuss them and then move on to what you do want to discuss.

The goal in these situations is to stop the bleeding. You want to make the story go away as fast as chalk on a driveway when it rains. You can't do that if you let others do the talking.

---

> You want to make the story go away as fast as chalk on a driveway when it rains.

---

Gone are the days when saying "I'm sorry" is enough, because it seems everyone eventually asks for forgiveness. Just watch Barbara Walters or Oprah. They probably hear more sob stories than a therapist. People want to know you mean what you say from deep down in your gut. Consider a few high-profile apologies and what we can learn from them.

## WILLIAM JEFFERSON CLINTON

|  |  |
|---|---|
| Apology: | The 42nd president of the United States insisted that he did not have "sexual relations with that woman." When he later apologized for lying under oath, his remarks were perceived as hollow. |
| Gut check: | Don't lie. |

## ALEX RODRIGUEZ

Apology:     The New York Yankee infielder was accused of using steroids to enhance his performance, which cast doubts about his achievements, but he owned up to the accusations and publicly admitted what he had done, which helped restore his reputation.

Gut check:   Don't lie.

## SENATOR JOHN EDWARDS

Apology:     Senator John Edwards apologized for making "a serious error in judgment" when he had an affair, but he denied fathering a child, then later admitted he was the dad when someone threatened to expose him.

Gut check:   Don't lie.

## ISAIAH WASHINGTON

Apology:     When the actor referred to actor T. R. Knight as a "faggot" on the set of a television show, he apologized, but then later denied using that word. He had to apologize again for lying.

Gut check:   Don't lie.

## ROGER CLEMENS

Apology:     Baseball legend and role model Roger Clemens fell from grace when he lied to Congress about using steroids.

Gut check:   Don't lie.

## DENNIS KOZLOWSKI

Apology:     You may recall when former Tyco CEO Dennis Kozlowski, who was convicted of using company money to fund his extravagant lifestyle, also apologized, but no one believed him.

Gut check:   Don't lie.

## BERNIE MADOFF

Apology:    Then there is Bernie Madoff, the former chairman of the NASDAQ turned investment fund manager. He apologized and pled guilty to an estimated $65 billion Ponzi scheme. No one believed his apology either.

Gut check:    An apology that is not believable is worse than not apologizing at all.

---

An apology that is not believable is worse than not apologizing at all.

---

The list of lies and apologies is almost endless, but you clearly see the trend. In the long run, coming clean will help you prevent more embarrassment than the scandal itself. How you handle a situation can also forever change what people think and feel about you, as these high profile examples illustrate.

Scandal:    Former New York governor Eliot Spitzer is disgraced and resigns after being linked to a prostitution ring when, as Attorney General, he had prosecuted prostitution rings and offenders.

Perception:    Arrogance.

Scandal:    U.S. senator and self-proclaimed family values advocate Larry Craig of Indiana leaves the Senate after being arrested in a sex sting with an undercover cop in a Minneapolis men's room and then denying it.

Perception:    Hypocrite.

Now, contrast the difference in public perception between late-night comedian David Letterman's admitted sexual affairs with women on his staff with news about Nevada's social conservative senator John Ensign's alleged affair the very same week.

Scandal:    News media reports Ensign was having an affair with a former campaign staffer who was married to one of his former legislative aides. Ensign denies the affair, which turns out to be a lie.

Perception:    Phony.

   Scandal:    Letterman was being blackmailed by a television news
                 producer about his sexual escapades but was smart
                 enough to come clean about the affairs.

Perception:    Victim.


It's easy to play Monday-morning quarterback when someone says
something that makes you ask, "what were you thinking?" (or not thinking, as the case may be). It is tough enough to think clearly, much less
communicate, when under pressure. Unfortunately, there is not always
time to implement well-thought-out plans when the media is at your
door and people are tweeting what they know or think they know. Regardless, it's still important to talk even if it's to say you have very little
information, but here's what you do know. How you respond to questions will ultimately determine the outcome.

This was evident while conducting a crisis communication training
program for an organization. As part of the squirming exercise we created, the media came calling before officials had a chance to gather all
the facts, determine a course of action, and prepare a statement. Officials
refused to comment until they had all the facts, so we did what any good
news crew would do. We gathered information elsewhere and started
reporting live from the fictitious scene. One individual was furious and
said it was completely unfair, to which our videographer, a former ABC
TV camera person responded, "Real life isn't fair and when events un-
fold, you don't always have the time you need." Here are some review
notes that followed the session.


- As the director of operations, you had knowledge that others didn't,
  and you could have offered important safety facts to reassure the
  community. You could have talked about security presence, your
  stellar safety record, what is done 24/7 to protect people, partnering with police, and you could have emphasized that safety is
  your top priority. I think you missed an opportunity to lead and
  communicate.


At another college communications training program, something similar happened. On the day we were there, a national story broke about
a college student who had died from overdrinking at another institution. In the midst of role playing, one of our coaches asked the president
what her policy was regarding drinking. She stopped the exercise in its

tracks, saying we were hired to create a mock scenario around a specific issue and they did not want questions about anything else. That's fine in a fantasy world, but training programs are designed to mimic real life and in real life, you don't get to script the questions.

To address those questions, think about how you might feel if you were affected by what was happening. You might be angry, frustrated, scared, or anxious. Here is a checklist to help you manage people's feelings, contain panic, and quickly correct misinformation. Ask these "Am I" questions to check your gut.

## GUT CHECK CHECKLIST

Am I putting anyone in harm's way?

Am I delivering accurate information as quickly as possible?

Am I using positive, reassuring words?

Am I speculating or sticking to what is confirmed?

Am I taking responsibility or blaming others?

Am I stating why I can't comment?

Am I using simple words instead of jargon?

Am I anticipating tough questions?

Am I conveying care, concern, and compassion for those affected?

Am I being argumentative or defensive?

Am I being open and honest?

Remember, if you're not under oath, you do not have to answer every question someone asks you. However, as an executive at a publicly traded company or a public official, stakeholders and the public will hold you accountable. Organizations that are perceived as thoughtful and caring perform consistent gut checks to best understand how their actions and words will ultimately affect outcomes.

As this book was being written, Toyota was struggling to protect its image amidst millions of worldwide recalls over safety concerns following uncontrollable gas pedal acceleration that caused numerous accidents and deaths. While the company was initially slow to respond, it was quick to take the public's pulse. In addition to traditional interviews, CEO Jim Lentz could be seen everywhere, including sites like Digg.com, where he conducted live video interviews.

Crisis consultant and principal of Amme & Associates, Rick Amme believes companies and institutions that stumble out of the gate can recover if they get their wits about them reasonably quickly and points to the movie *Saving Private Ryan* as an example. Captain John Miller's (played by Tom Hanks) last words to Private James Ryan (played by Matt Damon), for whose survival Miller and most of his squad have given their lives, says, "James . . . Earn this. Earn it." Amme says the quote applies to companies like Toyota that badly injure their formerly stellar reputations through serious operational errors and poor crisis management. He says the only way for them to retrieve their good name is to "earn it."

A little-known British company found itself with a very big problem when it issued repair kits for nearly one million strollers it had sold in the United States after 12 cases of children's fingertips being chopped off in carriage hinges was reported. Instead of immediately recalling the strollers, the company initially issued warnings to owners, telling them not to let children stick their fingers in the hinges when they opened the chairs. The public was outraged; Twitter was ablaze with livid remarks. While the company eventually issued a recall, it failed to think like moms and dads and unintentionally came across as mechanical instead of human. Whether online or off-line, many of the lessons are the same.

> Lesson 1:   To make people care, show them you care.
> Lesson 2:   Be willing to admit mistakes.
> Lesson 3:   Perception becomes reality.
> Lesson 4:   Convey a sense of urgency to make things right.
> Lesson 5:   Express empathy early and often.
> Lesson 6:   Accept responsibility.
> Lesson 7:   Avoid answering emotional outbursts with numbers and facts.
> Lesson 8:   Recognize problems so you are prepared in advance.
> Lesson 9:   Tell it all, tell it simply, and tell it quickly.
> Lesson 10:  No excuses.

Because online rumors and anonymous postings are as quick as the click of a mouse, you can't possibly manage everything that is said about you or your company, and you don't want to refute every comment either. There are monitoring services that can keep you updated on what's being said on the Internet so you can decide whether to take action. If a rumor is gaining momentum, if public safety is threatened, or if what is being said could negatively impact your brand or business, that's when responding can be effective. You should post your position front and center on your own Web site or blog, and, depending on the circumstances, you can also call traditional media outlets directly. Remember to keep your employees in the loop so they hear the facts from you first.

As more and more everyday citizens post personal experiences and opinions online, an increasing number of companies are building relationships with influential bloggers and podcasters the way they once did with mainstream media. Take what happened when Kevin Smith, a Hollywood actor and director who made headlines in early 2010. The self-described "person of size" booked two tickets on a Southwest flight from Burbank, California, to Oakland but decided to fly standby on an earlier flight on which there was only one available middle seat. After he was on board, airline officials booted him off the plane for fear he might infringe on the personal space of his seatmates. Smith, who has over a million Twitter followers, went on a tweeting and blogging rampage, then posted an online video claiming he was the victim of discrimination. The story was picked up by numerous media outlets, including *USA Today*. Not only did Southwest apologize to him, but the airline posted its side of the story on Smith's blog.

While it has become increasingly difficult to control the message in such an information-bloated environment, where lines between fact and fiction are often hazy, the importance of gut checking along the way cannot be understated.

No matter how good your public relations efforts may be, it cannot erase mistakes. Research shows that leading companies and products that fall victim to crisis and poor crisis management never completely regain their former status. The most important lesson is to avoid a crisis at all costs. If you are already knee deep, Amme advises doing everything possible to stop the bleeding operationally and through astute crisis management to prevent the crisis from defining you for years.


## GUT CHECK FIXES

**Plan for the worst.** When you approach a situation with the mindset of what can go wrong will go wrong, you will plan much more thoroughly and minimize surprises.

**Go to your audience.** If your audience lives online, then contacting the *Wall Street Journal* might not be the best strategy. Communicate in your readers' space.

**Sincere apology.** If you apologize, mean it. From your voice to body language to your words to your pace and pitch, every fiber of your being should convey your sincerity.

**Facts and emotion.** In the news business, we joked that sometimes the facts got in the way of a good story. Specifics are essential but must be explained in human terms with empathy and understanding for those affected.

**The how.** It's not enough to say you have great security or great people who are working on the problem. You must tell people how you are going to fix it and how you are going to prevent it from happening again.

**Big picture.** Look outside your walls to see the big picture and gain a greater understanding of what others are feeling in order to acknowledge and address their concerns compassionately and realistically.

**Full disclosure.** If you have a secret and someone else reveals it first, you will be ridiculed, labeled as guilty, and remain in the spotlight. Coming clean can squelch rumors and make it easier to forgive wrongdoing.

**It will pass.** Eventually, it will pass, but at what cost? Withholding information, lying, not answering questions, or misleading people under any circumstances will anger many shaping perception, which will become reality.

When Peter Drucker was alive, he created a published a self-assessment tool titled "The Five Most Important Questions" organizations should ask. The questions are very simple:

1. What is our mission?
2. Who is our customer?
3. What does the customer value?
4. What are our results?
5. What is our plan?

I suggest those same questions should serve as gut checks when dealing with adversity on- and off-line. If you stay true to your mission, customer, values, and the results you seek, you are less likely to waver from your well-crafted plan and more likely to consistently communicate in a thoughtful human voice.

**A thoughtful and truthful voice is a trusted voice.**

## REFERENCE

Ethan Watters, *CEO Survey: Lacking the Human Touch* BNET, http://www. bnet.com/2403-13058_23-173259.html.

# CHAPTER 21

# Fire Away

Sometimes the questions are complicated and the answers are simple.

—*Dr. Seuss, author*

On November 4, 1979, just three days before U.S. Senator Edward Kennedy officially announced his plans to challenge President Jimmy Carter for the 1980 Democratic presidential nomination, he sat down for a CBS TV interview with then correspondent Roger Mudd who asked, "Senator, why do you want to be president?" The normally quick and well-spoken Kennedy stammered and rambled as he tried to answer the now infamous question. Some say that single question doomed his bid for the presidency, and some critics blamed Mudd for bringing Kennedy down. I think it's not that clear-cut and pose this question for thought. Was Mudd's question the culprit, or was the answer to blame? I suggest it's the latter. Because the senator could not articulate why the top job in the land was so important to him, confidence in his ability to lead was compromised. This decades-old interview remains one of the best examples of the importance of answering questions directly, clearly, and from the heart.

In the nearly two decades that I have been preparing professionals for a wide variety of communications, I am always amazed at how some of the most basic preparation questions can elicit comments such as, "you were really tough on me." While preparing an energy executive to face a hostile community objecting to the construction of a new power plant, I asked why the company needed to replace the current plant if it's not even operating at full capacity and why it needed to build the plant so close to a populated city. The executive knew the answers but viewed these questions as hard-hitting when they were simply basic questions the public was asking and had a right to know.

While few of us will face questions on national television, the Kennedy interview underscores the importance of being able to respond effectively, even when you haven't prepared for or anticipated the question. It is one of the most valuable skills business professionals and spokespeople should have, yet often they blame others when they don't like questions or are caught off guard. Certainly, we've all been surprised by unexpected or unanticipated questions, but in my experience, almost all questions can be anticipated if you take the time to prepare in advance. And if the answer escapes you, answer from the heart. If Kennedy had responded by saying something like, "I love this country with every fiber of my being and am committed to helping each and every American have the best life possible," the outcome may have been different, for he would have appealed to people on a very human level. That's not to say he wouldn't have to answer the tough questions, but it would have framed the conversation and enabled him to move on to message points he wanted to deliver.

In our preparation sessions, we always advise people to make two lists to better anticipate questions. The first list is easiest because it includes every question you think you could be asked. For example, if you are preparing for an investor meeting, it is likely potential investors will ask about your strategies, current market conditions, competitive advantages, and how long it will be before they see a return on their investment. The second list is tougher because it should include all of the questions you fear, don't have answers for, or hope no one will ask. As always—and, most importantly—think like your audience so the questions are emotionally realistic. For example, when companies prepare spokespeople for specific events, communications professionals typically develop lists of anticipated questions and suggested answers. This usually includes standard questions as well as potential stumpers they want to make sure their people can answer. All too often, however, the preparation lists are missing emotional questions that get to the heart of the matter and questions that address what people really want to know.

## CASE AND POINT

While preparing spokespeople to discuss women's attitudes and behaviors regarding sexual health, a survey taken found a majority of women experienced issues but were reluctant to talk about them with their partners and health care providers. Below are sample questions the agency anticipated would be asked and wanted us to include when role-playing with spokespeople.

## FIRE-AWAY QUESTIONS

1. Why was this survey commissioned?
2. What were the key findings?
3. Where can women go for more sexual health–related information?
4. What's the significance of the survey findings?
5. Why did your company sponsor this survey?
6. Are your spokespeople being paid to deliver messages?
7. What are common sexual health–related problems you hear about from your patients?
8. What other aspects of a woman's overall health can be affected by sexual health problems?
9. Why do patients have a hard time discussing sexual health problems with their doctors?
10. Why do doctors have a hard time discussing sexual health problems with their patients?

All of these questions were well thought out and some were asked. However, the emotional questions below, which were missing from the preparation document, are the types of real-life questions that are more frequently asked because they are questions you and I would pose to each other in conversations.

## EMOTIONALLY CONVERSATIONAL QUESTIONS

1. What does sexual health mean? Is it how many times a week a woman wants to have sex?
2. What's considered the norm?
3. Is sex different for women as they age, and what are the most common sexual issues affecting women of all ages?
4. What was most surprising to you about these results?
5. Do you think women really have a problem, or is it just life? They have a lot on their plates—work, children, aging parents,

perhaps getting older themselves and libido is not what it once was—does that really mean they have a problem?

6. But just because a woman doesn't have desire, why does that suggest she go to a doctor?

7. The company that is sponsoring this campaign is trying to get approval for a female sex drug, so isn't this a way of promoting it to convince women they need help?

8. How do you differentiate whether the problem is lack of desire or problems in the patient's relationships—maybe someone isn't attracted to their mate anymore?

9. Are we creating diseases to sell drugs to fix them?

Whether you are in a board room, testifying at a hearing, participating on a panel, or being interviewed, your reputation is always at stake, so it's understandable why people are so apprehensive when it comes to fielding questions. What if you can't answer? What if you don't know the answer? What if you give an answer people don't want to hear? What if they think you don't know what you're talking about? You might be perceived as lacking confidence or leadership qualities. It's why the best and brightest frequently shy away from the spotlight.

I worked with a senior executive who is a strong, charismatic people person. He has no problem speaking to employee audiences or at industry events, but he confided to me that he is terrified to take questions or do media interviews because he doesn't want someone else to make him look bad. What he had not given much thought to is that questions can be opportunities to create dialogue, learn what others care about, provide information, showcase one's expertise, and turn negatives into positives. Easier said than done you, may be thinking, but like any other communication, it's all about preparation.

You should always begin with a clear understanding of your audience to help you anticipate the types of questions they will ask and objections you will need to address. To help you do that, I've divided this chapter into four parts:

1. Annoyers
2. Stumpers
3. Horses
4. Steroids

Annoyers are the kinds of personalities who seem to show up at events for the sole purpose of irritating you. Stumpers are the tough questions the methods you can use to turn the answers to your advantage. H-O-R-S-E is an acronym of strategies to help you think on your feet and handle tough questions so, like a horse, you appear strong and swift. Steroids are performance enhancers to boost your credibility when delivering answers.

## ANNOYERS

Annoyers are irritating. They seem to show up at meetings to tick you off, cause problems, or undermine your credibility. There are numerous types of annoyers, but these are the most common.

### BLAMERS

Blamers try to assign guilt, but they can't succeed without your help. The examples below show you how to advance your own agenda.

Q:  How could this happen if you put all these controls in place?

A:  We are working very hard to determine exactly what happened and how it happened, but at this point the cause is not known. It is important to point out that, in our 40 years in business, there has never been a safety issue.

Q:  Who is to blame for this?

A:  Pointing fingers and naming names is not in anyone's best interest. What's important is that we have learned from our mistake and have put controls into place to prevent this from ever happening again.

### HOGS

Hogs are noisy creatures who take up a lot of time and space at meetings. They keep talking because they think their ideas and opinions are more valuable than everyone else's. If you are leading the meeting, your job is to remind them that you want to hear from others as well.

### SUCK UPS

Suck ups only care about impressing the boss. They will disagree with you if you think that will impress someone, and, if you're not careful, they'll stab you in the back to get what they want.

## ATTACKERS

Attackers almost always disagree with your point of view just for the sake of being difficult. They will say things like "for argument's sake" or "just to play devil's advocate" and will then disagree. Sometimes they get personal to see if they can provoke you. It's important to stick to the facts and not address accusations with emotions.

Q:  Your competitors say you have done everything within your power to sabotage this project. Is this true?

A:  For whatever reason, Company X has decided to release information that we do not believe is accurate. The facts are as follows." Or "Let me share the facts with you."

## HIDE-AND-SEEKERS

Like attackers and blamers, hide-and-seekers try to make it appear as if you have something to hide. They typically imply that you purposely withheld information and seek ways to assign guilt. It's up to you to take the high road and communicate positively.

Q:  If you knew this was about to happen, then why didn't the company let employees and the surrounding communities know about the plant closing and upcoming layoffs?

A:  We felt that it was appropriate to release information only after a final decision had been made. Now that the decision is firm, we are providing information to you well in advance of the actual closing and anticipated layoffs in order to help people prepare.

Q:  Why won't you comment? Clearly, you have something hide.

A:  We want to make sure we deliver accurate information. Until we have all of the facts, we are not going to speculate. We are in the process of gathering that information, and, when we do have it, we will share it with you.

## GLOOMY GUS

Gloomy Gus is like a vacuum cleaner, because he or she sucks the energy out of the room. No matter what you say, Gus will tell you why it won't work or can't be done. It's important to poke holes in Gus's arguments by pointing to facts that back up what you say in an effort to help Gus and others in the room see your point of view.

### Show-Offs

Show-offs appear in the form of jokers, class clowns, and attention seekers. They conduct private conversations just loud enough for others to overhear, make inappropriate comments, frequently interrupt, and clown around when others are delivering information. While they may appear harmless, their jokes can be disguised putdowns, and their actions can affect the productivity of entire teams.

### Assassins

Assassins have hidden agendas and quietly wait for the right moment to fire. They are tough to spot because their motives are not always clear. By listening carefully to their tone and the types of questions they ask, you may be able to sniff them out. It's important to get these people to participate in the discussion at hand by asking questions to involve them and keep them out in the open.

### Silencers

Silencers don't say much, but it's hard to tell whether they are shy, uninformed, nervous, angry, or simply have no interest in the topic. These people can also be drawn out by asking them questions in an effort to involve them in the conversation.

### Ramblers

Ramblers are like birds. They fly off in many directions, are hard to pin down, and you rarely know where they are going. These people take forever to get to the point, go off on tangents, and drag down everyone in the room. Sometimes you have to stop them and politely ask them to give you the bottom line.

### Disrupters

Almost nothing is more disrupting than people texting, using cell phones, PDAs, or their computers and not giving their full attention to the meeting. It's up to the meeting leader to set ground rules in advance or tell them to stop.

## STUMPERS

I work with an executive who more than once confided that he loves to "stump the chump" by firing questions at people to see if he can make them squirm. While this may be mean-spirited, learning to handle tough questions without getting flustered can position you as a confident take-charge person who can control important conversations. For starters, remain calm. If you can't control your emotions, you will not be able to control the conversation. Second, be respectful of the questioner, even if he is not showing the same respect to you.

Here are common question stumpers and approaches to effectively handle them.

### HYPOTHETICAL

This question asks you to speculate, which can be disastrous. The suggested answers show you how to state and stick to what you know.

Q: What happens if you can't figure out what caused this problem?

A: These are the facts as we know them. In our clinical trials, we saw a, b, and c and believe that means the cause is either x or y.

Q: What would you say if I told you that I have it on very good authority that your boss is stepping down tomorrow?

A: I have no information to support your claim and will not speculate on what may or may not happen.

### YES OR NO

Sometimes a simple yes or no answer is all that is required, but often just answering yes or no can shut down a conversation, cause you to appear abrupt, and prevent you from adding to the discussion. When appropriate, look for opportunities to provide information instead of just one-word answers.

Q: Isn't it true that you have known for years that this factory did not meet FDA requirements?

A: We have been working very closely with the FDA to make sure we conform to the appropriate standards. It is important to know that, over the past few years, we have made significant improvements that include [state the improvements], because we take this very seriously and are committed to making sure our products are of the highest quality.

## EITHER/OR

This is a lose/lose, because either/or questions limit your ability to respond. Answering with message points you want to make helps you deliver information and take control.

Q:  Either you took the money or you didn't. Which is it?

A:  This is a very complicated matter. The real issue here is the people who are affected by what has happened.

Q:  What do you think your biggest mistake was—not expecting the amount of snow or waiting too long to salt the streets?

A:  We got a lot of snow—14 feet—and we were caught off guard because the forecast called for much less. But this department is working around the clock to clear every street in this city. In the past 24 hours, we have [state what has been done]. It takes time, so please be patient. We ask the public to help us by staying off the roads if it's not necessary to travel.

## LEADING QUESTIONS

Be careful not to allow someone else's question be perceived as your opinion. Instead of repeating her words, which can be negative, respond by stating the message you want to deliver. This allows you to choose your own words.

Q:  Don't you agree that it looks bad to hire celebrities for so much money when the costs of drugs are so high?

A:  By partnering with role models, we can reach far more people on a much bigger stage to create awareness about this life-saving treatment.

Q:  How much do you expect prices to go up next year?

A:  We are committed to making our products as affordable as possible for people who need them and will continue to do everything possible to keep prices down during these difficult times.

Q:  How much do you pay these people anyway?

A:  It is company policy not to discuss personal contracts.

## Personal Opinion

If you are speaking on behalf of your company, industry, or association, you should not offer your personal opinion. Think "we" instead of "I."

Q: Last year, sales and profits were down. The economy is still staggering and your company keeps losing money. In your opinion, can this company really survive?

A: It has been a difficult year, but *we* are very encouraged about the future. This quarter *we* have already shown a 30 percent increase and *we* are predicting growth as the year moves forward.

## Multiple Choices

Some people will ask several questions at once. If you choose to answer all of them, then say "let me take one question at a time" or "first let me address." Otherwise, just address the question you want to answer.

Q: You recently merged with XYZ Company, so does that mean you continue manufacturing all of their products along with yours and hire more employees to do so, and what about relocation? Do you plan to shut any of your factories down?

A: We have been in business for over 80 years and Bethlehem is our home, so we have no plans to make any immediate changes.

## Rumor Mill

You should never address rumors or information that is not familiar to you.

Q: We have heard that you will be shutting this facility down by the end of the year.

A: I am not aware of any plans of that kind. I can tell you that [bridge to your message]."

## Mission Impossible

In some situations, no matter what you say seems to say enough. Remember to have heart.

Q:   Your people arrived at the wrong address and demolished some-
     one's home. How in the world can you ever repay this family?

A:   What happened here today is tragic and nothing we can say can
     undo what has been done. We take full responsibility for what
     happened and are trying to do everything possible to help the
     family relocate.

## Don't Know

In most cases, if you don't know the answer, just say so, offer to
find out, and tell the person you will get back to him as soon as possible. Unfortunately, when people don't have an answer, they often try
to fake it and start rambling, which can position them as evasive. If
the question asked is essential to your work, answer it as directly and
honestly as possible by speaking to what you do know. The following
phrases can lead you to what you want to say:

- I do not have the specifics, but what I can tell you
- What we do know
- What this means is
- What we found
- What we saw
- What we learned
- The reason this is significant
- What's critical to point out
- This is key
- It's important to understand
- What we can't lose sight of
- What makes this unique
- The reason we are so encouraged

When hit with that terribly difficult question that you want to answer but don't know how to handle, always remember heart over head.
For example:

Question:   After what just happened, how can anyone believe you
            have their best interest at heart?

Heart: This is terribly difficult and upsetting for everyone involved. What happened is unfortunate and unacceptable. Like you, I also want to know what happened, when it happened, and why it happened, and we are doing everything humanly possible to get those answers.

There may also be opportunities to outstump the stumpers by gently firing their question right back at them so they have to repeat it—which they are typically happy to do, because stumpers like to hear themselves talk. You can say:

- I'm sorry, I'm not sure I understand the question, can you repeat it?
- Can you explain what you mean when you say [such and such] so I make sure I address your concern?

## H-O-R-S-E

The following strategies were designed to help professionals confidently handle challenging questions at important events such as FDA hearings, community protests, analyst calls, investor days, management meetings, and debates. The question-and-answer examples are from specific practice sessions.

### H for Headline

If the fire alarm went off and you only had seconds to deliver your main point, what would you say? By approaching your answers as headlines, you position yourself to answer the question directly by delivering the most important point first. You can then back it up with proof points, examples, and analogies that support your main point. It's important to understand that listeners won't always take what you say at face value. There is often a little voice in their head silently screaming "prove it!" The following coaching notes were provided to a medical director in preparation for a product approval that was ultimately successful.

### Coaching Notes

The most important thing you can do when you answer questions is come across as confident and sure of your answer. Even if you don't have the answer or know it's an answer someone won't like, you still have to respond with conviction and certainty in what you are saying.

You need to answer questions sharply, directly, and immediately with-out continually repeating the question, saying uh or um before the an-swer, or taking even a couple of extra beats to get to the point. Contrary to popular belief, it is important to not repeat the question or say "that's a good question" when you answer. Every question is a good question.

Based on the mock panel today, here are some examples: Q is ques-tion, A is your answer, and H is my headline suggestion.

Q:    Is this purely cosmetic?

A:    No it is not.

Headline:    The reduction in joint contracture is a very meaningful event.

Q:    Can you explain the benefit of xyz compound?

A:    Uh, I think it has some benefit.

Headline:    It has definite benefit [if that is the fact]. We included this because. Or the benefit is x and Mary can provide a more detailed explanation.

Q:    Can you provide another example about dose range?

A:    Well, the question about dose ranging . . .

Headline:    Hit it directly: We used x amount and this showed us . . .

Q:    Are you suggesting?

A:    Uh, we're not saying . . .

Headline:    Go straight to message: We are saying or We found. Don't repeat his words if they're negative.

Q:    So, only specific types of surgeons will perform this surgery?

A:    That is not true.

Headline:    Our target will primarily be these surgeons, but [then talk about others who will be able to perform and what type of training they will have].

Q:    What safety concerns should doctors be worried about?

A:    To answer your question, I don't believe there are any safety concerns.

Headline:    We specifically looked for xyz, and there were no safety concerns.

It is not necessary to constantly refer to their questions every time you answer. You repeatedly started your answers with phrases such as:

- Your question is
- To answer your question
- Your question is asking
- I guess the question about
- I can give you the answer
- This is a question about

There is no need to qualify. Just say what you have to say.

## O FOR OPEN ENDED

When used correctly, open-ended questions buy time, clarify what the questioner is after, and prevent misinterpretation by helping both sides better understand each other. Open-ended questions include:

- I'm not certain that I understand the question; can you give me an example?
- I'm not sure I follow; can you restate the question?
- If I understand what you are asking, you want to know . . .

When you ask for clarification, you are blaming yourself for not understanding a question as opposed to insinuating that the questioner is at fault. Pushing the questioner to rephrase the question or give an example also helps a spokesperson answer in his own words. At the same time, be careful not to ask for clarification every time a question is asked.

## R FOR REFUTE AND RESPOND

Refuting negative questions allows you to focus attention on what you want to address. This is especially helpful in responding to hostile or accusatory questions. As an example, when working with employees at a hotel chain, they were charged with explaining why high-speed Internet service at their properties was superior to what competitors were offering guests. Let's look at how negative questions prompt negative and defensive responses.

Negative Q:   Everyone offers this. Why would someone choose your hotel over another when this is available everywhere?

Refute:   It's not available everywhere, and if you took the time to look at our literature, you could see why we offer superior service.

It's normal for most of us to take questions personally when they seem critical of our work. Unfortunately, our answers are often emotional, which can make us appear defensive and even abrasive. Let's take the same question but positively refute it with facts.

Positive Q:   Everyone offers this. Why would someone choose your hotel over another when this is available everywhere?

Refute:   You are correct. High-speed Internet has become routine in many hotels, but let me tell you what's different for the customers when they stay with us.

In the second example, not only does the response come across as more thoughtful, but it doesn't dismiss or put down the other person's feelings. Responding nondefensively tells the questioner you're confident in what you're saying and can calmly back it up with facts.

## S for Stay Positive

When was the last time you said, "let's invite Mary to the party because she's such a downer"? People like positive people because positive people create confidence in others. The same is true of positive words. Look at the difference in tone and meaning conveyed by both negative and positive responses delivered by a financial executive who was preparing to talk with analysts.

Question:   Doesn't this show a lack of confidence in your ability to improve returns?

Negative:   No, this does not reflect a lack of confidence.

Positive:   We're fully confident in our ability to improve returns, which is why our strategy to do . . .

Question:   Don't you think patients will be lost to generic competition?

| Negative: | We don't think so. |
|---|---|
| Positive: | We have every reason to believe there will be substantial growth beyond generics. |
| Question: | Are you worried? |
| Negative: | No, not really. |
| Positive: | We are actually extremely confident and believe Product X will be the market leader. The fact that it has patent protection through 2011 predicts strong growth. |

Almost anything that can be asked negatively can be answered positively if you take a moment to listen to the question, avoid repeating negative words, and look for opportunities to respond with messages.


## E FOR ESCAPE

Media trainers commonly refer to this technique as the "bridge," because it helps you escape the question and transition to your message. Escape techniques can also be used to defuse inflammatory or negative questions in a wide variety of situations. This takes practice, because a bad bridge completely ignores the question and can make you sound phony. A good bridge briefly addresses the question before moving on to what you want to say.

An easy way to remember how to bridge is the A-B-C technique introduced in chapter 12. *A* is for acknowledging and addressing the question. *B* is the bridge to *C*, which stands for communicate the message. The ABCs can be used together or independently.

| Question: | So, you're throwing this person out of your facility? |
|---|---|
| A: | We have asked Mr. Jones to leave by the end of the week. |
| B: | What's important to understand is that. |
| C: | We gave Mr. Jones every opportunity to correct the situation but he has repeatedly violated the rules despite numerous warnings advising him of the consequences. |
| Question: | Why should anyone believe you are innocent? |
| A: | The amount of evidence presented here today is overwhelming so I can understand why people might doubt my innocence. |
| B: | However, I'd like to point out that. |

C:   When this trial is over, I am fully confident I will be cleared of any wrongdoing.

Other situations call for bridging (B) immediately.

Question:   Can you tell me how soon you expect the experiment to yield results?
B:   That is not my area of expertise, but what I can tell you . . .
Question:   I heard that you will be shutting down your main plant.
B:   Quite the contrary. We are actually adding jobs at that plant and talking about constructing additional facilities.

Politicians are particularly adept at dodging and deflecting questions, but they often do it by ignoring the question and saying whatever they want to say, which is not always advisable in business settings. In business, it is important to answer the question but also effective to communicate (C) the message quickly as possible instead of acknowledging, addressing, and getting stuck in the question.

Question:   Aren't you concerned that your actions will hurt business?
C:   We believe the steps we have taken will help business by . . .
Question:   Isn't it true that your company discriminated against women?
C:   Absolutely not! We do not tolerate discrimination of any kind.

Communicating the message as quickly as possible also prevents you from getting stuck in the weeds and tuning people out.

Question:   So, is the end result 28 or 7?
C:   It's 28 and here's why.

The following bridging phrases can help you smoothly connect two thoughts or transition to a point you want to make. Pick two or three that sound natural to your style of speaking.

- It's important to understand
- What you might find interesting
- That is not my area of expertise, but what I can tell you
- I can appreciate why you might feel that way, but
- That is a common misperception, so let me clarify
- Let me first say
- It's important to point out
- In fact
- Another important thing to know is
- The real issue is
- What you should remember is
- It's our policy not to discuss, but what I can tell you
- That is not true; the facts are
- Let me put it another way
- What we do know

## STEROIDS

Just like bodybuilders who use steroids to gain muscle, presenters can enhance their performance not just by what they say but by how they say it. Make no mistake, however: even the most superb delivery cannot substitute for lack of preparation. Preparation will help you think about difficult questions in advance so you can answer them clearly and confidently. Before we talk about performance enhancers, I want to share my single biggest pet peeve in an effort to urge you not to do this.

### Do Not Compliment the Questioner

People love to say "that's a good question." Every question should be considered a good question. Most listeners realize you are stalling in an effort to think about what to say. But more importantly, if you tell one person she has asked a good question but don't compliment someone else's question, does that mean his question isn't quite as good? If you feel compelled to say something to buy time, try to say "that's an interesting question" or "I've never thought of it that way," which sounds far more thoughtful and sincere.

PERFORMANCE ENHANCERS

- **Shut up and listen.** When you are being asked a question, just listen. Do not interrupt, look away, and continually open your mouth to talk or shake your head. Look directly at the questioner and give her your full attention.

- **Repeat the question.** Not only does repeating the question give you a moment to think, but in larger groups, you ensure that everyone has heard the question correctly. It's not necessary to repeat it word for word, but by paraphrasing the essence of the question, you can focus your listener on what you consider to be important. Additionally, when a question sounds more like a rambling statement than an actual question, repeating key words helps you get to the heart of your response more quickly.

- **Eye contact.** Eye contact has frequently been mentioned throughout this book. It is essential to look people in the eye when they ask you a question and when you address the question if you want to appear confident in your response. If you are speaking to a larger group, look directly at the person who asked the question as you repeat the question and first respond, then pause and shift eye contact away from the questioner to the rest of the group so everyone feels included.

- **Pause.** Try to pause for a beat before launching into an answer. This tells the audience you are truly listening to the question so you can answer it as opposed to just spouting off what you want to say. Pausing can also help prevent those ums and uhs frequently used to fill in silent spaces. Pausing after you deliver an important fact will also highlight that piece of information and make it sound more important.

- **Keep your cool.** No matter how rattled or annoyed you are by a question, it's important to keep your composure if you hope to maintain credibility. Take a deep breath and pause before answering the question. Look for opportunities to bridge to key points of your presentation, which will help you reinforce and include messages in your responses. If the question has already been asked and addressed, don't point that out and embarrass the questioner. Simply answer it again and do so politely. You should also keep your body language as neutral as possible so it doesn't convey your irritation.

- **Keep it short.** Keeping your answers as short and focused as possible maximizes the likelihood that your intended message is heard the same way by all.

It's important to recognize that question-and-answer sessions are not separate from your presentation but are a part of your presentation. Questions provide additional opportunities for you to reinforce key points, invite listeners to participate, and demonstrate your expertise. If you hope to continue to control the flow of information, it's critical to spend time thinking through the questions that will be asked in order to deliver fact-based answers with calm confidence. Additionally, sometimes the way we perceive a question is not the way it was intended. In our sessions, professionals often inquire about the "hidden meaning" or "what do you think she really meant when she asked that?" Quite often, the question had no hidden meaning and the questioner was sincere. You can win over more people than you might realize if you address their concerns as openly and honestly as possible.

**Sometimes we learn more from questions than we do from answers.**

# CHAPTER 22

# Electronic Engagement

*If you can't explain it simply, you don't understand it well enough.*
*—Albert Einstein, physicist*

A Google search for the words "social media" will yield hundreds of millions of hits. You'll find vast amounts of information on cool new Web sites, how to market your business, and how to leverage the social media explosion to your advantage. Even if you aren't social media savvy, there's a good chance you are communicating by e-mail, video conferencing, teleseminar, webinars, or perhaps using a service like Skype, which allows users to make video and voice calls over the Internet.

This chapter is not a user's guide to help you better navigate these applications. Electronic engagement will show you how to communicate clearly and effectively in an electronic world so you can interact with and engage others more successfully. Whether before the social media age or after, as with any communication, it is essential to keep it simple if you hope to be heard. Just because it's faster and easier to create and distribute content in so many forms doesn't mean it's easier to communicate. In fact, in some ways Web 2.0 has made communicating harder than ever. For example, in days past, public relations professionals pitched mainstream media to take messages public whether that meant getting coverage of an event or hoping a publication would voice an opinion by printing a letter to the editor. Today, journalists actively seek out bloggers and Tweeters who have something to say but are not always adept at crafting thoughts that are easy to follow and understand. Like compelling news stories, content must be clear, concise, and conversational and create an emotional connection with the audience. That's why communicating effectively in this new age requires thinking in billboards.

> Communicating effectively in this new age requires thinking in billboards.

If you're speeding down Interstate 95 at 75 miles per hour, would you be able to look up and read someone's rant on a billboard? Certainly not. That's why billboards boast visual images with few words. A good billboard touting an airline might inspire you to fly off to a vacation spot. When communicating electronically, you should strive for the same thing. By helping others picture and experience what you are saying in a way that is short, focused, and to the point, you create greater connections with your listeners. Like any form of communication, it's important to have something to say, but, unlike days past, mainstream communicating is no longer a one-way street. Blogs, video forums, texting, and social networks encourage feedback and constant interaction from others, just as a telephone conversation once taught us to do.

Critics complain that time spent with family, friends, or a good book is being threatened by texting, surfing, and posting. In fact, some psychologists believe social networking may kill emotional intelligence. I think nothing could be further from the truth. People often criticize when they are fearful or don't understand how to participate. Some people still don't use e-mail and will tell you they have no use for it, but that's like suggesting we travel by horse instead of car or that we revert back to phonographs instead of MP3 players.

Social media are social. They allow people to reconnect with old friends, gain introductions to new associates, post pictures of their kids online for family members across the world to see, find jobs, and join important conversations of our time with one click. Social media provide opportunities to interact with celebrities and public figures. Most importantly, engaging electronically encourages communication, which the free online dictionary defines as the exchange of thoughts, messages, or information.

This new electronic age won't harm our ability to communicate, because it is not an act of communication. It is a tool to help us exchange information and ideas on a global stage. If we learn how to do this more effectively, we will foster more transparent conversations that engage more people and produce richer outcomes. Let's start by identifying three essential electronic engagement keepers that should be applied across all platforms.

## 1: KEEP IT SIMPLE

Twitter is an excellent example of how social media have forced people to simplify communications. Because tweets are limited to 140 characters, which is roughly 20 words, communicators must make points in succinct headlines, which increase the likelihood of being understood. If you apply that technique to your own writing and speaking style, you will engage others more quickly.

## 2: KEEP THEM INVOLVED

Because we have more communication choices than ever before, it's important to involve listeners so they can visualize what you're saying. For example, when describing the 2010 record snowfall just midway through winter, a meteorologist put it this way: "It's like a football game where you score 84 points, and it's only the third quarter." Analogies, colorful stories, exercises, and questions keep listeners engaged and help them experience what we're saying.

## 3: KEEP IT PERSONAL

When blogging, podcasting, e-mailing, or conducting an online seminar, speak to one person as if that person is in front of you. Face-to-face encounters are more conversational, passionate, and ripe with appealing anecdotes that sound natural and conversational.

According to David Campbell, the creative director for FNUKY, a digital branding agency in Adelaide, Australia, it would take 412 years to view all the content on YouTube, which explains why cutting through the clutter is so daunting. More and more people are struggling to get noticed in a digital era when there are more demands on our time than ever before.

Organizations of all sizes can determine where they want to communicate and how they want to do it. When the Ford Motor Company was detoured by declining sales during the recession, it said no to federal bailout money and yes to social media. In an orchestrated campaign designed to change perceptions that the automaker was a tired clunker, management accelerated into Twitter, Facebook, and other influencers to change the way they communicated with customers and employees. During the initial campaign, the company reported making 11 million new impressions and having 4.3 million YouTube views. While Ford faced some criticism for using sponsored blogger conversations as a way to communicate with new customers, by opening up its products to comments from others, Ford said it fueled an atmosphere of transparency and candid conversations, which allowed readers to come to their own conclusions.

Online communication is enabling both small and big businesses to recognize employees, encourage innovation, and gain a better understanding of what goes on at their company. IBM, which started tapping into new communication platforms in the late 1990s before it was as popular, encourages employees to communicate through internal blogs, videos, social media, and its interactive employee directory, which receives more than one million page views each day. Adam Christensen, IBM's social media communications manager, blogs that "These platforms remove all of the artificial and geographical boundaries you find in organizations that lock up knowledge and information. Instead of relying on your office neighbors or reporting line as the sole source of information, you can reach anywhere into the organization—or out of the organization—to collaborate, learn, listen, and influence." Christensen says, as a result, people are doing their jobs better than ever.

The ability to communicate quickly and frequently is apparently motivating children as well. A National Literacy Trust survey of over 3,000 children observed that these communication vehicles have helped children become more literate. It also played a role in electing President Barack Obama, who embraced technology and social media to distribute his message to the masses. It wasn't simply engaging electronically that helped him sell his point of view. The president mastered the art of simplicity when communicating. If you think of Obama as the CEO of America, who took time to fully understand his audience in order to tailor his message to their concerns, then CEOs and corporate communicators who muddle the message with too many words should take a page from the president's playbook.

Engaging electronically is also opening closed doors. In the past, if you wanted to get introduced to a decision maker, you had to call someone who knew someone who knew someone else who might eventually introduce you through a cover letter and a stamp. Today, online business networking sites like LinkedIn make it easier to find common ground with strangers.

As an example, I've always wanted to do business with a company located about 15 minutes from my home, but I didn't know anyone there and my network of contacts weren't connected either. So I started clicking around LinkedIn and found the contact that would be most likely to hire me. According to her profile, we had six connections. As it turns out, they were actually connected to her through other connections and no one knew her well enough to introduce me. Case closed, right? Wrong. About two weeks later, I received an e-mail from a woman I barely know but who is great friends with the woman I want to meet and that they play golf together all the time. She tells me she once attended a program I conducted and would be happy to recommend me to her friend. I call and the golf buddy executive invites me in for a meeting. Because we were "linked," it was easy to communicate on a much more personal level about her interests and acquaintances we had in common. I now do work with her company and firmly believe the social communications component that allowed us to engage as friends made her more open to meeting me. Obviously, it's not always as easy as that, but it's a great example of how the online world has helped communications become more personal and connected.

In other instances, being able to communicate electronically has been a lifeline for people. When the Haiti earthquake struck, cell phones, social media, e-mail and Web-based phone systems like Skype were the only way those affected could communicate, because traditional communication systems weren't working. Twitter, Facebook, and blogs, online media were able to get the word out and bring in aid quicker than mainstream media. When you are forced by word limitation to be as succinct as possible, messages automatically become short, focused, and to the point. If we want to engage more effectively in an electronic world, we need to speak the same way.

Because there are so many types of personalized media and more emerge every day, it would be difficult to provide tips for each and every one. So I have selected a handful of the more popular communication vehicles to offer quick fixes on how to best communicate ideas and information through these media.

## ELECTRONIC ENGAGEMENT FIXES

### E-mail

Have you ever taken time to craft an e-mail and then wondered why the recipient didn't seem to read what you wrote? If your e-mail was too long, chances are they put it aside, skimmed it instead of read it, or even deleted it. With many people getting hundreds of e-mails per day, it's more important than ever to keep your message short and to the point. Start with the subject line. Often five to six words such as *Last Day to Join Our Club* will tell people why to read the e-mail.

In the body of the e-mail, start with a greeting such as Dear Karen. In the first line, state the purpose of the correspondence. Be as specific as possible so readers do not have to wade through lots of words to determine what you want. If it is necessary for the e-mail to contain a lot of information, break it up into paragraphs or bullet points so it's easier to read.

## Blogs

Short is still the advice, but in longer posts like blogs, organization is key. An emotional, stream-of-consciousness post that doesn't clearly hit key points, rambles, and is unfocused will be hard to read. Before you post, outline key points you want to make and examples you can share with each point so the post is structured and easy to follow. Just as a reporter would ask when writing a story, you should ask "what does this mean to my visitor and what can they do with this information?" If possible, keep it to one page.

## Tweeting, Linking, and Posting

How often have you heard someone say he doesn't want to know if someone is walking her dog or shopping? If you don't care about their everyday tweets, then why should they care about yours? Make tweets and posts valuable by sharing ideas and information that others can use. Post links to articles, interesting blogs, pictures, and videos that encourage conversation.

## Videoconferencing and Video Interviews

Online video meetings are a great way for companies to save dollars, but technology can't replace meeting in person. There are often lags in transmission, and people don't know where to look, what to do with their hands, or how to engage. Think of video as having a one-to-one conversation, but speak a tad louder so your passion comes through the screen. If you are speaking to other people in the room, look at them, not at the camera, so they can see you react and respond to questions.

Use your hands as you would in person to come across as animated and fully engaged.

### VIRTUAL PRESENTATIONS: WEBINARS, WEBCAMS, AND TELESEMINARS

Talking to people you can't always see or hear is tough. If you're on a webcam, think of being in a box, much like a closeup on TV. If you look up, down, or off to the side, it is distracting to your viewer and may give the impression that you're not confident in your message, so look right at the computer camera. Even though you are providing valuable information, it's tough to keep people's attention, which is why you need to keep it interactive if you want to keep their attention. Ask questions and pause for thought even if they can't answer. Like any presentation, use examples, stories, and visuals to illustrate your points and make it more interesting. Don't forget to remind them what slide you're on so they can follow along.

### YouTube AND ON CAMERA

In my television days, we used to say the best on-air people were those who could make love to a camera. That's why enthusiasm and passion rule whenever the camera is on. Like writing or presenting, think of the camera as one person, and make steady, direct eye contact with that person. Even if they can't see you, smile because they can feel you. If the camera shot is wider, you can use your hands to gesture, but avoid jerky and aggressive movements. It's important to enunciate; speak, not read, so you sound conversational; and slow down. Avoid rocking, swaying, shifting your weight, and bouncing.

For many, the quick-changing pace of a reality TV generation is daunting because, regardless of age or expertise, it's tough to keep up. But remember, these are tools that have revolutionized the way we communicate. The *how* we speak has not actually changed. Great communicators of past and present have infectious, passionate styles. They quickly get to the point and convey complex ideas in interesting ways to make others care about their message. They weave stories to inspire and create experiences that are relevant and memorable to listeners. Whether you're writing, speaking, blogging, tweeting, texting, linking, e-mailing, or connecting on Facebook, you can do the same.

**Reach out to reach beyond.**

# CHAPTER 23

# DOODY Principle

I just want not to suck at this.
—*Bob Doody, Assistant Director of Investor*
*Relations at Viropharma*

It was a rainy, chilly Chicago afternoon when room service knocked on my hotel door with the much-desired fresh pot of hot coffee. As the attendant set the coffee down, he looked at the many open folders scattered all over the desk and said, "don't work too hard." I smiled and told him I had to work hard because I was giving an important talk in the morning and wanted to make sure that I made a good impression, to which he replied, "make sure to smile."

It was such a simple piece of advice from someone who probably doesn't deliver too many presentations and isn't schooled in communication, but he may understand more about connecting with people than many of us who interact with customers and colleagues on a daily basis.

We do forget to smile. In our fast-paced, time-challenged environments, we are often so intent on just getting it done that when we actually arrive at the moment, we frequently plow right in instead of taking a breath, saying good morning, and smiling at our listeners so they know we are happy to have this opportunity to speak with them.

If you want to have a little fun at work, start counting how many times someone speaking at a meeting actually says "good morning" or "good afternoon." Then count the smiles. You won't count many, which brings us to the name of this chapter. Bob Doody is a cool guy who has worked hard to make tough talks look friendly and easy. As the corporate communications manager at Viropharma, a Pennsylvania-based biotechnology company, he frequently speaks to investors and potential investors. He sent me the following e-mail:

> My goal is pretty simple. I would like not to suck at this. I think I will do well, but I get real nervous the night before and my stomach will be in knots.

Like many executives who want to shine, especially when the stakes are high, they frequently approach the process with remarks like: "I just need some help with my delivery." While they often do need help with delivery, rarely is delivery alone the real problem. The difficulties typically include a laundry list of items such as poor preparation and organization, unclear message not tailored to audience concerns, lack of anecdotes and examples, as well as writing remarks to be read instead of heard. While there is no one-size-fits-all formula, there is a solution that applies in every situation. The better prepared you are, the better you'll be. Additionally, when you prepare remarks around the results you're after, you can then pitch with passion and personality, which is far more likely to keep people awake and increase the likelihood that decision makers will buy what you're selling.

## DOODY PRINCIPLE

The DOODY principle is a five-step delivery process designed to help you make your ideas sing so you can move them to action. But again, no matter how good you think you are, if you're not willing to prepare in advance, you'll never hit all the high notes. I've heard every excuse in the world. Perhaps some of these sound familiar: "This is the way we do it here," "I've done this many times before so I don't have to go through it," "Everyone says I'm a great speaker," "I just need some help with delivery." And my favorite: "I know this is important but I don't have time to prepare." That's like saying I'm going in the ocean but I don't know how to swim. Who are you kidding? Every audience is different, which means no two talks are the same. Failure to prepare can doom even the simplest presentation.

---

Failure to prepare can doom even the simplest presentation.

---

Consider a woman I'll call Donna, an aspiring partner at a risk management company. As part of the interviewing process, she has to spend 15 minutes telling the esteemed partners why she should be selected to join the inner circle. She worked hard on her script, but it was written to be read, not heard. Here are some excerpts from that first version and our revised version, which was tailored for the ear.

> Read:   At Company X, the CFO, having struck out with our competition, which offered a one-size-fits-all approach, was looking for insight and perspective on how to tackle enterprise risk management in their environment. I led numerous discussions involving the CEO, his key executives, and the board about Company X's strategy. The powerful combination of my practical experience in implementing risk programs and the audit team's in-depth of knowledge of Company X's culture and business resulted in a candid, pragmatic, across-the-table dialogue with senior management for a breakthrough engagement.

> Heard:   Company X is a perfect example. The CFO was looking for insight and perspective on how to tackle enterprise risk management challenges in their environment but wasn't having much luck. He struck out with our competition, who offered a one-size-fits-all approach. So I partnered with the audit team to bring a fresh perspective to the Company X leadership team and help them understand how we could manage risk. This included setting up numerous meetings and leading discussions involving the CEO, his key executives, and the board to eventually win the business.

Engaging your audience is essential in any form of communication, but speaking to be heard is very different than writing to be read. Enter the DOODY principle, which touts techniques to help you appear more animated, conversational, personable, and distinctive when you articulate what you've prepared. DOODY stands for:

*D*ifferentiate yourself
*O*pening strategies
*O*h boy!
*D*elivery techniques
*Y*es

## DIFFERENTIATE YOURSELF

Think about what you can say that only you can say. When I first toyed with writing this book, I shared some concerns with my long-time friend and colleague Suzanne Bates, author of *Speak Like a CEO*. Given that we have similar backgrounds and are now in the same line of work, I was afraid my book might mimic hers. What she said stayed with me, and I hope it stays with you. She said I couldn't possibly write the same book because only I could share my stories and experiences, which were different than hers. Aha! She made it so simple. That's because it is. Look for opportunities to showcase your expertise through personal experiences. For example, if you are a scientist, you might recall involvement in groundbreaking clinical trials. If you are a musician, you might talk about the time you played at Carnegie Hall. If you are a journalist, you can talk about stories you've covered. These experiences are unique to you. Sharing them showcases your personality and reminds listeners that you are an expert in your field, giving them even more reason to listen.

## OPENING STRATEGIES

A team of sales professionals was charged with empowering sales representatives to recognize an opportunity to be the market leader in their field. They started their talk by laying out what these sales people had done wrong and focusing on numerous opportunities that had been missed. It reminded me of trying to train a puppy without a reward. If the puppy performs a trick and isn't given a treat, then the puppy isn't empowered to do it again. So why would a group of salespeople—or any audience, for that matter—buy what you're saying if they don't understand what's in it for them?

Opening remarks are critical. It's where you set the stage, give people a reason to listen, frame your agenda, and create rapport with your listener. Saying "Hello, my name is Karen" is not an open. Reading an agenda is not an open. Whether you're providing an update at a meeting, delivering a keynote at a conference, conducting a breakout session, or speaking to investors by phone, typically, you have less than 30 seconds to grab them at hello.

There are many effective ways to open, which include beginning with an important statistic, sharing a story or anecdote that drives home the message and creates an emotional connection, and using memorable visuals to command attention. These are excellent techniques that I encourage you to use. But I want to step beyond what is traditionally taught and challenge you to deliver outcome-focused openings that create an understanding of the problem or issue so recommendations and potential solutions are more meaningful.

When a public relations firm created an educational awareness program to help women learn more about their sexuality and not be afraid to discuss issues they may have, we were called in to work with spokespeople who would eventually deliver the message to difference audiences. Without exception, each individual immediately started talking about what women can do to better communicate with partners and health care providers to achieve the sex life they desired, without stopping to realize that many audiences probably didn't even recognize that this was a problem. Look at the opening both ways.

## OPEN 1

Solution first: The educational awareness program offers tips and techniques to help women get the conversation started with their partners and health care providers so they can have a more satisfying sex life and communicate without feeling embarrassed. We've created a Web site to help them do this.

Clearly, you understand the words, but perhaps you're confused. Did you know women might not be sexually satisfied and aren't sure how to talk about it? Why is this important? Why do they need to visit a Web site to learn more? Let's look what happens when we try it differently and open by presenting the problem first.

## OPEN 2

Problem first: Surveys state 1 out of 10 women say they've experienced decreased sexual desire, which they find distressing because it impacts their relationships and self-esteem. Yet less than 18 percent surveyed say they rarely do anything about it, because they don't feel comfortable talking about it.

Solution next: The educational awareness program offers tips and techniques to help women get the conversation started with their partners and health care providers so they can address concerns for a more satisfying sex life and learn to communicate without feeling embarrassed. We've created a Web site to help them do this.

By helping people understand the problem and why it deserves attention, the solution is more important.

Here's another example. National account directors prepare to explain to select audiences why a newly approved therapy to treat a disease of the hand is important. Like the previous example, many of these people are too close to the information so they don't give much thought to helping audiences understand the impact of the disease. When they start talking, they launch right into the solution.

### Open 1

Solution first:   This therapy is the first FDA-approved nonsurgical treatment for people with this disease that works safely and effectively by breaking down the buildup of collagen in the hand.

Hear the difference when the problem is presented first.

### Open 2

Problem first:   Imagine not being able to shake someone's hand, brush your teeth, use your computer keyboard, or reach into your pocket for your keys. These are things most of us take for granted. But there are 27 million people in the United States and Europe who suffer from Dupuytren's disease, where a buildup of collagen prevents them from doing these things because they can't straighten their fingers. Until now, the only answer has been surgery, which is not always successful.

Not only do powerful openings frame arguments and set the stage, but those first few minutes can position you as an educator and problem solver.

## OH BOY!

In the case of chapter namesake Bob Doody, his goal was to make potential investors understand that there was an opportunity to dramatically change the way transplant patients are treated and that he was really excited about it. Unlike many business presenters who fear showing emotion will harm their credibility, Bob knew his excitement needed to be infectious if he hoped to maintain credibility and captivate attention. As importantly, he wasn't afraid to show his boyish enthusiasm, which reminded me of a little kid saying "Oh boy" when he gets a new toy. Yet Bob maintained his professionalism and did it without jumping around like a bouncy ball. Here are some notes from our session.

- Your enthusiasm is contagious so don't let the slides get in the way of the story. What's the oh boy? We can dramatically change the way transplant patients are treated, which is why we are really excited about this! (Oh boy!)

- Set up the problem. It's not enough to say it is "the most frequent viral illness post-transplant"; make it real. "It's important to understand that 80 percent of us have this, but when you are healthy it lies dormant." Then when you explain that a new, less toxic therapy is needed for those who are not healthy, it's clearer.

- Look for ways to personalize, simplify, and not get stuck in the slide. You are calm, credible, have good eye contact and really nice pacing, and you have a nice voice.

## DELIVERY TECHNIQUES

Listeners want to like you. In fact, in this post-9/11 era, when so much of what we used to believe has come into question, many are clamoring for authentic communicators in a greater way than ever before. If you appear overly rehearsed or robotic, you'll be hard pressed to warm up your listeners. If you seem uncomfortable, you'll make them uncomfortable, and if you aren't enthusiastic about your subject, you shouldn't expect others to be. Business audiences are no different than other audiences. They want the person on stage to be the same person off stage. Imagine meeting your favorite movie star, only to find out his on-camera image is nothing like the real him. How disappointed might you be? Real life isn't much different, but this delivery dozen should make a difference the next time all eyes are on you.

### Delivery Dozen

1. **Talk to one person.** How would you explain information to a friend or coworker? That's how you want to converse with a

group. It will help you pace, pronounce, pause, project, and vary your tone as you do in normal conversations.

2. **Practice out loud.** It's essential to practice out loud as if you are explaining this to a neighbor or friend so you sound conversational. This will also help you recognize and get rid of big words not typically used in conversation.

3. **Bullets and phrases.** Now that you've turned the written word into the spoken word, put that written word into bullet points and phrases so you can talk it, not read it.

4. **Eyes and body.** Make eye contact with as many people as possible and as often as possible to establish sincerity, credibility, and confidence. Additionally, make sure your body language conveys openness and self-assurance. Use hands to gesture; keep them out and open so you appear approachable, not in pockets or crossed over the chest. When possible, come out from behind the podium, which puts a barrier between you and your audience.

5. **First time.** Even if you've delivered the same talk 20 times, every audience is different, so you should approach every meeting, talk, or presentation as if this is the first time you've given it. It will keep you fresh, which in turn will keep listeners engaged.

6. **Involve your audience.** The definition of a lecture is "the act of delivering a formal spoken communication to an audience." That means you talk, they listen. But even if you're doing the talking, you can involve others by raising questions and pausing for thought. Bring examples to life by using metaphors that help people visualize what you're saying.

7. **Emphasize key words.** By repeating or punching important words, you call the listeners' attention to key pieces of information. For example, if you said "everyone is going home with a prize," everyone would be happy. But if you said *everyone* a bit louder, then dragged the word out and repeated it or paused for emphasis, the statement would have even more effect.

8. **Limit numbers and abbreviations.** It's hard to process lots of numbers, abbreviations, and acronyms. When using them, try saying what the numbers mean or providing context, such as "this represents one-third of all sales." If you want to abbreviate the name of an organization, state the full name first and then tell them what you will call it. For example, Karen Friedman Enterprises, also known as KFE.

9. **Breathe and pause.** Conversations ebb and flow, and talks should do the same. It's important to come up for air and pause between thoughts to give listeners a chance to take in what they're hearing. Try pausing in between slides or when you move to a new topic.

10. **Just tell them.** Don't tell them what you're going to tell them, just tell them! For example, instead of "today I'm going to talk to you about the weather," try "If you walked outside today, then you know how bitter cold it is. I want to share the latest information on climate change to help you understand what appears to be happening."

11. **Pace and pitch.** The next time you watch a TV show, notice how camera shots frequently change, how music pops up for effect, and how the pitch and tempo of actors' voices constantly varies. Effective presenters must also pace material to maintain attention. When appropriate, mix it up with video clips, music, props, visuals, and exercises.

12. **Um and uh.** It isn't necessary to say um or uh to fill the silence, though most people don't realize what they're doing, which is why audio- or videotaping your rehearsal with or without a coach is a good idea. It's okay to pause for a moment and look at your notes or slides to see what you want to say next. You will sound thoughtful and in control as opposed to hesitating, stammering, rambling, or filling in the silence with um or uh.

## YES

The *Y* in DOODY is for yes. Just like my favorite childhood storybook, *The Little Engine that Could*, say "yes I can, yes I can, yes I can" the next time you're offered a prominent platform, even if it's the last thing you want to do. Think of every occasion as an opportunity to impart knowledge that can make a difference for your listener. Albert Einstein once said, "If you can't explain it simply, you don't understand it well enough." So think simplistically to speak simply to address the concerns of your listeners who are pleading for ideas, information, and suggestions.

> If you can't explain it simply, you don't understand it well enough.

## COACHING NOTES

- You have a tendency to pick up speed with each slide and eventually become hard to understand because the words are coming so fast and furious. Remember to breathe! A pause and deep breath between sentences should do wonders.

- When you say it's a disease of the hand, remember that, depending on the listener, not everyone knows exactly what that really is, so even though you are going to explain it in more detail later, you want everyone on the same page from the start. Hold up your hand, point to the area, and elaborate a tad so they care. If they care, they'll be more apt to listen.

- If you have been given 15 minutes to talk, do not prepare 20 minutes of material, which requires you to cram it all in by speaking faster. Instead of speeding up, break your thoughts into chunks and pause at the end of each chunk to give your listener a chance to process what you said. Additionally, work on pronouncing words clearly to prevent trailing off at the end of a sentence or word.

- Delivery skills don't begin when you are in front of an audience, but should be shaped in advance as you determine who your listeners are and what they need from you. Even if the presentation is serious, try to be warm and smile when appropriate so they see that you are human too. If you make a mistake or lose your place, that's okay. The only person that will know is you.

- Let's work on eliminating excess words and delivering in a stronger, more definite manner. For example, instead of, "So, thanks for listening to me today," which is almost apologetic, how about, "Good morning. I want to talk to you about a devastating disease that has no cure. That's why our plan to do x, y, z is so important. In the next half hour, I will walk you through—" You had way too much information on the slide. Remember, less is more; you don't need all of that stuff to talk about the impact.

- You did such a great job. The pictures were excellent, and your opening was framed very nicely to set up why anyone should care. You told the story, and you tied it into the bigger theme. Quick point: When you say things like "That's why we come to work everyday," make sure to stop, look up, and look directly at the listener for impact. It's a powerful statement, so you don't want to be looking around or looking at the slide.

- Think about standing up to speak, so you project and give more emphasis to what you are saying. If your headline is "We believe our proposal is appropriate and here's why," then say so right up front. Don't beat around the bush. You can provide the minutia and details later. Keep it as simple as possible.

- It's important to remember that your listeners want what you want, which is far more than just being educated or informed. Memorable speakers who are experts in their field understand that they must find a balance between style and content to energize people and affect behavior.

As I was writing this chapter, I received an e-mail from a marketing firm urging small businesses like mine to hire them in order to better understand what customers need. It took me a while, though, to figure out what they meant, because they delivered their message with an opening line that said it was important for businesses like mine to focus on "Improving and Speeding New Offerings that Counter Commoditization." I'm not sure what that really means, but it meant nothing to me, so I hit the delete key. Don't let your delivery delete your message.

**Don't let your delivery delete your message.**

# CHAPTER 24

# Communicating Change

You can change your world by changing your words.
—*Joel Osteen, pastor*

It was a beautiful fall day as multicolored leaves fluttered to the ground while my friend and I lunched at a quaint neighborhood spot. Inside, the conversation wasn't so pretty. Her company had been swallowed up by a larger player that promised 20,000 layoffs. More than a change in weather was seeping in. Many people had already been let go, but most like her didn't know their fate and were scared. She said, "It's like being told everyone has cancer but just a select group will be lucky enough to get chemotherapy. Only no one will tell us who the lucky ones are."

Perhaps the analogy was a bit strong, but uncertainty can be terrifying in any situation. In this case, there had been numerous employee meetings, e-mails, and communications leading up to the deal, which is the way it should be. But once the ink was dry, she said it seemed as if old and new management alike forgot how to communicate, which enhanced feelings of anxiety, panic, and dread. She confided that during a meeting she scheduled with her new boss to discuss her role in the organization, the boss took phone calls, checked e-mails, and had conversations with others who stopped by her office. My friend said, "I felt invisible, as if I clearly didn't matter and was certainly not important to the new organization."

This woman illustrates the increasing number of friends and colleagues complaining about how management communicates change to employees specifically during uncertain times, when communicating is more essential and easier than ever. There are blogs, tweets, intranets, and social networking sites begging for conversations, which, when conducted correctly, could replace rumors with reassurance. As a former card-carrying journalist, I can tell you firsthand that when media learns something is brewing, in the rush to be first, they feed the fear machine by repeatedly printing and broadcasting gloom and doom, which is not always accurate, comprehensive, and balanced. Business communicators can learn something from the types of questions reporters ask when covering stories of change and how closed responses elicit very different responses than more direct open answers.

Question: How many people will lose their jobs?

Closed: That has not been determined yet.

Open: That has not been determined yet and we are not certain which departments or locations will be affected, but I have been told it will be approximately 20,000 people worldwide.

Question: How many sites will be closed?

Closed: No one tells me anything.

Open: We don't know at this time, but we have been informed that a decision will be made in the very near future. As soon as I'm informed, I will let everyone know what I know.

Question: You've opened a new building, hired more people, and have reportedly become the fourth largest employer here. Does this indicate a shift in business to more profitable cutting-edge production?

Closed: It indicates we're doing what needs to be done.

Open: Yes. In today's economic environment, it is necessary to compete and keep costs down.

Question: How much money will you save?

Closed: I can't say.

Open: I am not at liberty to discuss that publicly until the paperwork is complete.

Notice what's happening. Reporters ask the most basic five Ws and H questions typically learned in grade school—who, what, when, where, why, and how—to draw simple answers they can put into context so people understand what's happening and why. While business communicators more frequently speak to other professionals and not reporters, like a journalist, they should be able to acknowledge questions, tell people what they know, and openly state why they can't discuss certain items if they hope to manage messages and expectations.

For example, if a company says, "We are operating as a combined company and will be implementing changes over time until we are fully integrated," what does that really mean to employees? If it said, "The combination of our companies will allow us to streamline costs, eliminate certain units, and consolidate operations, which will result in the elimination of an undetermined number of positions before the end of the year," employees would still worry, but the message would be heard differently. By sharing what they know as soon as possible, management is better poised to tighten the leaky faucet of distrust and speculation by quietly conveying that they won't keep people in the dark.

> Communicating change does not come easy to most people. Neither does embracing it.

Communicating change does not come easy to most people. Neither does embracing it. But one can't happen without the other. If senior management doesn't talk to middle management, then middle management can't help the rank and file understand how the basic five Ws and H affect them. Like media reports, the story will be repeated and embellished by unconfirmed sources that fuel the fears and anxieties of others.

Without deliberate and well-planned communication at all times, leaders risk disengaging employees who are needed to help them accomplish their goals. Communicating is not a task, it's a continuing process. Being proactive and straightforward is even more critical to prevent problems from escalating. In the deal mentioned at the beginning of the chapter, employees claim much of the focus was centered around communicating on the day of the big announcement instead of helping people understand what will happen to them when the dust settles. To quote another colleague who asked to remain anonymous, "They failed to think about keeping people engaged, motivated and focused on new objectives and the company's new vision. Most people's point of reference during changing times is their manager and their team. Communications at a time of upset must be local, personal, and conducted with the highest degree of sensitivity."

> Communications at a time of upset must be local, personal, and conducted with the highest degree of sensitivity.

While leaders can't always control what happens, they can foster understanding, shape perceptions, and influence outcomes. When I ask people what leaders they recall who were greatly challenged during changing times, they unanimously name famous people such as Martin Luther King, Jr., who navigated change during the American civil rights movement, or President Roosevelt, who steered us through the Great Depression. You don't have to be famous to tell people, here's what we're doing, why we're doing it, and what it means to them. You don't have to be famous to say "I don't know," and you certainly don't have to be famous to put a human face on change. While volumes have been written on communicating change, here are 10 key game changers to help you shut up and say something to influence the end result.

## GAME CHANGERS

1. **Face to face.** The world may be technologically advanced, but nothing can replace face-to-face contact when times are tough. Even world leaders hold town hall meetings so they can deliver messages face to face. If you can't be everywhere, be visible. Schedule video conferences, Web casts, and in-person meetings to make a personal connection.

2. **O-B-M.** Focus on **O**ne **B**ig **M**essage and stick to it. When the Obama administration first tried to win public opinion in the controversial health care reform debate of 2009–2010, it lost control of the message because there were too many competing points and people didn't understand what they stood to gain. The O-B-M was actually simple: Costs are out of control, and we need to contain them to make coverage affordable for all. Once the O-B-M stuck, it was easier to add the details.

3. **Top down.** Top management may be making decisions, but it's important not to leave middle management and other communicators out of the loop. These people are tapped into the troops and can be strong supporters who can help you deliver your message and control the rumor mill on the ground.

4. **Make it quick.** As reporters, we used to open the newspaper in the morning, look at the gossip column, and joke with colleagues, "Whew, I'm not in the paper, I guess I still have a job!" No one wants to learn their fate from the media or through the grapevine. Even if you have little to say, say something so people hear it from you first.

5. **Two-way street.** You may be facing the same uncertainty as your employees, so it is important to keep the lanes of communication open and give people opportunities to ask questions and share concerns. For example, asking questions such as, "What are your concerns?" or "What can I do to help?" encourages people to speak up. Take time to listen even if you don't have answers.

6. **Positive attitude.** Lead by conveying confidence during changing times. Instead of blaming, bad-mouthing, or apologizing for something out of your control, try to help people understand how everyone will get through this together.

7. **Multiple channels.** Use e-mail, company intranet, social networking sites, newsletters, staff meetings, and every vehicle at your disposal to communicate as quickly and frequently as possible so people feel you're keeping them in the loop.

8. **Show empathy.** Let others know you understand what they're going through and convey your support. Be careful not to overpromise or mislead anyone to believe everything will be fine when the outcome is uncertain.

9. **Long haul.** Realize that open, honest communication must take place at all stages of change. Think of this as an opportunity to deliver accurate information, help people understand how change could benefit the organization, and empower them to positively embrace it.

10. **Pay attention.** Look directly at the person who is speaking to you. Put the Blackberry away, move away from the computer screen, ignore your phone, and tell others who stop by that they will have to come back. Give the person speaking to you your full attention.

My long-time friend and colleague Doug Petkus, former vice president of business and financial communications at Pfizer, advises communicating from the bottom up. Instead of focusing on grand gestures such as big town hall meetings, which he says can sound like corporate speak to many, Petkus urges top management to reach out to team leaders who can spread messages in smaller settings. "When you're in a conference room with your team leader, that's when the rubber hits the road. These are the people you need to bring on board to deliver your message," says Petkus.

When a colleague we'll call Ralph became the general manager of a laboratory in the Midwest, he was ecstatic to have an opportunity to institute changes and lead the company in a new direction. Unfortunately, not everyone shared his vision. Most actually opposed it. A popular long-time department head had been passed over for the top job and wanted nothing more than to see Ralph fail. In person, he was supportive and friendly. Behind Ralph's back, he complained to senior executives, bad-mouthed Ralph to employees, and spread nasty rumors that scared employees and threatened to sabotage Ralph's efforts. Ralph had no power to fire the man. It was a real dilemma.

As it turns out, the company's previous general manager ran the organization by intimidating and threatening employees, which created a toxic environment of backstabbing and lying. The man who had been passed over for the position was too busy empire building to notice that the company was heading toward a cliff. It had always flourished in the past and resisters wanted to stay in the past, fearing change would make things worse.

Ralph did everything right. He instituted a companywide survey, repeatedly met with his team, held company meetings, and reassured employees their jobs were safe. Via e-mail and newsletter, he kept people updated. Personal development coaches were provided for many. Still, it wasn't working. People didn't buy into the new business model and direction he sought to pull the company out of its slump. No one was aligned around a common vision. That's when he decided to provide ongoing communications guidance and coaching for the entire leadership team.

Resistant at first, it was important to get them to share their perspective, which was much bigger than Ralph. They appeared brainwashed by the former if-I-need-your-opinion-I'll-ask-for-it style of management, who saw no value whatsoever in communicating with subordinates. Ralph was telling them he would steer this ship differently so they needed to climb on deck, but he didn't fully understand that telling them wouldn't make it happen. He needed to communicate differently. Here are some notes to him following an initial meeting.

- Until they are on the same page, you will never get anything done. You must empower them by giving them tools to succeed.

- You have a vision. They won't buy into that vision just because you say it's the right way to go. You can't tell them to change their behavior. They won't. You have to get them to change their perspective. They're scared and they are not going to stick their necks out for you.
- You need to give them a safe playing field. Let's come up with specifics that tell them what to do, what actions to take, timelines, and how those actions will benefit them.

The first step was to create a plan and develop messages that answered questions. It wasn't enough to tell people they had a bright future and opportunities to form partnerships that would allow them to develop new technologies and increase profits. They needed to understand how that would happen, what was expected of them, how soon the company would recognize profits from new investments, and what the future looked like. Ralph needed answers to questions such as:

1. You keep telling us how bright our future is, but this company isn't manufacturing any product. What are we working on?
2. What is the next wave of product and how fast will it be marketed?
3. How many more partners are signing on?
4. How do we stay ahead of the competition, which appears to have more money and resources?
5. How will we launch new products and enter new markets?
6. Your job is to grow the company, so doesn't that mean if you grow it, it will be sold?

Little by little, the team prioritized common goals, audiences, and determined what information to communicate to each. Ralph insisted that each company division, which had always operated independently and celebrated milestones separately, would share highlights together. He hosted picnics and held a TV-style town hall meeting at a local movie theater, where I served as the talk show host who tried to cut through the clutter and facilitate open, honest conversations. Though some still looked for opportunities to rock the boat, within two years, profits increased fivefold. People began to see each others as colleagues, and the internal infighting that threatened to destroy the company subsided. Eventually Ralph left company but told me through teamwork and clear, consistent communication, employees eventually felt safe and valued and understood how they could float above the changing tide.

## COACHING NOTES

- Learning to ask tougher, more direct questions will help you identify concerns and create communications that address those concerns. Develop a list of focused, well-thought-out questions that go to the heart of the problem even though they will produce answers you might not like.

- The discussion or message must be delivered with empathy and compassion. Employees must be told that they are appreciated and valued so they feel that you are being honest, straightforward, and are not stringing them along.

- The owners obviously want to know how much money this is costing and what kind of damage or interruption these changes will cause with their vendors, especially given they have a relationship with many of these people. They are interested in overall value, how it will drive loyalty to their brand, and how the change you propose is truly a solution.

- While she may need to tone it down a bit when giving instructions to people so she doesn't come across as so bossy and abrasive, her ability to be direct is an attribute she can learn to use to her advantage. Here are a few suggestions:

  - Continue giving directions orally and in writing. To maximize the probability that she is crystal clear, ask the listeners if they understand. If they repeat back to her what they believe they heard, when they paraphrase, she will immediately realize whether or not she was clear.

  - Although it is time consuming, in instances where communications are difficult, she needs to follow up meetings or directions with an e-mail that simply states her understanding of what is to happen. Example: I'm glad we spent some time talking about such and such today as this is a priority for our department. Just to reiterate, you are going to do x, y, and z, which will be completed by next Monday.

- Make sure employees give regular status reports to their supervisors and these supervisors do the same with their managers. They should be meeting at least once a month with their employees to update them, field questions, and solicit feedback. Even if there is nothing critical to discuss, this creates an open, communicative environment and cultivates relationships between managers and employees.

- It's important to act on feedback from others. Write it down. Get back to them even if it's to say you can't do anything about the problem or suggestion at this time.

- Regularly hold meetings to celebrate major milestones. This helps people perceive what's important, gives them a sense of direction and fulfillment, and lets them know that management values their contributions.

- Offer context so residents understand why making these changes are important and will benefit them in the long run even if they are furious right now. If you explain that in the past five years, there have been 32 blackouts and that this is what's causing their continued power outages, falling trees, and damage to homes, they will understand the importance of cutting down all their trees even if they don't like it.

Seeking feedback and not acting on it can send mixed messages to employees. I used to work for a news director who would call mandatory staff dinner meetings twice a year. He'd wine and dine us and pull out all the stops, but it was a joke. People would voice concerns, offer suggestions, and ask for support in certain areas, to which he'd always agree but never act on. He never even wrote the requests down.

## COMMUNICATING CHANGE FIXES

**Frequent communications.** Communicate quickly, openly, and as often as possible so people can talk with each other about what is happening in the workplace. Facilitate the conversation so they feel included. If they are kept in the dark, they will never embrace your vision and work with you to change the culture.

**Worldview.** Help people understand how changes reflect the times and what is happening in the world around them so they understand the importance and necessity of actions as opposed to assuming you're changing things for the sake of change.

**Steps to success.** By providing tactics, you can help others visualize success. Lay out the changes in steps such as, here's what's taking place, this is the time frame, this is what you can expect, and this is what is expected of you. This might include a monthly reporting process with goals to check off along the way so people can see their advancement toward success.

**Avoid blame.** Be understanding and empathetic instead of complaining and blaming. Use phrases such as "I understand" or "I appreciate your concerns." If you say you understand, then look the part. When people are angry, give them a chance to vent. Most people want to be heard even if they realize you can't do much about the situation.

**Everything talks.** People communicate when they aren't talking. Closed doors, frowns, e-mails instead of personal contact, and not showing up at important events speak volumes, so be careful of how loudly your actions speak.

**Join the conversation.** Go to your audience instead of making them come to you. If they frequently communicate on company blogs, industry sites, or internal newsletters, that's a great place to join the conversations. If employees are tweeting, then consider tweeting key thoughts back at them to let them know you're listening.

As importantly, keep your communication as simple and frank as possible regardless of your audience. Instead of defending change, constantly look for ways to communicate what that change means to them. Instead of resisting, they may be more inclined to follow your lead.

**Look to your own words to help others change theirs.**

# CHAPTER 25

# Big No-Nos

Speakers who talk about what life has taught them never fail to keep the attention of their listeners.
—*Dale Carnegie, author and speaker*

I had my first big television news break at WAFF-TV in Huntsville, Alabama. For a kid from a large metropolis like Philadelphia, the words *culture shock* are barely descriptive. I remember pulling into the parking lot, opening my car door, and, as I was about to step out, I nearly stepped on a big, fat, slithering snake. Now, I may be a Yankee, as they called me down South, but I knew a rattler when I saw one. After I screamed and slammed the car door shut, I drove to the back door of the station and hollered for Doug, the engineer, to help. Ever so cool and calm as he tried to decipher my unintelligible Yankee gibberish, he climbed in the front seat of my car and we drove back up the hill to the scene of the killer snake. Doug got out of the car, stared it down for a moment and then said, "yep, that's a rattler alright." Then, as if he were yanking a stick of gum out of a package, he jacked up his pant leg, reached into his boot, pulled out a revolver, and shot the monster dead on the spot. That was how I was welcomed to my first on-air television news job a thousand miles away from home.

I learned a lot in the two years I spent at WAFF-TV covering everything from farm animals to the space program (the Marshall Space Flight Center is headquartered there). However, the takeaway that remains my mantra today is that good communicators always speak from their listener's point of view. Perhaps that isn't so startling. After all, Dale Carnegie, author of mega best-seller *How To Win Friends and Influence People*, was sharing similar wisdom before I was born. As a reporter, however,

I learned that every time someone opens their mouth, regardless of circumstance, they have an opportunity to educate, set the record straight, inform, entertain, inspire, motivate, or make someone see things differently. Not recognizing these opportunities is a big no-no.

This chapter identifies the top 10 big no-nos I've observed through decades in front of cameras, crowds, at events across the globe, and in countless conference rooms where executives muddled through missed opportunities. Many of these no-nos and the specific tactics to overcome them are repeated in various ways throughout this book as they apply to different chapter topics. This chapter will identify big no-nos, explain how they impact modern-day listeners, and provide lessons you can use in your own circumstances.

## NO-NO 1: OPEN MICROPHONE SYNDROME

Back in Huntsville, Alabama, I was anchoring the evening news with a fiery, outspoken redhead named Sarah Moquin. While trying to straighten out a problem during a commercial break, she uttered the F word under her breath. The microphone clipped under her blouse captured it for northern Alabama's deeply religious viewers to hear. As you can imagine, they weren't happy. While Sarah sincerely apologized on TV the next day, the offensive gaffe was attached to her name for a long time.

Impact:   At the time, Sarah's goof was only repeated in the local community. Today's world is rife with blogging, file sharing, uploading, and Googling. Even President Ronald Reagan's joke about bombing Russia that was made to radio technicians during a sound check back in 1984 can still be heard on the Internet today.

Lesson:   To borrow a phrase from Scott Monty, head of social media for Ford Motor Company, "Whatever happens in Vegas stays on Google."

| |
|---|
| Whatever happens in Vegas stays on Google. |

## NO-NO 2: I'LL JUST WING IT

No matter how good you think you are, winging it is not an option. I worked with the incoming CEO of a manufacturing plant who considered herself a good communicator. She was warm, enthusiastic, and personable. She knew her products backward and forward but refused to spend time preparing and practicing, which resulted in unorganized, unfocused ramblings devoid of examples and memorable points.

Impact:  Without preparation and practice, you miss opportunities to bring facts to life that help listeners understand how your product or service benefits them.

Lesson:  It is not the hardest-working or smartest people who make the best communicators. Those who are most prepared and rehearsed appear the most natural.

---

It's the people who are most prepared and rehearsed who appear the most natural.

---

## NO-NO 3: IT'S ALL ABOUT ME

Prospects and audiences aren't interested in all of your titles, accomplishments, and names you can drop. As the saying goes, they're just not that into you! They want to know what you can do for them. For example, if someone attends a financial seminar you're conducting, they're savvy enough to know you want their business. But until they have a clear idea of how you might make money for them, they won't be so quick to sign up.

Impact:  With so much information to choose from in a world that seems noisier than ever, if you can't quickly make others understand what's in it for them, they will hang up, tune out or find another Web site.

Lesson:  Review your Web site, blogs, printed materials, slides, and scripts. Do they contain a lot of "I" and "me"? Are they all about you, or do you address problems you can solve for others?

## NO-NO 4: HOPE NO ONE WILL FIND OUT

Burying your head in the sand and hoping no one will find out is like wishing for a snowstorm in the desert. Bad things happen to good people, but when scandals erupt, people want to know what you knew, when you knew it, and how quickly you did something about it. If you don't craft messages and immediately control the information, you risk letting others define the story for you.

Toyota is a perfect example of a bumpy ride that quickly accelerated. In early 2010, the Japanese car maker voluntarily recalled millions of defective vehicles with sticky accelerator pedals amid reports of accidents and a fatal crash. Weeks later, news reports suggested the company may have known about the problem for more than a year before taking action and could have prevented some of the problems.

Impact:  If it appears you were hiding something that could put other people in harm's way, your reputation is forever tarnished. Even when the problem is resolved, the negative stories will always surface when someone searches on your name.

Lesson:  No matter how expensive your problem appears, always put the best interest of others first to help you say and do the right thing. The price of not doing so is far more costly.

## NO-NO 5: A LITTLE LIE WON'T HURT

Former presidential candidate John Edwards admittedly had an affair. He isn't the first high-profile politician to admit his indiscretions, and he likely won't be the last. In fact, other than feeling sorry for his wife, I don't care who he sleeps with. But I do care that he lied about fathering a child with his mistress when appearing on ABC TV's *Nightline* program. While lying is a no-no, lying to a reporter is like jumping from a plane without a parachute.

Impact:  Anyone with an Internet connection can locate that video and help Edwards further damage his already tarnished reputation at the click of a mouse for eternity.

Lesson:  Lying to the media may not be a crime, but it's the same as lying to the public, because reporters are your mouthpiece to the community. When you lose their trust, you will very publicly lose your credibility and integrity, which may never be recovered.

## NO-NO 6: TOO MUCH DETAIL

I once turned in a story script to a producer who tossed it back to me and told me to get rid of all the three-syllable words. While he was teasing, the message was dead on. The producer understood the importance of keeping things simple so the listener gets the point. The more you say, the more room there is for misunderstanding and misinterpretation. Yet business speakers continually dump data like a dump truck unloads cement.

For example, an energy executive who was trying to convince a hostile community why they needed a new power plant spent several minutes discussing engineering grades, capacities, and volumes of cubic yards.

Impact:   His audience had no clue what he was talking about, nor did they care. He wanted the community to understand that the new plant would provide enough clean energy to keep their lights on and costs down.

Lesson:   If you "brain dump" without real attention to helping your audience understand how the information affects or benefits them, you may confuse them and lose them.

## NO-NO 7: NO HEART

When working with a pharmaceutical sales representative who delivered only the facts when giving a product presentation, I asked him whether he had any emotional connection to what he was selling. He explained that he got into the oncology business because his mother had cancer. When I suggested that perhaps he could share pieces of that story, he was adamantly opposed, saying that the workplace was no place to wear your heart on your sleeve. Eventually, he tried it, talking about how he felt, what his mom meant to him, and relating that to why he believes in these products that helped his mom and might help others. Speaking from the heart made him much more impactful.

Impact:   Delivering "just the facts, ma'am" without emotion or feeling can suggest you are unfeeling, uncaring, and, in some cases, arrogant.

Lesson:   When you convey concern and speak from the heart, listeners can relate to you because you appear to care about the same things they do. Without feeling, you're just spitting words. Speak to others as if you are speaking with friends.

Speak to others as if you are speaking with friends.

## NO-NO 8: BIZ SPEAK

Whether it's electronics, how to assemble a new appliance, or instructions for my car's GPS system, I'm not one to read instruction manuals. If a SparkNotes version exists, I'm all over it. Here's the problem. These manuals sound like gibberish. It's as if they're written for the person writing them instead of the person reading them. I once came across an airplane safety card that required a thesaurus for translation. Explaining who should not sit in the exit row, it said, "You do not have the visual capacity to assess conditions outside of the exit or perform any other function described without the assistance of visual aids other than contact lenses or eyeglasses." How about, "if you can't see, don't sit here!"

| | |
|---|---|
| Impact: | Biz speak, also known as jargon, is confusing, misleading, and makes listeners work too hard to figure out what you're saying, so, in all likelihood, they don't hear you. |
| Lesson: | Say what you want to say out loud to someone else. Ask him if he gets it. If he doesn't, say it again, but this time say it as if you were explaining it to a child. It won't diminish your authority. It will help you be understood. |

## NO-NO 9: I DON'T CARE WHAT YOU THINK

I once had a conference call with a human resource director and a top-level executive. The HR director said the executive was having a tough time getting his employees to follow directions. I asked him what he thought the problem was, to which he replied, "They constantly offer their opinions, and I don't care what they think. I just want them to do what I say."

| | |
|---|---|
| Impact: | People want to be heard, and they want to be appreciated. When you behave like a dictator, you create a hostile atmosphere where people gossip, are afraid to speak, and will sometimes go out of their way to sabotage your efforts. |
| Lesson: | Communication is a two-way street. When you allow people to state their opinions, you create an open environment where people feel valued. Treat people the way you would want them to treat you. |

## NO-NO 10: DON'T STEAL MY STUFF

Not only is this a no-no, it's unethical. In my opinion, stealing people's stories is criminal even if it's not against the law. A few years ago, my mother called to tell me she heard an incredible motivational speaker so I looked him up. Coincidentally, we were members of some of the same organizations. However, my mom said she was surprised when the speaker told one of my stories, to which I replied, "that's not possible, because all of my stories come from my personal experiences." But Mom went on to repeat a true but embarrassing experience I had at a gynecologist's office.

Having just moved to a new town as a TV news anchor, a friend referred me to her doctor for my annual check-up. As I was on the table being examined, the doctor looked up at me and said, "I watch you all the time, but you look a lot different in person." I was 24 and thought I would die on the table.

I can't imagine there are too many people who have had that identical experience, and I know the same thing could not have happened to a man.

Impact:   Using someone else's content without attribution or permission is stealing. If proven, in some cases, you can be prosecuted. It's also an ethical issue and if word gets around, you may be blacklisted from events.

Lesson:   Everybody can turn their own experiences into stories. There is enough material to circle the world for eternity. Don't use other people's stuff. You have your own.

Finally, even if you're not a well-known public figure or celebrity, you are still known in your neighborhood, office, place of worship, and organizations to which you belong. So when you think no one is looking, think again. When I was at a World Series game some years ago, I left during the fourth inning to find a bathroom. I found one, but it wasn't the one I was looking for. It was a temporary toilet created by a former major league baseball player whom I observed urinating on the pavement under the bleachers. He obviously thought no one was looking.

**If you think someone might see you, you're probably right.**

# CHAPTER 26

# Approachable Attitudes

 

When you look good, you feel good. When you feel good, you do good.

*—Josef R. Friedman, my dad*

I'm a big fan of health spas and have been to my fair share of them. For me, there is almost nothing quite as relaxing as a good massage or facial to melt the stress away. I've had a lot of great therapists, but, like any other professional service, some are better than others. When I walked into the lovely Ocean Pearl Spa at the Sheraton Carlsbad Resort outside of San Diego, where I had traveled for a client program, I knew the experience would be good. I just didn't know that Athena Hutchison, the esthetician assigned to my time slot, would have so much to teach business professionals about communication.

Typically when you go to a health resort, a therapist will come out into the waiting area, call your name, smile at you, and you'll follow the therapist back into the spa. But Athena was anything but typical. A proud, pretty Jamaican woman with a cheek-to-cheek smile and enough energy to power a nuclear plant, she walked up to me, looked directly in my eyes as she took my hand, and held it before saying, "You must be Karen. I am so delighted to meet you." Once we were situated, Athena oozed enthusiasm as she told me how much she loves her work and the people she gets to meet every day. She said she loves to make people feel good, because "if you feel good, you do good." It's what my father has been telling me since I was a little girl. My father, like Athena, is the type of person you want to be around—warm and approachable with a contagious attitude that is hard to shake.

So what do health spas and a father's advice to his little girl have to do with business communication? The vibe you give off is usually the one you get back.

> The vibe you give off is usually the one you get back.

Contrast Athena to a woman I'll call Marge, who is the receptionist at a doctor's office. When I handed her my new-patient paperwork, she scowled and told me to take a seat. When I asked whether the doctor was running late or on time, she replied, "He'll be with you shortly." So I asked, "How shortly is shortly?" Rather than answer, she simply ignored me. As I sat in the waiting room for the next half hour, I watched her deliver the same attitude to everyone who walked into the office. She made no eye contact, was abrupt, and seemed pretty unhappy with what she was doing and the people she was doing it for. Finally, after another half hour of waiting, I went back to the reception desk and politely asked if she could give me an update on the doctor. She huffed, "no idea," to which I sarcastically inquired, "Are you always this nice to everyone?" She glared at me and walked away. Well, at least she finally made eye contact.

We've all met people like this, but Marge is the first impression of that doctor's office. It is her job to promote his image to patients by the way she greets them. As it turns out, he was warm and personable, nothing like her at all. Think about the attitude you convey or the attitude that is conveyed about you by others. According to a Stanford Research Institute study, success is 88 percent attitude and 12 percent education. That's probably not surprising as positive people increase confidence in others and make them feel good.

Take Derrick, head of patient safety for a group of hospitals. His boss called me to help him with his presentations, which she said were way too complicated and detailed for her board of directors to understand. Derrick worked tirelessly to improve and please her. Following his next meeting, he called to say he received many compliments from board members and was really excited he was making progress. But when his boss offered feedback, instead of complimenting his efforts, she told him what he should have done differently. In an e-mail to me, he wrote, "She gave me the handout of my slides where one of the board members had written criticisms all over it. I can't win."

While constructive criticism is important, so is praise. It would have been far more productive if Derrick's improvement was positively recognized so he could focus on what he was doing right and be empowered to continue working at it. Instead, the negative reaction caused him to be nervous, self-conscious, and adopt an attitude of "it's not worth it because no matter what I do, they'll shoot me down." Think about little children or pets. When you praise their accomplishments, they squeal with delight and try it over and over again. When you scold them, they cry or run away with their tail between their legs.

In a paper titled "Why Does Affect Matter in Organization?" Wharton management professor Sigal Barsade, who studies the influence of emotions on the workplace, says, "Emotions travel from person to person like a virus." In long-term care facilities, her research found that residents who were exposed to positive attitudes experience less pain and made fewer trips to the emergency room.

While maintaining a consistent positive attitude may be easier said than done, I'm a firm believer that you and you alone determine your attitude and how you will communicate it. Certainly life will present difficult challenges, but, as William Penn once said, "The secret of happiness is to count your blessings while others are adding up their troubles."

---

> The secret of happiness is to count your blessings while others are adding up their troubles.

---

My dear friend Lisa Steinberg is a wonderful reminder of the positive attitude philosophy. She tells me that even when times are tough, such as when her husband was battling cancer, she would wake up in the morning and silently ask herself, "what kind of day do I want to have today?" The answer was always optimistic.

Yet too often people silently communicate the opposite without realizing they're even speaking. A colleague I'll call Kathryn is a good example. Kathryn runs a small communications firm that has some big-name clients. She wants these clients to think she's bigger than she is, so she refuses to answer her phone and waits a day or two to return calls. She once told me, "I want people to think I'm so in demand that they are thrilled to finally get on the phone with me." She believes this enhances her image and likelihood of getting hired. Perhaps. But it could also hinder her approachability and potentially cost her clients. What Kathryn doesn't know is that she once lost a client to me and I actually didn't find out about it until many years later. It wasn't because I was better or more qualified than her; she is an excellent communication coach who I admire greatly. The client, who works for a leading business school, told me she hired me because I answered my own phone and quickly returned calls when she left a message. She said she felt I was approachable and that was a trait she valued.

What makes someone approachable? Is it nonverbal behavior, such as body language and actions? Is it tone of voice? Is it demeanor? Choice of words? Or perhaps it's positive feedback? I suggest that it is all of the above. To determine whether you need an approachability adjustment, ask yourself the following 10 questions:

1. Do I make eye contact when I pass by someone at the office?
2. Do I smile frequently?
3. Do I stop what I'm doing to give someone my full attention?
4. Do I complain a lot?
5. Do I convey my message?
6. Do I use positive words?
7. Do I show concern and empathy for others?
8. Do I sound like I know it all?
9. Do I mirror the behavior of others?
10. Do I communicate the same on- and off-message?

If you answered no to any of the above, you may need a slight adjustment. Applying these tactics to each question should give your attitude a little lift.

1. **Eye evasion.** Have you ever spotted someone across the room and purposely avoided eye contact so you didn't have to talk to them? In reality, you are talking. You're silently saying, "please don't speak to me." While customs vary among cultures, making direct eye contact not always appropriate, eye evasion can convey aloofness and lack of approachability. If you get on an elevator with someone, even an acknowledgment glance is better than a vacant stare.
2. **Smile.** Smiling, like laughter, is a universal language that says I'm approachable, but it must be genuine. When President Obama

delivered his first state-of-the-union address and smiled when he declared he had never been more hopeful about America's future, critics and bloggers painted his smile as phony. He may have meant it, but some suggested the expression in his eyes did not match the upturned corners of his mouth.

3. **Stop and listen.** Songwriter Bethany Dillon writes, "Stop and listen. It's the same slowing down lesson we all learn." Yet many of us fail to look up from the Blackberry or remove the headphones from our ears so we can fully listen and participate in the conversation instead of conveying a message of indifference to our listeners.

4. **Stop whining.** Think about the people you know who suck the energy out of you. Chances are they constantly complain. The only people who probably like to be around them are other complainers. Instead of grumbling about everything that *isn't*, look for ways to be optimistic about what *is*. You got stuck in an airport for 45 hours. Yes, that stinks. But you got to party on the company's dime at an amazing resort on the beach in Honolulu. You're sick and tired of your long hours and need a raise. I understand. But there are plenty of unemployed people who would work harder and longer for less pay.

5. **Match the message.** Do you sound like one of those customer service recordings that keeps repeating, "your call is very important to us" while you wait and wait until someone finally answers? Clearly, your call isn't that important. Set the example you want others to follow.

6. **Winning words.** Every morning when I stop into my local bagel shop for a cup of coffee, a man named Steve is sitting at the table. I say, "how are you today?" and he says, "I'm great!" or "Couldn't be better!" No matter what has happened in his life, he always speaks positively. What if Steve said "lousy" or "don't ask"? To be polite, I probably *would* ask, but positive words energize others, and most of us want to do business with optimists.

7. **Convey concern.** Just the other day, a human resources executive complained to me that she was sick and tired of answering people's questions about sensitive topics she wasn't free to discuss. I asked, "well, what do you tell them?" She said, "I tell them I don't know, but I wouldn't tell you anyway." How's that for attitude? What about saying something like, "I know things are

uncertain right now, but we will get through this. I'm simply not at liberty to discuss specifics."

8. **Get over yourself.** I received an e-mail promotion inviting me to attend a speaker's rather pricey conference on corporate book promotion, so before writing a check, I contacted him to learn more about the event. Specifically, I wanted to know how many people were permitted to attend so I could determine whether this was a small, intimate venue or a large convention-type meeting. Here are snippets from our e-mail correspondence, which ultimately cost him in a variety of ways.

> Me: I am very interested in attending your event, but before I make the investment, I want to know how large of a meeting this is.
>
> Speaker: We do not release numbers to the public.
>
> Me: Okay, but I would like to talk with one or two other people who have attended.
>
> Speaker You can find testimonials on our Web site.
>
> Me: With all due respect, I'm sure your programs are great, but no one puts bad testimonials on their Web site. Is there anyone I can call or e-mail, just as I'd want someone to check me out if they signed up for my program?
>
> Speaker As a policy, we do not ask our former students to become sales agents for our business. I believe the testimonial videos on our Web site are sufficient.

Normally, I would have stopped the e-mail train in its tracks, but I was ticked, so I sent one more and then told some of my other author colleagues to stay clear of this egomaniac.

> Me: Your remarks have really turned me off, and it is clear you are far more impressed with yourself than those you allegedly serve. References are not sales agents. They are a standard way of conducting business. One-way communication and testimonials on a Web site do not answer specific questions someone might have about a seminar or the person leading it.

There is a saying that people buy people, not companies. In fact, a national survey that examined why salespeople fail reported that

50 percent responded that salespeople fail due to lack of a positive attitude.

> All the advertising, slogans, buzzwords, and promotional campaigns can't mask a business that isn't truly focused on the customer.

Author and sales guru Jeffrey Gitomer put it another say. He said, "All the advertising, slogans, buzzwords and promotional campaigns can't mask a business that isn't truly focused on the customer."

9. **Mirror on the wall.** Let's say you schedule an appointment with your financial advisor to discuss depressing business problems. How would you feel if the advisor also sounded down, slouched in his chair, and agreed that your situation was hopeless? True, the advisor can't always fix what ails, but he can craft a plan, show you where positives trump negatives, and try to offer hope. Conveying a positive attitude often leads to brainstorming new ideas.

10. **Soccer field approach.** NBC *Today Show* anchor Meredith Vierra radiates approachability. Colleagues say if you met her at a soccer game, she'd be no different than she is on television. Who do people see when they see you? Are you the same on and off the field? In an interview with *More* magazine, Vierra said, "For me the message is get in touch with who you are, with what you want and try to shape everything else around that." I believe that's good advice in any workplace.

Most of us can likely remember middle school or high school, when the thought of approaching a certain someone we admired was akin to jumping out of an airplane without a parachute. In some ways, social media have changed that, because it's easy to contact practically anyone and engage thought leaders in online discussion groups. Even those groups can be intimidating to some people if they don't convey a welcoming attitude.

When you sign up for most groups, you'll get an automatic response that thanks you for joining. So imagine my surprise when I joined the Public Relations and Communications Professional Group on LinkedIn and received a more personal automated response. I sent organizer Janet Lawson a quick appreciation note and learned that she has read over

30,000 profiles and personally sent out over 20,000 responses. I was astounded, to which she replied, "It only takes a moment, and I feel it's important to let the people who are taking the time to participate in the group know that it really is appreciated—like yourself, for instance!" That's what I call a great attitude!

## APPROACHABLE ATTITUDE FIXES

**Enthusiasm.** If you are enthusiastic or excited, let people see it and hear it, especially when you are on the phone and they can't see your facial expressions.

**Empathy.** Let people know you're a human being first and a manager or associate second. If they're having a tough time, lend an understanding ear.

**Praise.** Look for positives, not just negatives, if you want to cultivate positive attitudes. If you only tell people what they are doing wrong, then they will focus on those negatives. If you want to help someone correct behaviors, offer constructive ideas or alternatives.

**Talk to people.** If you've hired people because you believe in them, then talk to them. Ask about their children, vacation, or a project they're working on. You don't have to engage in long, personal conversations, but taking a little interest in their lives will make them feel good and make you much more approachable.

**Have lunch.** At candy maker Just Born, home of the Easter PEEPS, located in Bethlehem, Pennsylvania, co-presidents Ross Born and David Schaffer take turns having lunch with employees at least once a week.

**Open space.** More and more companies are doing away with ivory tower mentalities of private floors, offices, and lunchrooms. By removing closed doors, people work side by side to promote a more open, approachable atmosphere.

**Seek suggestions.** Let people know you are open to suggestions and feedback so they are empowered to work hard, grow the business and help you succeed.

**Do what you say.** If you say you will look into something and get back to someone, then do it. Too often, employees feel forgotten or ignored when the boss says one thing and does another.

**Remove barriers.** Just as I would encourage you to come out from behind a lectern when speaking, if possible, come out from behind a desk or table when someone is speaking to you. If you sit closer to someone and face them directly, you will signify that what she is saying matters to you.

**It's not personal.** It's important to keep your emotions in check and not react to someone's tantrum or negatives. Listen, stick to the facts, voice your concerns, make suggestions, and do not scold someone in front of others. Even if the outcome isn't pretty, it's important not to rob people of their dignity.

**Create fun.** Instead of deciding what you or your staff might think is fun, ask them. This demonstrates that you are open to fresh ideas and want to do everything possible to make the workplace fun.

One of the biggest complaints we encounter when working at companies is that senior management doesn't listen and seems resistant to new ideas. This was the overwhelming complaint at a worldwide technology company that was struggling to keep its stock afloat. Repeatedly, employees confided that management was totally unapproachable, and some said they felt sick to their stomachs on Sunday night because they hated going back to work on Monday.

In a correspondence to the CEO, I offered the following observation: "In my opinion, the lack of open, meaningful dialogue and inability to communicate in real and personal terms has held your company back, contributed to low morale, mistrust, negative attitudes, and potentially contributed to your net loss. People say management is completely unapproachable, and some say they feel sick to their stomachs when it's time to come to work on Monday." I suggested there were huge opportunities to change through more effective communication. He never responded, and I've never worked there again.

When I'm asked what leaders and managers should do to cultivate a more positive workplace, I always attribute great attitudes and morale to great communication. My dad, quoted at the beginning of this chapter, has another saying. He always told me that garbage flows downhill. I've come to learn that means behavior by example has to start at the top.

**Positive attitudes breed positive results.**

# APPENDIX A

# Quick Tip Resources

The following tips and checklists are quick, at-a-glance reminders reinforcing techniques to help you communicate clearly, crisply, and concisely to overcome important business communication challenges.

## SUCCESSFUL MEDIA INTERVIEWS

A media interview is an opportunity to share information and inform the public. It does not have to be confrontational or frightening. These tips will help you prepare in advance to shine in the spotlight.

- Know the reporter's audience and talk to them.
- Empathy, concern, and compassion should be the primary focus when people are affected by something that happens.
- Determine your key messages in advance.
- Get to the point quickly.
- Weave key messages into the interview even if the reporter doesn't ask a specific question to trigger your message.
- Develop examples, analogies, and visual images to simplify information and make your messages memorable.
- Put yourself in the seats of the readers, listeners, or viewers, and ask yourself what you would want to know if you were them.
- Anticipate every question you think you might be asked and determine how you will answer.

- Keep your answers short and to the point.
- Do not repeat negative words.
- Never speculate. Stick to what is confirmed.
- Do not criticize competitors or elaborate on their products.
- Never say, "no comment."
- Speak in simple, nontechnical language.
- Be sensitive to cultural and religious issues.
- Appear positive, energetic, friendly, and interested.
- Personalize and humanize the facts.

## Questions To Ask in Advance

- What is the story you hope to share with your audience?
- What made you call us?
- What is the best possible way I can help you, and what information can I provide?
- Is this part of a series or a stand-alone article?
- What is the format of this program?
- Is anyone else being interviewed?
- What is your deadline?
- Can you share the types of questions you'd like me to address?
- Will the interview be broadcast live or taped?
- Do you need props or visuals?
- Who will be asking the questions?
- When will it air?
- When will it be printed?

## Should You Say Yes or No to an Interview?

## Ask the Following 10 Questions

1. Will it compromise me or my company?
2. Is this within my expertise?
3. What can I gain from this interview?
4. What do I hope to accomplish?
5. Will I increase public awareness?

6. Will it jeopardize my job?

7. Who is my audience, and how can this information help them?

8. Has the reporter or media outlet been negative toward us in the past?

9. Is this a potentially negative or positive story?

10. Am I doing this to benefit the audience, or do I just want to see my name in print?

## Crisis Catchers

These are the types of questions you should expect and prepare for while managing issues and navigating critical communications.

1. What happened?

2. How did it happen?

3. When did you know about it?

4. What did you do about it?

5. How quickly did you act?

6. Is this an isolated incident or are there other issues you're not discussing?

7. Has anyone been hurt?

8. Has this happened before?

9. How can this happen if you have such stringent safety procedures and regulations?

10. What could you have done to prevent this?

11. How can you prevent this in the future?

12. Did you notify authorities or did they call you?

13. How are you communicating with stakeholders?

14. Are you going to put any new policies or processes in place?

15. Do you feel that the reputation of your brands has been compromised?

16. Will you make any changes?

17. Is the public in jeopardy in any way?

18. Are your products/services safe?

## PRESENTATION POINTERS

Sitting in your listener's chair will help you prepare an audience-focused talk or presentation. Begin by asking the right questions so you can frame your ideas from your audience's perspective.

### QUESTIONS TO ASK IN ADVANCE

- Who will be in the audience?
- What do they care about?
- What is the one thing you want listeners to take away when you are done speaking?
- What should people think, feel, know, or do when I'm done speaking?
- If this talk is a huge success, what would that look like?
- What is the room setup and seating arrangement?
- How much time do I have?
- How much time can I allow for a question-and-answer segment?
- Have I checked and tested audiovisual needs in advance?
- Have I checked blogs and articles to see what others say about this organization and industry?
- What are the three greatest challenges or problems faced by attendees?
- Is the audience culturally diverse? If so, explain.
- What styles of presentation have been most successful in the past?
- Have you ever had a terrible speaker? If so, what was it about the program you didn't like?
- Can you share any humorous stories, case studies, or incidents that might be relevant to this audience?

### DELIVERY SKILLS CHECKLIST

Audiences want to like you. If you're uncomfortable, you'll make them uncomfortable. If you appear friendly and approachable, they are more likely to relate and forgive any imperfections.

- Talk, don't read.
- Have a conversation.

- Pronounce words clearly.
- Use facial expressions, open gestures, and natural movement.
- Vary pitch and pace.
- Pause for emphasis and to give listeners a chance to digest information.
- Project to the back of the room.
- Practice out loud in advance.
- Make consistent eye contact.
- Eliminate jargon and buzzwords.
- Know your opening and closing, but don't memorize.
- Smile when appropriate.
- It's okay to be nervous.

### Bringing Talks to Life

Just the facts ma'am doesn't cut it, even in today's time-challenged workplace. To breathe life into messages, use the following connections:

- Examples
- Stories
- Analogies
- Anecdotes
- Case studies
- Powerful numbers
- Comparisons and contrasts
- Visual images
- Acronyms
- Problems and consequences
- Then versus now
- Three things you must know

## CONNECTIVE COMMUNICATION

Whether talking to employees, financial audiences, or colleagues or navigating tough times, the following strategies will help you connect in every situation.

### Believe that You Believe

- People don't have to agree with you. They need to see that you believe in what you are saying
- Attitude is always key. Friendly, upbeat, personable people help reduce tension, overcome challenges and improve the attitudes of other
- Create an honest, transparent, and positive experience, even during down times.

### Personalize the Story

- What can you say that only you can say because you're the expert?
- Draw on your own experience to tell the story.
- Speak from your gut to make others care.

### You're Always On

- Someone is always watching and sharing in the digital age.
- Maintain steady eye contact, project pleasant facial expressions. and use open gestures.
- Exude passion and personality.

### Manage the Message

- It's about them. How does your message impact, benefit, or affect the listener?
- Highlight three or four points to condense complicated information into bite-sized nuggets.
- Keep it simple.

### Talk to Grandmom

- Convey context and perspective.
- Use short phrases and real-life examples.
- Avoid too many details and complex explanations.

### The PS Approach

- Present the (P) problem first so the (S) solution is more impactful.

- How does the problem impact their workplace, community, or life?
- How will the solution make their workplace, community, or life better?

### Wrap It Up with a Bow

- People remember what they hear first and last.
- Deliver key messages at the beginning and the end.
- Don't leave conclusions to chance. If you want something, ask for it.

### Authentic and Honest

- Communicate quickly and honestly.
- Deliver bad news even if it hurts.
- Address fears and concerns.

### Prepare and Practice

- There is no such thing as not enough time if you are committed to doing a good job.
- Practice out loud.
- Visualize your own success.

## FINESSING FINANCIAL PRESENTATIONS

### Face of Your Company

- Create a positive experience by showing enthusiasm, excitement, and optimism.
- Let them *feel* your confidence so they are confident in your company's ability to deliver.
- Every part of you delivers a message, so it's important to set the tone through facial expressions, body language, voice, and eye contact.

### Tell Your Story

- Investors want to know whether there is a market for your ideas; whether you can meet challenges; and whether you have the resources, knowledge, and ability to overcome obstacles.

- Highlight three or four of their most important issues and support those issues with examples, data, and charts to show them how you will solve problems and tackle challenges.
- Include track record and credentials, and share your vision that will make them successful.

## Show and Tell

- Limit data, slides, spreadsheets, and numbers.
- Use pie charts, colored graphs, models, and pictures to show what the numbers mean, how they predict trends, and why they are important to the listener.
- Save the details for handouts.

## Get to the Point

- Briefly state what you will discuss, the problem you will help them solve, and what decisions, results, or outcomes might be achieved.
- Hook your listeners immediately. Articulate what's in it for them and why they should care.
- Begin with a story, case study, powerful number, or example that drives your main message home.

## Provide Direction and Vision

- Know what your audience wants to accomplish, how they perceive your company or product, what positive or negative attitudes they have, and what hurdles they face.
- Address their critical issues and vulnerabilities to create credibility and rapport.
- Help them make decisions by helping them understand how the information can be used and what the numbers mean to them.

## Mock Q and A

- Conduct your own mock question-and-answer session in advance.
- Think through potential questions and write out your answers to prevent surprise questions.

- Practice the answers out loud to sound polished, confident, and assured.

## Don't Get Stuck in the Question

- It's important to answer questions, but it's equally important to look for ways to insert messages into answers.
- When responding, emphasize what you can do instead of what you can't do.
- If you don't know, say so. If you can't tell them what they want to know, tell them why.

## Don't Wing It

- Executives who wing it are setting themselves up to fail.
- If the numbers are bad, say so, then tell them what's positive.
- Rehearse out loud.

# APPENDIX B

# Recommended Reading

Ailes, Roger. *You Are the Message.* New York: Doubleday Business, 1988.

Bates, Suzanne. *Speak Like a CEO: Secrets for Commanding Attention and Getting Results.* New York: McGraw-Hill, 2005.

Begala, Paul, and James Carville. *Buck Up, Suck Up . . . And Come Back When You Foul Up.* New York: Simon & Schuster, 2003.

Carnegie, Dale. *How To Win Friends and Influence People.* New York: Simon & Schuster, 1964.

Fugere, Brian, Chelsea Hardaway, and Jon Warshawsky. *Why Business People Speak Like Idiots: A Bullfighter's Guide.* New York: Free Press, 2005.

Gallo, Carmen. *10 Simple Secrets of the World's Greatest Business Communicators.* Naperville, IL: Sourcebooks, 2005.

Heath, Chip, and Dan Heath. *Made To Stick: Why Some Ideas Survive and Others Die.* New York: Random House, 2008.

Hoffman, Judy. *Keeping Cool on the Hot Seat: Dealing Effectively with the Media in Times of Crisis.* Clayton, NC: Four Cs, 2008.

Quebin, Nido. *How To Be a Great Communicator: In Person, on Paper, and on the Podium.* New York: John Wiley & Sons, 1997.

Scott, Susan. *Fierce Conversations: Achieving Success at Work and in Life, One Conversation at a Time.* New York: Berkley Books, 2002.

Segal, Edward. *Getting Your 15 Minutes of Fame and More: A Guide to Guaranteeing Your Business Success.* New York: John Wiley & Sons, 2000.

# Index

## About the Author

KAREN FRIEDMAN is an international communications expert who has worked with executives on four continents. An award-winning top market television news anchor and reporter for 20 years, her breaking coverage of local and national events has aired on ABC, CBS, NBC, CNN, the *Today Show*, *Good Morning America*, and *Nightline*. She now leads Karen Friedman Enterprises, Inc., which teaches business professionals, spokespeople, newsmakers, and celebrities across the globe how to make the most of important interviews, appearances, meetings, and presentations.

Friedman's expertise in message development was first recognized when a U.S. delegation led by former First Lady Hillary Rodham Clinton tapped her to provide media and political training for women in South and Central America. She continues to counsel key opinion leaders across the world and has rolled out speaker, media, crisis, and communication training programs in numerous countries, including China, England, Singapore, Malaysia, Uruguay, Argentina, Colombia, Trinidad, Canada, and Puerto Rico. She has also delivered keynote speeches at many of these events.

Since Friedman launched her firm in 1996, businesses have been relying on her to help them develop powerful messages and field tough questions to communicate more effectively during a wide variety of challenging situations, including nationwide educational campaigns, manufacturing shutdowns, congressional hearings, product launches and recalls, analyst and investor presentations, hostile community meetings, employee issues, chemical spills, and the drug approval processes. Her firm has counseled a number of prestigious Fortune 100 and Fortune 500 clients.

Frequently quoted by publications such as the *New York Times*, *Wall Street Journal*, and *Harvard Business Review*, Friedman is a professional speaker who has received many top-rated speaker awards. Her articles on leadership and communication techniques are regularly published in business magazines and online sites, and her popular monthly communication video tips are viewed by thousands of subscribers. She coauthored *Speaking of Success* with several best-selling writers, including Stephen R. Covey (*Seven Habits of Highly Effective People*), Ken Blanchard (*One Minute Manager*), and Jack Canfield (co-creator of *Chicken Soup for the Soul*). She has also developed numerous communication training manuals and a host of related audiovisual tools.

Friedman earned her degree at the Pennsylvania State University and furthered her studies at the University of Manchester in England. She developed and taught a journalism broadcast course at the University of Wisconsin-Milwaukee and has lectured at prestigious institutions, including the Wharton School at the University of Pennsylvania. She is a member of numerous organizations, including the National Speakers Association, International Association of Business Communicators, Public Relations Society of America, American Society for Training & Development, and the Healthcare Businesswomen's Association, where she has conducted a variety of workshops at conventions and leadership conferences.

Friedman lives in the Philadelphia area with her husband, two sons, neurotic dog, and ornery cat.

She can be reached at the company Web site, www.karenfriedman.com.